Alexander Raleigh

From dawn to the perfect day

Alexander Raleigh

From dawn to the perfect day

ISBN/EAN: 9783741177996

Manufactured in Europe, USA, Canada, Australia, Japa

Cover: Foto ©Andreas Hilbeck / pixelio.de

Manufactured and distributed by brebook publishing software (www.brebook.com)

Alexander Raleigh

From dawn to the perfect day

FROM DAWN

TO

SERMONS

BY

ALEXANDER RALEIGH, D.D.

AUTHOR OF 'QUIET RESTING PLACES'

EDINBURGH: ADAM & CHARLES BLACK
1883

PREFATORY NOTE.

THE Sermons in this volume, selected from Dr. Raleigh's manuscripts, are the last of these that will be published; and they owe their publication to the feeling that it was scarcely right to allow materials of possible practical value to remain unused. It is believed that there are some to whom his words, coming once again out of the past, will not be unwelcome.

M. R.

LONDON, 16th *October* 1883.

CONTENTS.

	PAGE
THE COMFORT THAT COMES INTO THE WORLD WITH CHILDREN	1
WHEN OUR CHILDREN ARE ABOUT US	15
CHRISTIAN NURTURE. (*To Parents.*)	34
ENTRANCE MINISTERED ABUNDANTLY. (*To the Young.*)	46
THE BROAD WAY AND THE NARROW	62
THE CORN OF WHEAT.—LIFE OUT OF DEATH. (*Easter Sunday.*)	75
STRAIGHTWAY	87
GIRDING ON THE HARNESS	98
NICODEMUS—THE LESSON BY NIGHT	108
COME WITH US. (*For the New Year.*)	123
THE PARABLE OF THE TREES (*To Young Men.*)	132
TO LIVE IS CHRIST	153
THE BLADE, THE EAR, THE FULL CORN	166
THE RESURRECTION OF CHRIST HISTORIC. (*Easter Sunday.*)	178
THE WAY WHEREIN WE SHOULD GO	190
ON CHRISTIAN GIVING	204

	PAGE
DIVINE EXPULSIONS	219
ON THE MOUNTAIN	230
THE FIRST DISCIPLES	250
THE GOSPEL BROUGHT INTO EUROPE. (*An Exposition.*)	265
THE HUMILIATION AND GLORY OF CHRIST. (*An Exposition.*)	282
RECEIVING THE GRACE OF GOD IN VAIN	297
THE CREED OF CHRISTENDOM	312
QUENCHING THE SPIRIT	327
STRENGTH AS THE DAYS. (*For the New Year.*)	337
PAUL, TIMOTHY, AND EPAPHRODITUS	347
"JESUS CHRIST THE SAME YESTERDAY, AND TO-DAY, AND FOR EVER"	361
OUR YEARS. (*Watchnight Address.*)	379
THE GENERAL ASSEMBLY WRITTEN IN HEAVEN	388
THE LOT AT THE END OF THE DAYS	401
THE GREAT HOPE AND ITS EARNEST	413

I.

The Comfort that comes into the World with Children.

"And he called his name Noah, saying, This same shall comfort us concerning our work and toil of our hands, because of the ground which the Lord hath cursed."—GENESIS v. 29.

"NOAH" means rest or comfort; and his parents, we see, gave him this name, expecting by his means, in some way, or probably in more ways than one, the fulfilment to them of the happy meaning of the name he bore. We cannot say, in the absence of any information in the Book, how definite their expectation was regarding their son. Perhaps they themselves hardly knew exactly what they were expecting. They were sure, however, and not by parental instinct merely, but evidently as the result of some divine intimation given them concerning this child, that he would be a comforting helper. He would help them in their labours on the stubborn soil; he would help them in their resistance to the rapidly-increasing violence of society around them; it is possible that they might have had some hope that he might even prove to be the Messiah. Following the history of this child, we find that he was actually noted for improvements in husbandry; that he was the discoverer or inventor of wine; that he was a preacher of righteousness in a very unrighteous and lawless time; that he was a true prophet, although unheeded, as most true prophets are; that he was a shipbuilder on a gigantic scale; that he thus became the preserver of his family, and in them of the whole human race; and that he was manifestly, in some of these respects, a forerunner and a type of Christ, the true Noah, the giver of rest and consolation to troubled and weary souls.

Now this passage, although in itself no more than a mere glimpse into an old, old world—no more, indeed, than a scene from the family life of that old world—yet, either expressly or by implication, tells and teaches us a good deal, if only we are wise enough to learn it.

The hardness and difficulty of life.

This our human life is full of hardship. Put in familiar phrase, this world is a hard place to live in. It was so then; it is so now. I am not asking *your* opinion, young people; you cherish your bright hopes, which I would not darken, and your unconquerable impulses towards exertion and enterprise, which I would not suppress or daunt. But you have not got the materials for a full and intelligent judgment. Observe, these words are the words of parents. Father and mother speak them—not son and daughter, not young man or maiden. They are the words of Lamech, and they are remarkable as coming from a man bearing that name; for Lamech means "powerful." He seems to have been a strong, robust man—like the evil Lamech in this (for there were two of the same name), but unlike him, happily, in temper and disposition. That Lamech sang to his wives of his own crimes and excesses. This Lamech also is a poetic singer, and mournful enough is the strain when he speaks of hard toil, of sterile ground, and of divine curse. But the strain of comfort, also divine, gives the tone to the little poem. It is strange, or at least worthy of note, that such a man should have to sing such a song, and should sing it in the prime of his life. He has hardly reached his prime; but the hundred and eighty and two years of his life have at least brought to him unexpected difficulties, as well as dangers and hardships quite unknown to him in youth. Not that we can regard him as a vanquished man, but evidently he has, in some things, been disappointed. He is weary now at times; strong man as he is, the truth begins to come home to him that we cannot fight this battle of life single-handed; that even strong men cannot. At any rate, for himself, he is not ashamed to confess that he needs "comfort;" and when this child comes to him he accepts him as a divine gift, as a commissioned and competent, as he is a thrice-welcome, messenger of comfort from God. He seems to say to his wife and to his friends: "We have been feeling greatly of late the strain of life. Our testimony to God and truth has not been of much account among evil and violent men. We have not been getting much from the ground. Our eyes have been sometimes dark, and our hearts heavy; but now—'this same shall comfort us.'"

Is it not so still? This world is a place in which somehow the strongest men grow weary; in which men of the happiest temperament come to be in need of relief, and ease, and of all that is implied in the word "comfort." The soil of this world is, so to say, yet stubborn and hard; the weeds in it are many, and they have their roots far down. The seasons are uncertain, the harvest is sometimes scant. To put the thing without a figure: to live well in this world among men, and continuously well; speaking, acting, enduring; in success, in misfortune, through days and times bright and dark; in some measure of calmness and constancy—all this is, to use a familiar phrase, "hard work." It is noble and hopeful work beyond all other, but it is hard; and the strongest Lamech anywhere to be found in the world, whether toiling in its fields, or trading in its cities, or travelling on its highways, speaking in its assemblies, or living quietly but strenuously in any of its families, need not be ashamed to acknowledge that now and again "comfort," as it is not unneeded, would not be unwelcome.

The comfort that comes into the world with children.
Days are dark, and limbs are weary, and hearts are heavy, and the family lamp seems almost going out, for hope has not been there of late to trim it; when the wailing voice of a little stranger is heard, who comes, at least to outward appearance, not with relief and

largess, but in sheer helplessness, and with demand for constant service, and who yet is hailed as a very deliverer, and welcomed as a comforter. "*This same shall comfort us.*" In thousands of homes all over the world, every day, fathers and mothers are saying this in substance. They are feeling it in their hearts, and that is saying it. Strange enough it seems that some fathers and mothers should feel so. Even when they are poor, or in precarious circumstances, or have hard work and many children already, the little one is still accepted with thankfulness and greeted with a hopeful welcome. These words of Lamech are the permanent inscription in the horoscope which parents, everywhere and always, see over the cradle of the latest born. In the monarch's palace, while guns boom welcome; in the merchant's city home, where careful feet walk over thickly-carpeted floors; in the workman's street, groups of faces in neighbouring doors showing true, if homely sympathy; in the country cottage, from which the doctor drives away in his gig with a cheerful face; in the gipsy's wayside tent, the swarthy kindred scattered about the neighbourhood, or lying under clumps of trees on the warm earth—"*This same shall comfort us*" flames out in golden light; and for the time "sorrow and sighing flee away," while joy and gladness take possession of the house.

Thus we see the weakest and most helpless creature in the world, which certainly a new-born child is, become almost the mightiest. "Out of the mouth of babes and sucklings God ordains strength." Giant

Lamech—toil-worn, disappointed, weary with living—bows down at the crib of a sleeping infant, who, although asleep and helpless, takes up the significance of his father's name, just when his father seems losing it—and the best meanings and purposes of his father's life—and becomes a Lamech in moral influence and helpfulness. We sometimes hear the wish expressed that children who are being nourished and brought up by their parents with great pains, and through many difficulties, may live to repay them when the parents are old and helpless in their turn. And it is a beautiful sight to see the second childhood nourished and soothed by those who express in this way their thankfulness for the care that was once lavished on them. But this is a payment which is far from certain. A great deal will happen before the settling-day. The parents may not live to receive the reward; or the children may not live to give it; or a hundred things may arise to complicate the issues. It will be wise, therefore, to secure the surer recompense, if there be one; and there is, to all who are open-hearted and unselfish.

Payment for toil, and care, and never-ending watchfulness! *It is here*—in the house—in the hand. The living, growing children are themselves the payment for the care and trouble they bring. Strength, comfort, hope, come with them. The very solicitude we cannot help feeling, sometimes to painfulness, is part of the payment; for it likens us to God, and it aids us in being ourselves children in His larger family.

"Like as a father pitieth his children, so the Lord pitieth them that fear Him;" or, looked at from the other side, and in its deeper aspect, we may render the text, "Like as the Lord pitieth them that fear Him, *so a father pitieth his children*," and cannot but hope bright things concerning them, cannot but drink in comfort in beholding them.

For myself, I cannot help finding almost a system of theology, at any rate a clear, bright prophecy of God concerning the future, in this invincible hopefulness of the parental heart. But stay: here is a statistician, and he has something to say. He says it pitilessly, in a hard, scientific way, yet not untruly from his own point of view. He says: "All this is a matter of calculation. Your prophecies and auspices may be pleasant enough, but they can have little or no influence on the events. A certain number of those who, when they are infants, excite those hopes in parental and other breasts do not verify them. They are not in any deep sense a comfort to almost anyone; they bring discomfort and distress to many. Some few come to the saddest ends. Many, stopping short of that, yet fail in life; and very few are helpers and comforters of their kind by great and good living. It is for you to estimate these probabilities for yourselves, and then say whether you are justified in keeping that fanciful inscription over your child's cot, '*This same shall comfort us.*' You cannot certainly know that the very opposite of that may not turn out to be the truth. It would be as appropriate, therefore, to write in imagination, 'This same shall grieve us,' 'This same shall disappoint us,' or 'This same shall ruin us,' or worse than all, 'This same shall shame us, and draw burning tears from our eyes, and heavy sighs from our lips.'"

Something like this might be said, and said honestly enough, from the hard, scientific ground. The doctrine of mathematical probability settles the proportions almost exactly for the whole, and there is room for contingency only in regard to individuals. One even hears a strain like this in the pulpit at times, religiously put and accompanied with appropriate warning and instruction. Nor can it be said that teaching like this has not truth in it, if we are to be honest and upright all round. True? It is as true as winter, as true as night, as true as the law of gravitation! But what is the whole result in the parental heart of mankind? All this is known by fathers and mothers everywhere. Few of them, perhaps, trouble themselves with any philosophic views or calculations about the facts; but the facts themselves are as clear as human history and as open to view as human life. Surely it is an interesting and even a scientific question; what is the practical effect of this knowledge of moral averages upon parents as they welcome their children into the world, or see them growing up under their hand and care? Would this darker view, set strongly before any father or mother, at all sensibly affect the feeling of uncalculating hopefulness and invincible love, with which they bend over the bed of their sleeping infant, saying in their hearts, "Some way or other this same shall comfort us." Not in the very least. There is an unfathomable fountain of hopefulness in the human breast, and the springing of it cannot be repressed. It is not a partial or chance impulse. It is universal and continuous, and is therefore something to be estimated and appraised in any view of human nature which professes to be scientific. The really scientific view must embrace *all* the known facts; and this is one of them, that parents *will* hope good regarding their children as they come to them, and never will be persuaded that they ought not to welcome them with song and thankfulness. If other impulses and affections are divine, this too must have its meaning and use in the education of humanity and in the economy of the world. Can we be wrong in thinking that part at least of its meaning must be this—that by-and-by the great stream of human life is destined to run clearer; that in an increasing number of instances this prophecy of the parental heart will be fulfilled; Lamechs will bend over every cradle, Noahs will be born in every house; and at length the world, like a wayward, wandering child, shall return and find comfort, after all its weary "work" and the long "toil of its hands," in the fatherhood and motherhood of God?

What is thus true of parent and child may be transferred to a far wider scene, and applied to the successive generations of men. "One generation passeth away and another cometh." This is the unchanging order of God for the whole terrestrial life of man. The generations which are farthest on have much to say to the generations which are growing about them and following closely. The utterances are not all of one kind; they are diverse, they are even discordant. Distrust, displeasure, impatience, even denunciation, may be heard spoken by the lips of the retiring generation to and concerning that which follows in immediate succession.

But I seem to hear this old tone which welcomed Noah into the world clearer and louder than any other. We see the generation that has now almost gone—that is visible to us in only a few remaining representatives—standing as in shadow, and speaking to us by symbol and not by voice; by bent forms, by withered cheeks, by gray hairs. They say: "We are weary now with travail and hard work; but you, our strong sons and daughters, who are filling the field of life we are leaving, you comfort us, you console our disappointments, you soothe the sorrow of our going away." While we, in our turn, the sons and daughters of those who are now nearly all gone, conscious of our own disappointments, feeling our own wounds and griefs and failures, look for comfort to the fresh spring world that is growing about us, and to the younger world yet that is being born.

And so the tale runs on through the generations and through the families, "because of the ground which the Lord hath cursed," because of the hard conditions of this human life. Observe it well, however, there is no curse on *the labour* of the tillers of the ground. There is no curse, but all blessing, on the endeavours we make to master the circumstances of our own lives and turn them to the best uses. Yet, on the other hand, it cannot be denied that everywhere in life there is "thorn and thistle," consuming heats by day, cutting frosts by night; seed rotting in the ground, sheaves carried off by floods; hard stubborn soils, needing much overwork for the growing of the best things—the loamy softness of Eden all gone from them, and the nourishing warmth and the dewy fragrance—or rather, we may say, such never came to them, for Eden was better than the outlying world; "the gold of that land was good." The rough world beyond was for the education, the discipline, the victory of those who were driven out from the privileged condition of the garden. Trust and toil and obedience will bring men back to a better Eden. But meantime there is no evading the "curse" which is here said to be in "the ground." It is something which can never be measured or weighed. It may be largely negative—simply not "blessing." We need not aim at being more definite than God Himself is. It is enough that we feel it. We feel it without and within. It is in the earth; it is in the air. Still more is it in the disloyal conscience, in the mean disposition, in the selfish breast. And the thing we have to do is not to talk about it very much, discussing it, and defining it, and deepening it by our quarrels over it, but to match ourselves against it with all our strength, renewing them from the fountain of the strength that is "everlasting."

Toil-worn and sorrow-laden brother, be sure of this, that whatever the curse be, heaven has an alchemy which evermore changes curse into blessing, and desert into garden of the Lord. The golden age shall yet come back. The breezes of Eden shall fan and freshen the cheeks of weary toilers on land or sea. One generation shall speak to another with still lessening apprehension as the ages pass, and with still rising hope and confidence, saying, "This same shall comfort us," until the voice from heaven shall say, "It is done. Behold I make all things new."

The security we have for all this in the great fact of our redemption.

The foregoing train of thought is not only pleasant and welcome to the benevolent affections and hopeful tendencies of human nature, but it has in it an argument which grounds itself ultimately on the wisdom and veracity of God. God is true—true in all His works and words and ways; true, therefore, in human nature, the chief product in this world of His power and Spirit. The organic powers, affections, and instincts of the human race are from Him. And when we see the same hope and instinctive faith reproduced and continued from age to age and in every country in the world's parental heart, the conclusion we reach is, that after all this fatherly and motherly hoping and believing, there must be a corresponding realisation yet to come.

Yet I freely confess that the argument would be inconclusive and uncertain without some clearer and firmer support. It would, in fact, be little more than a religious philosophy; and a religious philosophy, although engaged about the highest themes and interests, must yet take its chance with other philosophies, and is apt, at particular points, to come to grief. We can imagine a thoughtful person to say: "I am not disinclined to accept what you are now advancing; indeed I could believe it if you were able to confirm it by any living instances—if you would even bring *one*, if it should be only one, really complete instance of the fulfilment of your theory. I could believe it if, amid the myriad births in human homes, there had ever been born one perfect 'Noah'—one rest-giver to all the weary about him, one comfort-bringer to all the sad and sorrowing, one strong soil-subduer to cheer the faithful worker, one calm master of all the confused elements and aspects of this tumultuous and ever-changing life—*then* we might hope that this parental prophecy, which never dies out of human hearts, is really to be fulfilled in the end."

This is exactly what we can do. We do need the substantiation of fact, and we have it. Our Noah has been born: true Rest-giver, strong Burden-bearer, grandest Worker, gentlest Comforter, surest Helper, most faithful Friend, all-pitying and all-sufficing *Saviour!* That last word implies all the rest. If He were not Jesus—Saviour—from first to last—He could be none of those other things. Noah was a preacher of righteousness; but Jesus Christ brings and gives righteousness, instilling it into every believing heart. Noah was a preserver of the world in his own family from a temporary flood; Jesus Christ makes this world itself the ark which He commands, steering it through this "great and wide sea" of space and time in safety.

Noah was a successful cultivator of the soil and an improver of husbandry; Jesus Christ feeds His disciples with bread from heaven; is Himself the Bread of Life; Himself the Vine which holds all strength and sweetness, and all divine purity and consolation. It is He who says "Come unto me, all ye that labour and are heavy-laden, and I will give you rest." Is it wonderful there should be always groups and gatherings of the weary around Him, and a laying down of the burdens of toil and care at His feet? Will it not be strange and sad if our burdens, whatever they may be, are not cast down among the others, if our weary souls are not refreshed with the Saviour's rest? That rest will be ours, according to His own sure promise, if only we seek it in the right way—by coming to Him—not in passive helplessness merely to be healed and soothed, and almost sent to sleep—but with all our active powers to be enlisted and engaged in His service. This is the ultimate comfort, the full abiding rest; not only that we come by grace into a state of safety, and into the enjoyment of God's forgiving love, but that we find full scope for our best powers, and that we have them continually refreshed and strengthened in the service of God and man. "*Take my yoke upon you, and learn of me,* so shall ye find rest unto your souls."

II.

When our Children are about us.

> " Come to me, O ye children !
> For I hear you at your play,
> And the questions that perplexed me
> Have vanished quite away.
>
> " What are all our contrivings,
> And the wisdom of our books,
> When compared with your caresses,
> And the gladness of your looks ?
>
> " Ye are better than all the ballads
> That ever were sung or said ;
> For ye are the living poems,
> And all the rest are dead."

LONG ago, in the dawn of the world's history, in a distant country, there lived a man who had once been prosperous, happy, respected, in a very high degree; but who, all at once, fell into great poverty and trouble. He lost all his property, all his children, and well-nigh his own life. He stood one day, or sat on the ground, bemoaning himself among his friends, recalling with a fond sadness vanished scenes and bygone years. He talked much and long—as men are apt to talk, in hours of confidence, with listening friends about them—of what he had been and done in other days. It is a melancholy tale of departed glory—a dirge such as, happily, very few men can sing over their own life. We listen the more eagerly to his wailing, because the sorrow is so vast and so exceptional. He mourns like a king discrowned and exiled. He lights up for us, in melancholy reminiscence, the palaces of pleasure that had been darkened, and the high walks of honour and usefulness he has now ceased to tread. He speaks of a "secret" once with him, now lost; of a "candle" which once shone in his tabernacle, but which now burns no more; of a Divine "presence" sheltering, sufficing, which then "preserved" him, but from which he seems now cast out. Then ran the oil out of the rock for his anointing; then butter washed his steps. When he went, in those days, to the gate of the city, there was reverence; when he took his seat in the street there were the tokens of a universal regard—young men standing aside, aged men rising up, princes keeping silence. As he moved about from place to place the air became vocal with benedictions,—the poor, the fatherless, and the widow joining in sweet chorus to his praise,—and so on through the multiform aspects of a prosperity now withered and dead like autumn leaves. Who can but listen when so great a mourner speaks? Who can fail to sympathise with him in reverses so entire and desolating?

"But probably he has some chief comforts remaining. His children will be about him, to soothe his griefs and beguile the sense of his losses. They—young and fresh —will stay their father in his great need, and ere long they will make life green about him again." Ah, no!

This touches the tenderest point in all his sorrow. He takes up *their* names also into his lament. He tells us that they are all gone; and he secures, as he could in no other way, the freshest and homeliest sympathy of every true father and mother in the world, just by one short, thrilling note in his long sad dirge of grief—"*When my children were about me!*" Is not that the tenderest touch of all? Does it not take us in a moment to our own homes, and back along the line of past years, and away to churchyards far and near, and up to heaven? Let us linger for a little on an expression so full of suggestiveness, and—not forgetting the patriarch who gives us the seed for our thought—let us apply his words in different ways to ourselves.

When our children are children we should really have them "about us."

Job's children (for by this time we all know that *he* is the mourner) were "about him" in the days of his prosperity. I do not know that we should be justified in supposing that he had his children in much closer personal association with him than was usual with godly parents of the time. It is certainly worthy of notice that they are named particularly at the opening and the ending of the book. We are told the number of his sons and the names of his daughters. He tells us, too, how "fair" they were, and we seem to see the sheen of their Arabian beauty. He tells us of "sons," and of "sons' sons," even to "four generations." He saw them all. We feel that he took *delight* in seeing them, in having them "about him," when he was a young father and when he was an old patriarch.

The highest and godliest nurture still is that which keeps the children beside the parents through the earlier years of life, in the fresh formative time, when there are beginnings of things that will never end. When the little birds are in the nest the parent birds are seldom far or long away. The human instinct prompting to love, and care, and nourishment, ought to be as strong. It usually is so for a while. But in many cases *only* for a little while. Many things arise to interrupt the continuity and impair the energy of parental presence, and the influence of that presence on the children. Many things—some of them without our will, some of them directly the fruit of our will or state.

The occupations of life with capable men and women are numerous, engrossing, and very exhausting. So that even a loving father, who is toiling for his children all day long, coming home spent at night, is not sorry to find that his children are two stories nearer heaven than he, and that he is not likely to see any more of them for the day. In the morning he must "take time by the forelock," and business by its opportunities, and men as he can find them; he has no leisure for the children. So comes and goes many a precious day in which little hearts are forming themselves, and little lives are taking shape in character, thoughts growing into principles, feelings becoming settled emotions—all *without* so much as there might be of that calm and great thing—a parent's presence. Such a man has his children in his house, but he has not got them "*about him.*" Nobody in the world would think of them as neglected children. All the neighbourhood knows them to be as clean as the morning and as fresh as the rose. The only pity is that father, and perhaps mother too, do not see so much as they should do of the beauty of the growing; do not catch the morning and evening and noonday fragrance of their own children, and do not shed on them more of that sweet and priceless element in a child's education—a parent's *present* care and love, so that the beauty may not fade, so that the fragrance may not die.

The child's education in many cases, surely in too many, brings on an early separation from home and parental presence. It is found not to be convenient, or judged not desirable, to have home and school together —going to school in the morning, coming home at night. But it seems to me that, where this is at all possible, it is by much the best arrangement for at least the earlier years of youth. Undoubtedly absence from home has its own advantages to the young. The power of such absence is sometimes wonderful, in developing character, increasing self-reliance, vivifying early memories, endearing the home from which absence is something of a daily banishment. But if that absence comes too soon, the probability will be so much less that the young scholar has in him the germs of right character to be developed; the youthful memories will be the fewer; the resistance to temptation will be the less; and the moral result of the whole more doubtful. It is God's way that the children, while young, should be "about" the parents. That was the way in the olden time. Happily it has been the way down through all time. It has ripened the richest fruits of goodness in human character. It has made the noblest men and women. It will be found still in all but exceptional cases, that home—be it tent of the desert or house of the city—and daily presence of father and mother—be they of high or low degree—are more for the child than any other persons or things that can be substituted. They are great days for after meaning, and far-off power and influence, the days when "our children are about us."

When our children are about us we should consider with Job that we are prosperous.
We have at least this element of prosperity, although the rest may be wanting, or may not be in such fulness as the patriarch possessed them. The rivers of oil do not flow for you perhaps. The city streets do not give reverence. No one refrains from talking because you are present. You are very *un*like Job in some of these outward respects. But you are like him at least in this, that "your children are about you." And because they *are* yours, they are as much to you as his ever were to him. Perhaps you have one as bright as his Jemima (although Jemima was not born when he spoke thus, and the children mentioned here were all dead and gone),—as bright as Jemima (the day); one as fragrant as Kezia (cassia), shedding perfume through

the house; or one as plentiful in goodness as Kerenhappuch. *You* know what your children are; strangers do not. Nothing is more common in society than pleasantries about the partialities of parents; but perhaps few pleasantries have in general less foundation. That there are parents who can see no faults in their children, although these faults are patent to every one else, and who therefore allow them to grow up self-willed, rude, a nuisance to all about them, is unfortunately true. Such parents generally have, soon or late, in these very children, full punishment of their own blindness. But we are persuaded that the case in general is rather this,—that what strangers or unobservant neighbours would hastily call a parent's partiality, is really only a feeling produced, or a course of conduct drawn out, by a parent's better knowledge. Only those who are in close relations with children can tell what they are. How they are tempted! How they struggle! How they overcome! How they do their noble acts, and also sink into their own little meannesses occasionally among the toys—in the playground—with their lessons! How shall a stranger or a friend presume to conclude that your boy is rude because he is salient? As well call the clematis rude that *will* climb over the wall; or the little burn that *will* have its leaps before it is quenched in the silent river. How shall he say that your girl is forward because she is frank—or stupid because she is shy? He had better be careful, and not quite so sure. Children are great mysteries. Friends do not understand them. Teachers do not understand them. Theorists do not understand them. Foot-rule experience will never measure them. Nor can the parental experiences of bygone times serve much for living parents and children. Each child is a new problem to be solved. Each child is "a new thing under the sun"—the only new thing there is. All else is old. Matter is as old as creation; spirits are as new as the moment of time, or the creative inspiration of God from which they were born. Each child comes into the world charged with manifold life, gifted and dowered with faculties, forces, laws, affections, sublime possibilities. A child is a great mystery, as yet unrevealed to any; but the nearest approach to an understanding of the mystery is just that thing which is called slightingly "a parent's partiality." No doubt there is the instinctive feeling which accounts for much. But there is also the better knowledge.

The children are about us thus, as a part of our prosperity. So regard them. So enjoy them. Take heed that the affection which we justify is not merely human, but divine. Put them where this now childless man puts his, in the vivid but mournful picture he draws of his vanished joys, *in divine presence* in the house—"the Almighty with you, your children about you!" "Lo, the children are an heritage from the Lord, and the fruit of the womb is his reward." The blessing of the Lord is making you rich—rich, indeed, if you have "the secret," if you have "the children."

Children are not only a blessing, they are also a

trouble and a care, and many parents dwell mostly on that side of the children. They see them through the shadows of the cares they bring. They are vexed with their thoughtlessness. They are wearied many a time, as they well may be, with all the toilsome and ceaseless attentions they require. They are discouraged by their little naughty ways. "Let us pass over to the other side," and see them in the light of the land from which they came, and to which, by God's help, we may lead them back. Look at the glory on their faces. See the sweet blossomings of better things, which *may* indeed be nipped, but which may also ripen, and all the more surely if you will think so, to richest fruit. Looking thus upon them from the side where "their angels" see them, "who do always behold the face of our Father in heaven," you will forget the toil, and the worry, and the care; you will not remember against them former transgressions; you will forgive them all their sins; you will bring them up with you as into the old patriarch's tent, as into Jacob's Bethel; you will present them all, "the infant of days" included, before the Lord. And as a prosperous man or woman, as one whom the Lord hath blessed, you will say over the old words: "When the Almighty is with me! when my children are about me!"

When our children are about us we should tend them very carefully, and train them up in the way they should go, that when they are old they may not depart from it.

Everything else that constitutes any considerable part of a man's prosperity requires to be kept and nourished—his house, his pictures, his garden, his fields, his money, his friendships, his position in life, his character—all need watching and nourishing continually. Let him play the sluggard with any of them, and they are so far lost. For they are parts of a world that "never continueth in one stay." It is eminently so with the children. We lose them every day, even when we have them, if we do not keep them as a man keeps his treasure. They can only be kept by training, growth, development. They are houses—little "banqueting-houses"—where our loves and hopes have sweetest entertainment. But if they are not kept, you will soon see the weather-stain, the gaping rent, the incipient decay. If the house is to wear and retain "the similitude of a palace," it must be "polished" day by day. They are little pictures, fairer than human hand ever painted, in which the gazing eye will find far depths, rich colourings, the endless play of light and shadow, the mantling of the individual expression, and a living beauty through the whole that cannot be described. But as the most valuable pictures grow vile with blots when hung within touch of the rude and careless, or hideous with cobwebs and dust when left in a deserted room, so those sweet living pictures soon catch the stains of rude commerce and careless society when too much exposed to them; soon darken and degenerate, if they are but neglected. They are gardens, fairer and more fragrant than Solo mon's, in which he "planted trees of all kinds of fruit." But you will soon see the weed, the wildness, the overgrowth, if you do not dig, and cut, and bend, and train, and water. It is instructive that the best flowers and plants of the garden are mostly the *ultimate* forms and products of far simpler and wilder things. The beauty and the fruitfulness, the deeper colouring, the double blossoming, the affluent size, the luscious flavour—these are all refinements and elaborations of skill and taste. Well, a family is just a garden of God, where are those living immortal plants called children (who all have something of the wildness of nature in them), and by gracious help we are to nurture and raise them up into the finer and nobler forms of grace. We are to labour until we have them so, that we can ask our best "Beloved" to "come into his garden to eat his pleasant fruits." If a garden be too fine an emblem for all conditions of human life, take the plainer emblem of the field. How beautiful and how bountiful is a harvest-field when the corn is yellow-ripe, and the glad farmer walks behind the long row of reapers and watches the busy sickle and the falling swath! But what ploughing was in that field long ago, when the day was short and the snow was falling! What harrowing of the clods amid the chill spring showers! What plentiful sowing during seed-time! What anxious watching days when the weather was fitful! *Now*, "when the children are about us," is the time for the ploughing, and the harrowing, and the sowing, and the watching. By-and-by "cometh harvest," bringing over-payment of all toil, presaging the richer garnerage of heaven.

All Christian training is summed up in this: "Bring them up in the nurture and admonition of the Lord." This general exhortation has so many parts in it that we cannot even name them. But these are some.

Look to the health of the body, for that is the basis in this world of other things. No studies or accomplishments should be allowed to injure that; for that, when injured, will affect injuriously all the higher things.

Consider, as far as may be, the temperament and peculiarity of each. There is a divine individualism of each soul, before which, when we find it, we should bow down as in the presence of a pure work of God, and to which we should yield, as we do to His great steady laws.

Give the mind knowledge of proper kinds, in due measures, at seasonable times.

Develop the affections, truly and tenderly, under the leadings and breathings of the royal law of love.

Try to put habits into the life of industry, carefulness, and benevolence, from the very first, that the powers may work by these more easily.

Provide for times of recoil and relaxation. Never be afraid of play—of what even might seem idleness to another—if you are sure that it is wholesome rest. When are children to learn to think, how are they to get the *love* of prayer, if they have not their little spaces of quietness allowed them like others? Some of them, I fancy, have no great affection for "the little busy bee" that is always brought humming about their heads as a teacher. They will be apt to like the owl quite as well, which does nothing but *look* as he sits up on the tree, hooting at the silent night. But the bee herself is as idle and luxurious as any creature can be for more than half the year. Let the bee be a winter teacher as well as a summer one, and join relaxation to activity.

Above all, try to secure the whole heart for God. Everything must bend to that. The whole manifold culture should grow up into that. Throw around them, as you may instrumentally, so much of the Fatherhood of God, that they shall not be able without a tremendous and distressing struggle to leave it, and when at last away from it shall not be able to live without it. Let them know, without mistake, from your own lips in face-to-face communication, that the good Shepherd loves them, is watching them with kindly care, is calling them by name, and waiting for their following. When they *follow Him*, you may sing in gladness and thankfulness of heart. You may consider that God has given you plentiful harvest.

"When our children are about us" we should be careful, not only to teach, but *to learn the lessons which they can teach us.*

Children teach lessons which are taught in no other school than the one they keep; or at any rate in no other so well. They are professors in Christ's College. He gives to each a chair; and although their audience sometimes is but scant, and their prelections little heeded, they go on teaching still. Since the day when that little child—unknown by name to the world—in fame immortal, stood up in the centre of the eager group at the Saviour's bidding, and by his ingenuousness and simplicity gave his lecture to Disciples, Apostles, Pharisees, Fathers and Mothers, and all listeners, the children have been teaching in the kingdom; and they will teach until the last returning sinner enters "as a little child" into the kingdom of heaven.

They teach faith. What believers they are! They hardly ever doubt. How they trust your word, your wisdom, your strength, your love, as soon as you give them the least occasion! Your little boy or girl would cling to you in utter simple trust, and lie in your arms a little believer, if you stepped from the Table Rock at Niagara, or from a vessel's side into the sea.

They teach contentment. For they are pleased with little pleasures. They are happy when the sun shines; and if the day is dark, they can find happiness under the clouds. They have not "*learned,*" as yet, "in whatsoever state they are, therewith to be content." But they *are* content, if the outward conditions of life are tolerably pleasant. They have no remembrance of the sorrows of yesterday, no apprehension of the tears of to-morrow.

They teach humility. For they do not "exercise themselves in great matters, or in things too high for them." Their plans are short and small. If they misgive—well, never mind, they can build again. There is plenty of sand on the shore.

When our Children are about us.

Ah, how well were it if we could learn from them in these respects! There is a whole group of virtues which our children, while yet they are about us, are teaching us, whether we are learning them or not. It is beautiful, and yet sad, to see the children teaching when the parents and others are not learning. The parents perhaps have their plans of social ambition, and are striving hard to rise. The children are content if the sun is bright, if grass is green, if flowers are pretty, if bread is sweet and water cool, if the floor is firm enough to walk upon, and the bed is soft enough for sleep. The parents have their cares and their fears lest they should have to go downward in the social scale. Because they are a little poorer than once, they are going to lose some of their friends. (What worthy friends they must be! and oh, what a sorrowful pity to lose them!) Or, they are going into a smaller house, because, perhaps, they do not any longer need the larger, or because it is now a little above their circumstances. They will go away sometimes into another neighbourhood, just that they may go down that little incline unseen. "The children" all this time would take any friends that were pleasant—cottagers' children, workmen's children, would do quite well. A few hours would suffice to begin a real friendship. They would go to any house that sheltered them, and be pleased with the little rooms as a nice change from the larger. Nay, they would go with you if you had not got a house to go to at all. They would wander with you, cheerily enough, along country lanes, and beside hedgerows and old walls. They would sleep with you by hayricks and in harvest-fields, or under the shelter of the trees, soothed and rocked to rest, unless the weather were too chill, by the music of the pines, and pleased by the new lamplight of the stars.

If it be said that a good deal of *such* contentment is the result of sheer ignorance, and therefore cannot be seriously proposed to reasonable persons for their instruction or imitation, a good answer is, that the cares and anxieties of grown-up people are largely the fruit of mere imagination and mistake. They conjure up difficulties which have no real existence; they fear evils that never come; they are poor often in imaginary poverty; sick with pains they never feel; dark when the sun is shining; dying and dead a hundred times before the real dying and the one only death "appointed" come. Surely, therefore, it were well if the care-furrowed faces of father and mother could in any way catch at least *a little* of the smoothness and openness and "sufficient-unto-the-day" look of their "children when they are about them."

When our children are about us we should anticipate the time when, as in the case of the patriarch, they will all be away.

> "How the children leave us, and no traces
> Linger of that smiling angel-band—
> Gone! For ever gone, and in their places
> Weary men and anxious women stand."

Watch, and within the brief circuit of a year, sometimes even in the course of a few months, you will see a change in the little faces. Take photographs of them, and if you happen to lay them by for a few years, and then open the book, you will have a surprise. You will have something like the feeling—" Why, I have lost these children. Surely they have gone from me. Has God taken them?" No. They are "about" you still. They are beside you now, looking at the pictures, much amused that they should be pictures of themselves. *They* can see no resemblance to the image they see every day in the glass. So they vanish from us, even when they live, and we see them no more. The infant is the infant but for a little. The little girl with the ringlets is a wayfarer who is tarrying with you only for a night. She will go on again in the morning towards womanhood. And the sunny boy will keep her company on the way to his manhood. Very soon now you will see touches of the manhood and the womanhood on their faces. Then will come their loves, their marriages, their cares, their children—and you will be grandfather and grandmother before you know. Many are taking these honours continually while yet they are not old. Their children conspire to crown them without their leave, although, generally, much to their delight. Then a few years more, and your children's children will leave you as they shoot up into men and women. You will have to reach across *two* generations then to find the children.

Nor can we forget that there are always some who far outstrip the rest—who do not glide away on feet along the earthly ways, but who have wings woven in silence, on which they fly up to the fields of heaven. We have spoken of the facial change as children grow to be men and women; but there is another change which sometimes comes on a young face, which betokens a growth quite out of this world, and a putting on of the beauty and glory of another. A change this, sad at first to see, sorrowful exceedingly to our earthly affections. Yet a change growing more and more fair to look on, a rebuke to our sorrow, a life-long memory to our love.

> "Have we not caught that smiling
>   On some beloved face,
> As if some heavenly sound were wiling
>   The soul from our earthly place?
> The distant sound and sweet,
> Of the Master's coming feet.
>
> "We may clasp the loved one faster,
>   And plead for a little while;
> But who can resist the Master?
>   And we read, by that brightening smile,
> That the tread *we* do not hear
> Is drawing surely near.
>
> "Then gently enters the Master;
>   Through the room His garments sweep,
> And our trembling hearts beat faster,
>   And our eyes forget to weep:
> For now we can hear Him say,
> 'Thou shalt be there to-day.'"

And so we lose them. And many a Job stands amid the relics of the past, looking back, and plaintively or thankfully recalling the days when the children were about him. Well, look forward. Antedate the time. Anticipate the inevitable severance, and work for the formation of the deeper, the immortal union. If you have wealth—heart property—in these children, *as children*, know it now; for the riches will "make to themselves wings, and flee away." If you have nurture to give them suitable to their tenderness, preparation for their strength, give it now; in a little while they will be too hard and strong in nature's growth to take it. If there are lessons which the Master would have you learn of them while they are yet young, and which they cannot teach, nor you learn of them, when they are older, learn the lesson now, for soon the little faces will be seen no more at your table, the patter of the light feet heard no more in your rooms.

III.

Christian Nurture.

"The children whom the Lord hath given me."—ISA. viii. 18.

(*To Parents.*)

WE speak of our children as especially "ours." We hold them as a dear possession, and if we are Christian parents, our affection reinforces our religious convictions, and fires those gracious impulses which lead us to seek for them the best spiritual blessings. There are some things which I desire at least to name, and which, if we can give them place and power in our own lives, will have great influence in enabling us to carry on and through our work as parents to a blessed issue of success.

These words may be resolved into four:—*Be faithful—Be tender—Pray,* and *Hope.*

Faithfulness.—The meaning of this word is explained by the resolve of the Psalmist when he says :—" I will behave myself wisely in a perfect way; I will walk within my house with a perfect heart." Always when we try to do good to others we are thrown back upon ourselves; we are reminded that high work must have fit instruments, and that our influence is likely to be as our character is. As the man is so will be his strength. This is peculiarly the case as between us and our children. They know us much better than others, are much nearer to us, see us more clearly. We cannot make them believe anything about our temper and spirit, our purpose and desire concerning them, that is not true. They will know inevitably whether we mean all we say, desire all we pray for, and are all we profess. We who are fathers and mothers must have the root of the matter in ourselves, planted in our deepest consciousness, "the love of Christ shed abroad in our hearts by the Holy Ghost which is given unto us;" and our whole life must be ruled and quickened by the principles and powers of the Gospel. We ought to seek not only, or not so much, that our children shall be brought, in some intense experience, out of one kingdom into another—despairing and repenting, believing and rejoicing, all in a few days; as that they shall drink into our own spirit day by day, and feel as life goes on that we have given them Christianity in its essence—the sweetness, the quietness, and the power of it, and the breath of its eternal love. As we train our children, and talk with them, and pray with them, and go in and out among them, until some of them find peace and joy in believing, let us remember that we are not only instrumentally forming Christ in their hearts, the hope of glory, but that we are reproducing *ourselves* in them—our own Christian character, our own life-hope, our own deepest, dearest loves and joys. What *we* think of Christ in our closet will colour and give tone to what they think of Him too. It is an awful, yet a blessed law. It allures us to the higher goodness for reasons beyond the personal ones. For our children's sakes we are bound to be the best we may. Nothing that we can say or do will have half the force of that invisible and almost irresistible power which comes right from our souls, and goes at once and straight into theirs. This power, issuing from the depths of our own being, is an involuntary thing on our part. We cannot make it this or that by an act of will. We affect others, and especially our children, by what *we are.* And they know what we are. O they know it! They feel it, if it be for good, thrilling them, helping them, warning them, winning them—shading their way sometimes like a very presence of God. And they feel it not less if it be for evil, or not fully good—chilling them, hindering them, coming with dark shadows between them and God. We must love Christ dearly ourselves if we are to show His loveliness to them. We must say to them by our life, not "go, seek the great and distant God, if haply you may find Him,"—but "come with us into His loving presence, for He is here."

This sincerity on our part ought to take as one of its forms *a firm, steady family rule*—an exercise of wise parental authority. Much is said in Scripture about this. And just now—in an age of theological relenting and softness, when much less is said in pulpits and books about the terrors of the Lord than used to be spoken in former times—when nearly all law is resolved into love, it is well to have the Scriptural idea of authority in the family brought clearly into view. " I know him (Abraham) that he will *command* his children after him." "Set your hearts unto all the words which I testify among you this day, which ye shall *command* your children to observe to do."

There are some who exercise authority in the family, not the Christian authority, which is a calm, just, beautiful thing, but mere human self-will. They are always commanding, requiring, checking, restraining. Such a habit does not engender in the child any spirit of true obedience to God and truth, and to the parent, as representing these; it rather irritates and evokes a spirit of opposition, or what is even worse, it depresses and discourages, and spreads a kind of hopelessness over the young life, which it is a very sad thing to see. In such an atmosphere of fault-finding, I am afraid some children do give up in a kind of despair: and there is found in the little bosom no longer the glow of a noble purpose—the hope of pleasing God! That is put away among the far possibilities of future years; and the young life, which might be pure and happy from the beginning, like the life of Samuel, somewhat even like the life of Christ, is cast down, becomes a loose unregulated thing, moulded by circumstances, driven hither and thither by accident or chance.

On the other hand, and perhaps at present this is the more common mistake, parents mar their own influence, hinder their prayers, and injure their children, although they are very far from meaning it, by over-indulgence. They never command—never rule calmly and firmly—all is softness, liberty, or even license. Such parents tell us in defence of their system: "It is not for us to command; our best influence is, as has been said, that of personal character; if that be not right, commands from us will be of little use; if it be, they are not needed. Influence will win them to goodness, while mere authority will fail." On the same principle it might be said that God does not need to command; that He only needs to reveal to His creatures what *He is*, and they will love and serve Him. He has revealed Himself to us. He has opened the heart of infinite love. What has He not given! His dear Son—His Holy Spirit—His everlasting Heaven—His own fulness, and all without money and without price! And yet this same God, this Father of mercies, commands, legislates, and duly brings penalty upon those who do not obey. Law and love, these make the whole revelation of God. Not the law without the love; that would fill the world with despair. Not the love without the law; that would fill it with selfishness and misrule; both in union will yet fill it with God's obedient children. Be followers of God in this. Be rulers in your own house—not by checks and shocks, by pull and strain, by collision of wills, and trial of strengths—but gently, as the moon draws the tides up the shores; or as the sun lifts the ocean exhalations into the rain-clouds of the sky.

But lest there should be any mistake, let us take the next word.

Tenderness.—Here is ground where one almost fears to tread. A mother's tenderness! It is one of the continual wonders of the world. It is really a greater thing than a father's constancy, a soldier's courage, or a patriot's love. It is a marvellous thing; and yet the world is full of it. "Can a woman forget . . . that she should not have compassion?" Yet, just because it is so strong, there is some danger of mistaking the natural feeling which glows in every unsophisticated heart, for that gracious and spiritual affection which is baptized in thoughtfulness, and animated with faith. There are living and growing things which are present to the mind of a Christian mother, and which awaken a tenderness more delicate and sensitive than ever touched the heart of one who did not love the Saviour. Think of the great interests at stake; of the principles now being formed; of the habits that will result from them; of the characters you are moulding; of the gladness or the grief, the light or the dark, that will be in future homes as the result of what you are doing now in yours; and of the issues to be revealed in the eternal world, and walk tenderly, as you would among flowers in early Spring; as you would move in a room filled with articles of rarest value; or as, on some day of solemn sweet memorial, you would go into the temple of God.

Such feelings will lead to *Prayer.*

Prayer is the instinctive action, the natural inevitable flow of a gracious soul. "This is one of my deepest convictions, I will go and tell it to God." " I am yearning over a son, a daughter: I cannot tell my thoughts, and fears, and hopes to them. I will go and tell them all to Him." "He, my Father, has had far more loving care, solicitude, and trouble with me than I with them. He will understand it all, and I shall understand the case better when I have told Him. I cannot but tell Him. I have no secrets from God. It would be a violation of the covenant between us if I kept anything back—my soul, with all its secrets and sorrows, thirsteth after God! These strong affections which He gave me, He will not deny and crush them when they lead me to Him. This prayer—which gathers in my soul when I stay away from Him, like water that finds no outlet—He will hear it, and honour it, and answer it." So the heart will drink in divine tranquillity and reassure itself in faith.

Again, in prayer for our children we are putting ourselves in the line of God's laws. We work as He works. So the farmer acts, in harmony with law when he tills his land and sows his seed in right season. So the builder does when he lays a sure foundation, brings sound material, and builds by line and plummet. We are in the fields of grace, watching for the springing of the good seed and waiting for the early rain. We are trying to "bring them up in the nurture and admonition *of the Lord.*" It is not *our* nurture, it is His, and in prayer we cast it over on Him. He is never weary of His nurture; He never ceases from His admonition; He makes registry of the birth; He is present at the baptism; He teaches the child to go, taking it by its arms; He soothes its sorrows, lifting it up into His own. Our nurture of our children is soon over. A few years, and they are gone. His nurture never ends. They are children in His hands all their days, and we do well to cast them on their Father's care, on the tenderness of His nurture, and the wisdom of His admonition.

Are some of your children far away? To bear their names in your heart to a throne of grace, will it not in a true sense be really going to them, giving them your best and purest presence, and your most effectual help? Every morning you may greet your daughter away in the far West. Every night you may lay your hand on the head of your sailor boy as he swings himself into his hammock, and touch and purify his heart with thoughts of home; and light will arise in the darkness as you name the prodigal's name, and commend him too to the great Father. This is the true electric line which goes first to heaven and then round all the earth. Nothing but an entire surrender, a full and unreserved communication of the whole case to God, will fill your heart with peace. You will feel that the mysteries of your lot lie clear on the plan of His wisdom, and that your prayers have gone up to Him in memorial, and have been or will yet be returned in showers of blessing on you and on your children.

We are thus naturally led to the last word—*Hopefulness*. We ought to cherish a feeling of cheerful confidence in God as to the result of our endeavours for our children's good. Discouragement, and despondency even, will come to us soon enough, and darkly enough, if we will permit them; and perhaps in some such ways as these.

A certain ideal is formed in the mind as to the manner in which the grace of Christ is to operate, as to "the way of the spirit," and such an ideal is seldom fully realised. A child is expected to develop into graciousness this way, and he develops *that* way. *This* is to be the time of decision, and it does not come; *this* the occasion of serious thought, and there is nothing but airy frankness. Moods of seriousness come, and then mysteriously they go, leaving parents to think of "the morning cloud and the early dew." Then perhaps we see other children drawn into the better life, whose training has been apparently not different from that of our own home. Their day of decision has come, while our children stand doubting still.

Now we have no right as Christian parents to give any encouragement to these moods. We have the one thing to seek—that our children shall be new creatures in Christ Jesus; but we have no right to require or expect the attainment of this in any particular way. We must not dictate to the Spirit of God, or infringe His rights and royalties. Let Him come as He will, as breeze or whirlwind, as fire or dew, He will be welcome. Without choosing, without presuming to regulate the matter by the measuring-line of our thought, we must go on hopefully day after day, doing the best we can, always sowing the seed and always cheerfully expecting the harvest. Christian parents, you continue in this work amid the very sanctities and breathings of Divine Love. Surely you will not despond? Surely you will not weary? You are working a quiet work, but a work which, if well done, will be the fullest and noblest upon earth. There is no work greater than the consecration to God of immortal beings from their birth. The great Christian field offers much harder work, enterprises connected with greater difficulty and more danger. In one sense it may be said to be a nobler thing to go and tame a savage, or to throw down the altars of idolatry and set up the throne of God; to go and preach Christ in the regions beyond the reach of civilisation; to go where Satan's seat is. All this has, of course, in it much more of the chivalry of the Christian service than is found in training the youth of a family, and in the silent and gentle cares of the home-walks of life. But after all, in some aspects this work is higher than that. It comes at a more advanced stage of human progress. After Paganism is abolished, what then? After the idols are thrown to the moles and to the bats, what then? Then there must still be the Christian nurture, the raising up of families in the fear of the Lord—*i.e. the keeping of the ground that has been won*, and the covering of it all over with the beauty and the affluence of a Christian vegetation. This is a calmer, but in some respects it is a higher work. Indeed, unless this work is done with increasing thoroughness and effect, one fails to see very clearly how this world is ever to be won and held for God. If the struggle is to be perpetually renewed—if no territory is to be won and *kept* by Christ—how is the world to be His at last? If the children are not to be born in His kingdom, and reared in His nurture, how is *the race* to rise to serve Him? Surely if there is a field in all the world where we may look with confidence to the springing of the seed sown in faith, that field is the Christian family. If promises are fulfilled anywhere they will be fulfilled there. When God is weary of His own Fatherhood He will forget ours. When He forgets to give His consolations, and His tender mercies, and His pity—He will forget the mother's cares and tears and prayers. When He looks no more on His own dear Son with joy and love, He will cease to care that you follow yours with hopes and benedictions and prayers.

To despond in the midst of such divine influences; with such promises; with the spirit of adoption in your heart; with the brotherhood of Christ revealed; and with the Fatherhood of God over you; it would be almost like feeling despondency in Heaven! No! I will not be cast down. I will trust my children where I trust myself. I bring the little boy, the little girl, the youth, the maiden, to Jesus, "that He may teach them." I must have them in the house; I cannot leave them out in the cold! I must see their faces in the light. I cannot let them stay in the darkness! I must believe that they are loved by the Lord, and that He will bring them into His house and lead them up through its many mansions, until they feel that they are for ever at home. Amen.

IV.

Entrance Ministered Abundantly.

"For so an entrance shall be ministered unto you abundantly into the Everlasting Kingdom of our Lord and Saviour Jesus Christ."—
2 PETER i. 11.

(*To the Young.*)

I CAN imagine, my young friends, that you are a little surprised, and even almost disappointed, on hearing this text chosen. It looks like a text for the aged. But you will be the aged in a little while if you live, and if these words are to be fulfilled in your experience *then*, the fulfilment must *now* begin. It looks like a text for the dying. And must we not all die, and be "as water spilt upon the ground that cannot be gathered up again"? If death is to be to us an entrance to something better beyond, we must begin now to tread the way that leads through the death-gate to life and joy. "*So* an entrance shall be ministered"—(the words run) in one particular way, as the result of one kind of life; and the whole course of that life, from first to last, is sketched in outline in the passage which is closed by our text. I have chosen the words at the end of that description, not because *you* are at the end of the way, although any of you may be far nearer that than you suppose, but rather because you are at the beginning, or not far from the beginning of it, and may now so design and shape and animate your course as to come at length to this abundant entrance to immortal life and felicity.

Going back to the beginning of the chapter, which is also the beginning of the Epistle, we find the usual salutation, and after that the first thing that arrests our attention is the announcement or proclamation of an immense benefaction—a great gift of God to men.

"*His divine power has given us all things that pertain to life and godliness.*" We follow the order of the passage in giving our attention first to this. Here is a stupendous boon; a great heavenly giving. Here is the assertion that God has revealed Himself; that He has spoken; that He has acted; that He has come to us with salvation—with life, power, glory, in His hand. You are just awaking, year by year, into the full consciousness of intellectual and moral existence, and it is an untold advantage for you to know assuredly, and of infinite importance for you to accept the knowledge, that there is in this world, and happily in your hands by the Scriptures, an actual communication to you from the Father of your spirits. You have not been born into a dark and silent world. This world is dark enough in many ways; but there is light shining in the darkness. There is silence and mystery on many questions. But there is speech of God on the things that most nearly concern us. The divine communications are so real that they have become parts of human history; and they are so interwoven with that history, that if they were taken away there would be little but confusion left. The history of Redemption is the main thread of the world's history, and the fact of that Redemption is the chief cause of the world's progress. "Great is the mystery of godliness, God manifest in the flesh, justified in the Spirit, seen of angels, preached unto the Gentiles, received up into glory." All this stupendous agency for redemption, all the blessings of a full salvation are here in the world, and were here before you were born—sent by God. "His divine power hath given us all things that pertain to life and godliness." Nothing really needed is lacking. Forgiveness, renovation, strength, light, comfort, divine companionship, prospect of eternal joy and glory, all are given. And I meet you now with the express message that all this is for you. Of course it is for millions besides you. But all this would be needed for you alone. If you *only* were to be saved among men, you would need for your salvation the manifested God, the cross of Christ, the indwelling Spirit, and the Forerunner in heaven. I am here to tell you that all these things are yours, not only as being generally available, but as being really intended for you *personally*, and one by one, so that unless God should name and call you, as He did Abraham, and as He did the child Samuel, you can have no more distinct invitation.

Here, then, is the solemn yet delightful state of the case: that you, in the flush and bloom of your young life, are met by this definite intelligence, by this almost startling message, that God has come down hither from the realms of light and beauty in the heavenly world, where He shows His glory and carries on His highest affairs: down through the shades of a sinful darkness which have gathered about this world, by a marvellous humiliation, in order to reach and save it: that He has come to save *you*. "He has given you all things that pertain" to this new life: truth for your thought; beauty for your imagination; moral excellence for your affections; Himself in Christ for your eternal portion.

Now, to follow the thought of the passage, when you accept these overtures, you become, in the high and beautiful language of the Apostle, "Partakers of the divine nature, escaping the corruption that is in the world through lust." The world is full of lust, of inordinate desire; not of one kind alone, but of all kinds that are possible—lust of power, of place, of property, of pleasure, of fame, of all that is desired by men. This is our depravity. This is the hunger that cannot be satisfied, the thirst that no one can slake. This thing called "lust," of which the world is full, is, radically considered, just the perversion of that immortal principle of desire which God alone can satisfy. When a man turns away from the creature, from the whole world as a broken cistern that can hold no living water, to God the fountain of all goodness and purity, then satisfaction begins. This is called "escaping the corruption that is in the world through lust." Every instance of religious decision is an instance of "escape." The world-prison opens its gates and the prisoner comes out into the day. The world-snare breaks, and the soul, as a bird, flies heavenward. Or, to put it in the form it bears in this passage, the escaping soul becomes "partaker of the divine nature." This, in fact, is the positive form of the escape. The escape from evil can only be attained by becoming and being good, by putting on the image of God; that fair, lost image, traces of which may yet be seen in every man, however low he has fallen, the beauty and completeness of which begin to appear in Christian people. "Partakers of the divine nature!" One with God! Ah, that is it! To be in our human measure what God is, in regard to truth and right and purity; to duty and love and self-sacrifice. To be in His moral world of calmness, majesty, and beauty—not in the *im*moral world of passion, of fever, and of insatiable desire—that is salvation begun.

Let us see now how this salvation goes on, for it is a moral growth; a life-movement from less to more. It is always so represented in the Bible. There is death and life in one and the same moment beneath the soil, deep in the hidden, almost unknown consciousness of the individual; and then the trembling blade of green; then the ear; then the full corn in the ear. A new child is born in the great Christian commonwealth or divine family. It is brought into sight, a babe in Christ, and the milk of the kingdom is given to it; but the babe grows, becomes the young man, then the perfect man in fulness of stature. It is morning, and in the dim uncertain light the pilgrim begins the journey; but as he goes on, the light shines "more and more unto the perfect day." A new racer has entered the lists; he has thrown aside his heavy clothing, he has put himself under the law of the course. But see, yonder, far off, is the goal he must touch before he can be crowned; and if he takes the longer circuit, round and round again, as though living many lives in one, he must run "with patience the race that is set before him." A warrior has just come in to the armoury. He is fitting the helmet on his head; and trying on the breastplate, and girding the sword; and lifting up, not without some difficulty to his young arm, the great broad shield. And all this is not for a review day. He is going out to the battle, nay, to the campaign; and, perhaps, many years of conflict and of watching must elapse before he stands war-worn and weary yet triumphant, on the hill that crowns the whole earthly life, saying: "I have fought a good fight, I have finished my course."

Or take this progress in the form in which we have it here. This new life develops itself by means of, and along a line of beautiful qualities, the one growing out of the other, linked as in a chain; or, literally, led up as in a dance or musical chorus, hand in hand, in a stately and majestic order. Faith is the leader of the train. There can be none of the virtues without faith. All the graces may say of her what we sing of the Jerusalem which is above, "She is the mother of us all." This fountain-grace sends forth all the streams. It is not only that faith saves. It is not only that faith is the first act and quality of the new life, but it is a fountain, and rivers flow from it; it is a stem, and has branches, and leaves, and fruit; a mother, with a beautiful and numerous family; a choral leader in a divine song of life, in procession towards glory and heaven; with a bright attendant train, wherewith she sweeps away to the "entrance" of the everlasting kingdom.

The first-born of this queen-grace, faith, is "*virtue.*" By virtue we are not to understand here a universal moral goodness. In that sense all that follow are virtues too, and there would be no intelligible reason for naming this one as distinct and first. The original meaning of the word is *courage*, and that is probably its meaning here. "You have faith," says the apostle, "have courage too. Manfully express your convictions. Give your faith a tongue that it may speak; an arm that it may work; feet that it may travel. Put instruments in its hand wherewith it may operate. Put armour on it wherewith it may fight." For just as certainly as you find your own new life in Christ you will find a manifold opposition to be overcome. No young man can find his manhood, in the Christian sense, the manhood that expresses itself in faith, without meeting enemies—enemies of the Cross of Christ. To go through the world at peace with everybody and everything is to be a traitor. That old word, "Only be thou very courageous," is still the battle-call, and the prophetic victor-song of the true disciple. "*Add to your faith courage.*"

And to courage "*Knowledge;*" in its higher and still advancing measures; in order that your courage may not be blind force; that your zeal may always be tempered with discretion. There is a first general knowledge that precedes or accompanies faith; there is a higher knowledge that guides and tempers firmness and directs the energies of practical life. Go on to the higher discoveries, make the finer discriminations, take in farther and yet farther reaches of the good land which God has given you, "Grow in grace and in the knowledge of our Lord and Saviour Jesus Christ;" then your zeal will be calm as the morning light, and your strength will be soft as the dew.

And to knowledge "*Temperance.*" Temperance means here, and often elsewhere in the Scriptures, self-government. It has no special reference to drunkenness or to any one kind of excess, but signifies that power of self-control which holds under mastery all the appetites, passions, and affections. This self-rule is not for great occasions only, but is largely to be attained and kept by the small self-denials of common life. The yielding up of the cherished desire that the desire of another may be fulfilled, because "Christ pleased not Himself;" the little hardship met silently for love's sake; the ready obedience to a call of duty at some cost of ease or comfort: these things brace the spirit and bring about it fresh airs of grace. Begin at the beginning of the day; you meet the family of which you are a member in the morning. Is there an hour fixed, but perhaps seldom kept? It may seem a little matter to fail in this, but it may easily be great in its moral consequences; repeated and repeated still, such failure will weaken your hold upon yourself and undermine the noble royalty of the will in your character. If you can overcome yourself in this—face the cold, master the weariness, keep the hour, meet the duty, and enter into the privilege—you will gain a point in self-government which will stand you in good stead when sterner demands come. Observe, this self-discipline, which includes both great and small things, is to be a fruit of the higher "knowledge" and the wider experience. You are beginning to distinguish and discriminate? Then know *yourself*; judge yourself; rule yourself; have the secret reigns always in hand. Look to the motives and springs of action; to the hidden ways and forming habits of the soul, and never think that your knowledge is true and good, or more than a vain and idle thing, if it does not enable you to rule your own spirit and your own life.

And to temperance "*Patience;*" or patient endurance in afflictions and trials. Since you never know how many or how severe these may be! How the providential weather may change! How dark the day may become! How bitter the cold! How long and dreary the winter! *Patience.* "He that endureth to the end shall be saved."

And to patience "*Godliness.*" That is to say, this patient endurance is not to be a mere stolid determination to hold on; a merely stoical and feelingless persistency, as when people bend to the blast they cannot resist, and wait, with closed eyes, and sometimes in no very amiable frame of mind, until it blows by—but a devout, submissive, God-filled resignation. Nor is it yet that you have touched the last link in the chain, or seen the last of the choral procession of the graces. "Godliness" is high, serene, and beautiful; but, like the rest of the virtues, it must be tried by what it can produce. Godliness (so-called) might be moroseness—a sullen, solitary habit of life—calling the mind away from human sympathy and common fellowships. Godliness is not to escape so, and still bear its name; it is not true godliness if it has not humanity in the heart of it. Add then

To Godliness "*Brotherly kindness.*"—Nor is brotherly kindness, in its higher Christian form of affection between one Christian and another, the last link in the chain, the last virtue of the illustrious company. The whole ends appropriately in an all-embracing, universal charity—the love that overlooks distinctions, that surmounts all bound and limit, and, taking pattern and inspiration from the fontal eternal love in God, has regard to every creature and to everything, except sin.

Such is the train of virtues brought before us by the Apostle; but there is no reason to think that he means to give anything like an exhaustive list of Christian graces. There are many excellent qualities of the Christian character not named here. Nor does he mean to put them into fixed and invariable order. There is no such order. But the central and continuous idea of the whole passage is this, that Christian virtues and qualities do not exist in isolation; one involves another, glides insensibly into another, until the whole bright company are drawn out to view. And this development of the germ of goodness and Christliness into all the variety of strength and beauty which it enfolds, can be accomplished only by watchfulness, and care, and pains —as it is expressed here, by giving "diligence to make your calling and election sure." Our calling and election is to an everlasting kingdom, that of our Lord and Saviour Jesus Christ; and we make that calling and election "sure" by accepting the grace that fits us for it, and by beginning at once that course of obedience by which our preparation will be completed, and by which we may hope to win at length a joyful and abundant entrance into that kingdom. "*So*—an entrance shall be ministered"—when the process is complete, when the generation-work is done, when every hour of the life-day has been filled with honest labour, when the traveller, having gone all the way, presents himself at the gate—then will the abundant entrance be "*ministered.*" The word exactly answers in form, although our translation does not express it, to the words in the fifth verse which describes the virtues advancing in a kind of festal procession. As if it had been said, "So furnish forth the graces in your life, so lead them up to the gate, and I will meet you there, with fitting ceremony, with harp, and palm, and welcome." "After the war is over comes the triumphal entrance into the city, and nothing shall be wanting to make it joyful. After the work the wages, and they shall be enough.

After the long journey the feast, and I know," saith the Lord, "how to furnish forth the banquet." "*Ministered*," every fitting symbol of gladness shall be there—every needed angel—every beloved predecessor in heaven, perhaps, will stand in beautiful array at the gate to give you welcome; and there shall be the heavenly harpers, and the swell of the new song, and far vistas of a blessed progress, and the sweep of the celestial movement onwards still to the Saviour's very presence —an entrance shall be "ministered."

But again, I hear you say, "What is the special use of bringing this subject before *us?*" What you say in exposition of the passage may be true. It is solemn. It is delightful to those who are in a certain state of Christian progress, or to those who are far advanced in life; but it is not very suitable to us. On the contrary, my young friends, you are the *only* persons, as a class, in the condition to get the whole application and benefit of this passage; you, and such as you, who have begun the Christian life in youth, and who have been going on steadily ever since. Can we speak of an abundant entrance ministered to a man dying in the prime of life, but who has given all his strength to the world, and who is only now, amid the shadows and agonies of death, beginning to turn to the Lord? He would say: "Tell me of mercy—tell me of Him who saves 'to the uttermost.' Read to me of him who found mercy at the eleventh hour. Say nothing to me about song and triumph at Heaven's gate! I have nothing corresponding to that in my life; *I* have never linked the virtues together, and led them on through long years as in joyful march. I have burnt precious life to ashes. I have covered it with blackness. I shudder to think of it all as lost and dead. If I can get in at all, as I hope I yet may, it must be in quietness, or with only the murmur of the publican's prayer on my lips—'God be merciful to me a sinner!'" Or, can we speak of an abundant entrance to quite old people who have turned late to the Lord, and who, with a long lost life behind them, are going away, through the mercy of God, to begin anew? Or to those who, although they began early to live the Christian life, have not lived well; who have put frivolities and passions among the virtues, and darkened and disordered the beautiful harmony of grace? No. The one highest kind of life is described here, and you, who are young, with life all before you, have the opportunity of making it that one thing, and you cannot have that opportunity later. It is strange that a statement so evident, and so universally accepted in all other departments of human action, should need enforcement.

You want to speak the language of a country to which you are going. What means do you take? Do you, having plenty of time before you, neglect the literature, the grammar, the very alphabet, saying, "I shall at the last catch up a phrase or two that will get me in at the gate of the frontier city?" If you were a husbandman with wide, rich-soiled fields lying about your house, from which you wanted a great increase in harvest time, would you loiter all through the crisp spring days, while your neighbours were busy with plough, and harrow, and seed-bag? In summer would you spend your weeks smiling among the flowers or lounging under the trees, and then on an early day in the autumn, when the corn is yellowing fast in other fields, would you come out as a sower into your own? If you were captain of a ship, with orders to make direct across one of the great oceans, and if you wanted to get into port without having lost a spar, your sails all set, and your colours flying, would you in the first instance steer your vessel away from your course to the stormy north, and spend a year among the ice?

I am not sure that the most tender and beautiful parable that was ever spoken, that of the prodigal son, has not sometimes done harm by a partial and one-sided reading of it. Such an air of romance has been thrown around the poor ragged creature, and his home-coming has been so dilated upon and glorified, that the half-thought may have entered the mind of some young people—" Is it not almost worth while to be a prodigal to realise all this?" No, no, it is not worth while. The prodigal lost, in his prodigality, what he never could regain. He never lost his Father's love, but he lost for the time his approbation. He never really lost his home, but he left it, and it could never be the same to him again, even when he came back to it. He lost his simplicity. He lost his purity. He lost his self-respect. True, he got these back, as far as might be; but still the loss was loss *for ever*, in a very real sense.

And he lost all the time he spent in the far country, and *that* he never got back. What did he get when he came? Everything that *could* be given. A wonderful welcome. The Father's arms. The open house. The best robe. The ring. The shoes. The feast! But oh! how little to be desired is it all compared with this— "Son, thou art ever with me, and all that I have is thine!" Oh, my young friends, be wise. Begin the life-work in the morning. Do it honestly; fully; without scamping it; without leaving it; without wearying in it; and your reward will be the highest and best—such as you can find *only* so.

I tell you again, if you want abundant entrance, you must show abundant diligence in order to gain it. If you want your life to be all saved, you must give it all to God. You have no time to lose; you have no strength to spare. Begin at once. To the undeclared and to the undecided I say, "Now is the accepted time, now is the day of salvation." To those who have just begun, or who are now beginning, I say, "Cast the lines of your purpose high enough, far enough. Take the noblest view of the possibilities of your own life. You believe in God—believe in what God says. You believe in Christ—believe in what Christ promises to do and to be to you. Believe in going from strength to strength. Believe in a light that shines more and more. Believe in glory, honour, and immortality. This is a busy fretful age, but find time and make quietness to read sometimes about the golden city, and the robes washed white, and all the glory that life here borrows from the life celestial; or, what will perhaps do as well—read such a passage as that we have been considering—read it again and again; and then again and again, day after day, rise up afresh and go along the line it opens. Do, and be as far as you can, the thing that is here described, and then? I do not say that even then you will feel that the virtues are all in march along the line of your life. You will groan, being burdened, many a time; you will struggle hard for the freedom that does not seem to come; you will sigh for the love that does not seem to warm your breast; and look sometimes with dim and tearful eye for the city that will seem for the time to have disappeared. But you will struggle on. If you continue faithful you will always be on the gaining side; and God, on His part, will be faithful to His promise. He will develop His own divine nature in you. He will see the graces in you that you cannot see, and, as His own gift, they will be owned and crowned in the peace and triumph of your latter end, and in the "entrance ministered abundantly" into the Everlasting Kingdom.

V.

The Broad Way and the Narrow.

"Enter ye in at the strait gate: for wide is the gate, and broad is the way, that leadeth to destruction. . . . Strait is the gate, and narrow is the way, which leadeth unto life."—MATT. vii. 13.

WHAT contrasts have we here! What pictures of human life are here presented to us! What interests are involved, and what stupendous issues are indicated! There is a strait and a wide gate. A narrow and a broad way. Life at the end of the one path. Destruction at the end of the other.

Movement.—Certain inevitable movement of human beings is implied in the whole passage. Our Lord regards the multitudes around Him as all in motion— none quiescent, none fixed and centred. And if He should speak to the living myriads of human creatures now, would He not speak to them just as he spoke to the crowds of Galilee, of "gates," and "ways," and enterings in, and goings? This transiency and mutability of human life can neither be doubted nor denied; and yet, practically, it is a truth little realised, and which requires continual enforcement. In the world of men, you shall find many, probably the majority, who, while they are quite willing to allow the evanescence of human life and of all human things, yet are actually deceiving themselves with imaginary conditions of stability and permanence yet to come in their own life. They are working on every day in the hope of achieving *something* that shall last for a while, unharmed by the great river of time with its waves of change. But the truth is—not that happy picture we may be painting in our imagination, of what we shall have, and do, and be— but this, that we know not what shall be on the morrow, except that we shall not be where we are, how we are, nor what we are to-day. And to-morrow will be as much under the law of change as to-day is—taking us on to another morrow beyond. We shall be lifted on the broad bosom of the ever-shifting time and carried away to the everlasting worlds. We are not dwellers, we are travellers. We do not possess outward things by any title worthy of being called ownership—we are rather measurers of things as we pass ; we inscribe our names here and there as we go ; then others come behind us, read them and blot them out, and write their own names there instead. We are all on the way —we are not stopping even here and now. I see the staff in your hand ! I see the dust on your sandals ! I hear the tread of a thousand feet! Onward and away each one goes, by the way that he chooses, and he shall never rest—not in deepest sleep, not in stillest midnight —for one moment, until he passes through the gate of death to some way everlasting.

Moral progress is also constant.—This is a far more serious and important kind of progress. If we could stay our *spirits* amid this universal vicissitude, and keep them in fixed conditions, the outward change would be of less moment. But the moral progress is as constant, and infinitely more important, than any change that can be apprehended by the senses. Probably all moral creatures are subject to a law of development, growing better or growing worse, and this law is in force among men. There are counteracting and modifying elements in human life of both kinds. The good is not so good and the evil is not so evil as it would be if "that which lets" were taken out of the way. Still, there is a moral issue of the whole. That is the tremendous thing, that each one of us is being saved or lost, that each one is putting on the image of God, the eternal beauty, and wearing more and more the everlasting strength; or losing both, falling into vileness and weakness, although it may be by slow or even imperceptible degrees. It is a solemn thought that the one process or the other is going on in every one of us, without the intermission of a day or an hour.

True, many a man does not *feel* himself to be growing either better or worse sometimes for a long time; and therefore he yields to the delusion that it is really so. Vessels that are in the habit of trading on the great rivers, going up and coming down, stay at this port or that, sometimes for days, trading or waiting. The waters sweep past them, but they are motionless, anchored in the river or moored to the quay. So some men are under the delusion that they can moor themselves, as moral beings, to certain circumstances and states, in such a manner that there shall be no difference between yesterday and to-day, between to-day and to-morrow. They seem to think that they can anchor moral character in the stream of life, and hold it in the same place for months or years. It can never be done. Our souls as well as our bodies are on pilgrimage, our spirits as well as our feet are on the way. And here the question arises : *What Way ?* How many are there to choose from ?

There are only two ways.—The broad and the narrow. Along one or other of these has every mortal pilgrim gone. By one or other of these is every living man travelling now. And when time shall be no more, when all the generations of men have come and gone, and there is not a solitary human footfall heard on the earth, it will be found that each one of all these vast multitudes has come through the strait or the wide gate—has passed along the narrow or the broad way.

Let us look now at these two ways. Take the broad way first, if for no other reason because it *is* the broad way. It is the most manifest and obtrusive, and the nearest to us naturally. Begin at the beginning of it. It has a gate. A gate is a place of entrance—to a city, or a field, or a country. As a religious term it means the beginning of a course or onward career. Being a figure, there is no need to attach to it a narrow inelastic meaning, but it does point to the great moral truth, that there are critical and decisive points in life to which men come. There are gates of decision, narrow or wide, through which they pass into the course which lies within. It might indeed be said that we enter upon the broad way when we are born : that birth is the wide gate, and natural life the broad way. There is truth in that ; but it is only a half truth. It is also true that we may be born in the narrow way, may pass, as it were, through the strait gate in our nurture as infants ; we may tread the narrow way in our Christian training, and leave it only by our own act and choice. Manifestly, our Lord is not entering here upon that question. He is speaking to reasonable and responsible men of their acts of choice, in the decisive times and places in life. He is speaking of the entering in at either gate of those who know that they so enter.

And yet the knowledge may not be very express or clear. From want of reflection, from want of observance of the real character and consequences of things, men may go on from youth to age without being aware that they pass through "gates" at all. They live as they list, or as they can. They take life as it comes ; and they are not conscious of points of transition. They see no gates in life, pass through none to their own consciousness. To-day is as yesterday, and tomorrow will be as to-day ! Precisely so. All this is consistent with the spirit of the passage " *wide is the gate !*" One may go through it and hardly know it is there. No one needs to jostle another in passing through ! No one needs to ruffle his garments or to lay anything aside or leave anything behind; no one needs to part from his companions, all can enter together, for the gate is wide.

And *the way* is broad. If there is amplitude even at the entrance, or at the critical points of life when the gates are passed, we may well expect that there will be space, and allowance, and freedom in the way. All kinds of persons may walk in it. The man of the world may work out his schemes, gather his money, and achieve his position. The pleasure-seeker may eat and drink, and dance, and sleep, and sing. The sensual man, who kills his moral life and vilifies the divine image within him, may pass on unchecked. The formalist may count his beads, and say his prayers. The Pharisee may draw his garments away from the sinner's touch. The sceptic may think his doubting thoughts; and the crowds of persons who never think, who live without a purpose, who do good or evil as the case may be, may all find a place here.

These persons are not all alike. Some are much worse than others, some are on the darker side of the road, some are on the side nearest the narrow way, "not far from the kingdom of God." They cast many a look to that better way, and perhaps some day they may enter it. In saying that there are but two ways, we do not abolish the distinctions of morality. Let them all stand. They do not touch the essence of the truth that a man is going *in the main* one way or another. As a moral being, having in him the element of progressiveness, he must, on the whole, be either rising to life or sinking to ruin. "Destruction" is the word our Saviour uses—an awful word—and signifying surely on His lips a yet more awful thing! The nature given in trust at first, is lost at last. It takes a whole lifetime and the whole length of the broad way to lose it, but it is lost in the end. As the character of the persons passing along is not the same, so the destruction at last may vary in degree. Scripture leads us to think so. But the momentous thing is, that the fact is true in every case. A man who has finished his earthly course, neglected the opportunities of salvation, resisted the strivings of the Spirit, and kept his footing on the broad way to the end, when that end is reached comes into the realm and state of "*destruction*," whatever may be the unknown meanings of the word.

Again, following our Lord's description, we come to a gate, and He calls it a "strait gate." There is thus an undisguised difficulty in salvation. There is a difficulty at the very beginning; indeed, it is never so much felt as then. The way is narrow, but the gate that gives entrance to it is narrower still. The beginning of some great enterprises among men is sometimes very easy and imperceptible. A great palace is to be built. The beginning of the work is, that a man lays a measuring line quietly to the ground, or a workman with a spade turns up a piece of turf. A company of men start for the ascent of Mount Blanc. But they do not go up at first, they go down by a river side, then their path slopes gently up through the pine woods, and it is not at the beginning of their undertaking that they find hardship and toil. But *this* work of returning to God, in the case of one who has not kept the narrow way from the first, is most difficult at the beginning. To every one who knows that he has to begin—to set his whole nature to obedience and newness of life—the beginning will be found to be more hard probably than any part of the progress. The gate is straiter than the way. The most miserable and agonising moment to the prodigal son must have been that which preceded the resolution to arise and go to his father. He found the strait gate *there*, when one kind of life was ending and another about to begin. So it will be with you, although you may not at all have gone to his excess. Perhaps in the outward aspect of your life you are not like him—quite the reverse. But if you have never before been in the way of holiness, and if now you resolve to enter it, you will find the gate strait.

The question occurs: How is this? Is it by divine arrangement? In one sense it is not. "God will have all men to be saved." "He is not willing that any should perish." The way, which *to us* has a strait gate and is practically narrow, is, in fact, as made by Him, wide in its gate and broad as a way; while, on the other hand, the way, which to us is so broad, seen from the heights will seem narrow. So much depends on the point of view! The angels looking down on the broad way may see that it is really narrow. They may say: "*How strait the gate!* What a pressure upon conscience to get through! *How narrow the way!*

Girded with penalty, overhung with danger, ending in death!" Looking at the narrow way they may say: "*How wide is the gate!* Wide as the divine nature. *How broad is the way!* Broad as the everlasting love of God—penalties all exhausted, promises hanging like ripening fruit, and helps ready at every step of the progress!" But our point of vision is not the angelic one. We need to know what the way is *to us*. Christ stands on our own plane of life when He describes the way; to us, practically, it is narrow, and the gate of entrance to it is strait.

To lay aside figure, the gate can be none other than repentance—the leaving of one life behind and entering on another. It is impossible to conceive of one coming from the wrong way into the right, without repentance or change; without conversion or turning. And the turning and the change are the greatest that can possibly be. The *principle* of the life is changed. The affections must follow the principle. The habits must follow the affections. It is a change throughout the whole being: "Old things pass away, and all things become new."

Therefore, the gate is strait! O how strait, when a man sees that he cannot pass in with one allowed sin, not even a little one! O how strait, when a man cannot even take in a single virtue, however fair to sight and fondly regarded, but must see that it is all stained and impure—to be cast aside as "filthy rags" unfit to be worn in God's sight! And not only is the gate strait, but the way is narrow. It is not merely that there is a moment of pressure in getting through—a brief, although complete, renunciation of self and the former life—and then relief, allowance, latitude, self-indulgence. There must be a continuous watchfulness, and a self-denial as long as life itself. Again leaving the figure, that word *self-denial* goes far to explain the narrowness of the way. That is the peculiar principle of the Christian obedience. It is the counterpart or complement of the principle of love to Christ and obedience flowing from that love—the self-love, overborne and denied, the common sinful self-rejected and left behind. The one is the right affection, the other the corresponding antipathy. Love makes all easy and pleasant, in proportion as it prevails; self to be denied, makes some sense of continuous difficulty, and explains the narrowness of the way.

"*Narrow is the way.*" True, it is not so narrow to most Christian people as it ought to be. It is not so narrow to *any* traveller on it as it ought to be. Selfishness is the most subtle as well as the most powerful principle of our natural life, and to get that principle denied, beat down, and rooted out is no easy work; it is, in fact, the labour of a lifetime. One person attends to this much more than another. It is possible for even a Christian man or woman, amid the easy graces and comforts of our civilisation, to lead a life of considerable, if almost unconscious selfishness. We have all degrees of self-denial, from the slightest to the most profound; and so the measuring line that goes across one man's Christian way is too long or too short for that of another. And, I fear, the measuring line which is common, which would stretch across the average Christian life of these times, would be too long by much for the narrow way of Christ. For we have fallen upon an age of harmonies, of conciliations, of great eclectic powers—an age which prides itself on having made the discovery that "the way" is, after all, not so narrow as had been supposed. We have found out that *every*thing has a sinless use and function—everything that God has made. And this is true. We make here no covert insinuation that it is *not* true. Architecture, painting, music, floral beauty, amusements—all these have place and function. But the danger is, that in the universal recognition of this there shall be a forgetfulness of the principle and continuous duty of self-denial. Self-denial, let us remember, is not merely the denial of ourselves in things that are unlawful, but in things that are lawful. It is not only that we shall keep the hand, the foot, the lips, the eye, and the spirit, in all circumstances, from what is wrong, but that we shall keep them more or less from what is perfectly sinless *in itself*, for the sake of attaining some higher good, a firmer self-control, or for the sake of others. Those fiery coursers the passions, and our strong self-will, need to be kept in with steady hand, and to feel the pull and check of a resolute self-denial, if we would not have them become our masters and trample our manhood under their feet. No man can lead a truly great Christian life who does not deny himself in some lawful things. No man can be in a spiritually safe progressive state who does not feel now and again that the way is narrow. And, on the other hand, no man can realise the narrowness of the way, and fit himself to it in will, purpose, and endeavour, without achieving a blessed advance, throwing barriers of safety around his steps, even as the guardian mountains stood around Jerusalem, without rising to dignity and strength, and a full salvation.

We shall close by naming three inducements to walk in this narrow way.

First :—

The gate is strait, but *it is always open*. You come to a nobleman's park, and you look in through the gate. The gate is massive, high, broad, and beautiful. But *it is shut*. You can look through the bars of it, but you cannot get in. All its width and magnificence avail you nothing as a means of entrance. Passing on, you come to a little wicket-gate which opens into a narrow footpath over rugged ground, but which leads up and away to the hills where the light is shining. That little wicket-gate is open, day and night! A child can go through. A beggar can go through. The blind man can be led through, and the lame man can limp through, or, if he cannot walk, he may be carried. Even the dying may be taken through on a couch, if he wishes to die within the gate or on the side of the hill. *Always open*—is this gate of grace that leads to the narrow way! and strait as it is, there is not a man living who cannot, if he will, get through.

Secondly :—

The narrow way is narrow; but *it grows wider as*

you go on. It grows wider, lighter, pleasanter, easier—that is the law of the road. Not that Christians ever cease to deny themselves, but that the self-denial becomes easier, more full of recompense, more the normal law of life.

The very opposite result takes place on the broad way of self-indulgence. That becomes narrower and darker and more full of peril as men go along in it. When sensation of pleasure is wearing out; when the penalties begin to come; when the prospects have faded; when the life is rushing fast to the dark bourne—how narrow becomes the way! On the other hand, when self has been long denied, when the good Master has been long served, then the pleasures arise, we may say, with the moments! And the compensations are given! And the secrets are revealed? And the air is crisper! And the light is clearer, and the way at length becomes broad and fair!

Finally:—

The end is everlasting life. Who can tell the meanings, hidden in the heart of God, that these words contain? It "*leadeth unto life.*" Ah, is not that enough to reconcile us to it all—its straightness, its narrowness, all its steeps and roughnesses? Is not that enough to draw us into it as by the gravitation of Eternity—*The end is "Everlasting Life"?*

VI.

The Corn of Wheat.—Life out of Death.

"And Jesus answered them, saying, The hour is come that the Son of man should be glorified. Verily, verily, I say unto you, Except a corn of wheat fall into the ground and die, it abideth alone: but if it die, it bringeth forth much fruit. . . . If any man serve me, let him follow me. . . . Now is my soul troubled; and what shall I say? Father, save me from this hour: but for this cause came I unto this hour. . . . And I, if I be lifted up from the earth, will draw all men unto me."—JOHN xii. 20-33.

(Easter Sunday.)

THERE came up to worship certain Greeks—not Hellenistic Jews, but Gentile Greeks, speaking the Greek language, and possessing perhaps, some of the Greek culture. The old heathen religions had at that day mostly sunk to the lowest point of degeneracy and had lost all hold over devout and thoughtful spirits. The coming of these men up to the Jewish passover, and their earnest inquiries concerning Christ, are very touching. It is probable that they had both seen and heard Jesus, but they wanted to "see" Him in another way, to have introduction to Him and conversation with Him on the things which lay deepest in their minds. With this view they betook themselves to

Philip of Bethsaida, the bearer of a Greek name, and probably therefore having Greek affinities and connections.

Philip, at first, did not know what to think of the application. He could not venture at once to take them into the presence of his Master. Some difficulty, not easily explained, seems to have made him hesitate. He consults a friend whom he can trust, and, having talked the matter over, they do the wisest thing they could have done—they go themselves to Christ to tell him the whole case. As to the result, there is no evidence that our Lord received these Greeks, as there is certainly none that he repulsed them. We may be sure that he consulted their best interests, and that he provided for their future instruction and salvation.

We pass from the narrower questions concerning the individuals to the broad and far-seeing teaching of Jesus Christ to which their request gave rise. His eye sweeps the circuit of the world, takes in the long coming ages of earthly time, and travels up to heaven. These Greeks are to him, for the moment, the whole Gentile world. It is all waiting. It is all at the door. And to that Gentile world and to these individual Greeks He says, in effect : " Wait but a little while now ; the very hour is come ; the mystery will soon be explained ; the gates of the future will soon open. These men shall see something far greater than they ask for. They shall see me on the cross. They shall see the glory of God —His thought, His purpose, His mercy, His relation to themselves—in my death and resurrection. 'I, if

I be lifted up from the earth, will draw all men unto me.'"

Let us look first at what is deepest here—at the profoundest meaning of this passage, for there is evidently a deep foundation-meaning running through all these verses. Our Lord Himself tells us what this meaning is; dimly, it may be said, and yet clearly enough to us now, when we read the words in the light of their fulfilment. There is perhaps no other passage in which our Lord so clearly refers to the significance of His own death as in this. It, therefore, has a peculiar interest and value. It confirms strongly the subsequent teaching of the Apostles in regard to the mysterious propitiatory character and sacrificial power of the death of Christ. Here, in His own words, before He had yet died, is a declaration of the great evangelical doctrine of atonement as strong and deep, if not so clear, as any in the whole New Testament. Let us look at the particular expressions of the passage, and at the course of thought in it, and see how inexplicable it all is if the great idea of sacrifice be dismissed.

"*The hour is come*" (23.)—The culminating hour of His life—that hour which is to explain all that has happened, to reveal all that is unknown. "The hour is come that the Son of Man should be glorified." So far well. The glory of the Master, although as yet they had poor ideas of it, was what His disciples were desiring and expecting above all things. And now He tells them it is come. Welcome the hour! Welcome the tidings from His own lips that at length it is come! And *how* shall He be glorified? If there be no divine purpose of sacrifice and atonement in His life—if we dismiss that element altogether, and look upon Him simply as a pure and spotless being who has come to the world to teach truth, to manifest goodness, and to gain moral influence over men—we should say that He will be glorified by a complete vindication of His character, by a great augmentation of His influence as a teacher, by ascending a moral and spiritual throne; if not that visible and earthly throne which shone too much and too soon in the carnal hopes of His disciples. But not a word of all this falls from His lips! And not only so, but His express intimation is the very reverse of all this. *"Verily, verily!"* These are the moral pioneers that go before and break up the way through misconception and prejudice. " Verily, verily!" Let my words strike deep beneath the roots of all your thoughts and desires for me. "Except a corn of wheat fall into the ground and die, it abideth alone." In that vegetative process of disorganisation, decomposition, and utter loss, you have the symbol and pattern of the method of my glorification. Without the death of the seed there can be no increase. Without *my* death there can be no glory. But the question arises: Why not, if the doctrine of sacrifice is not assumed? Would it be well for all good men to die young? Would it be well for all teachers to die before they are understood? Would it be well that a cloud of misrepresentation should shadow the close of every virtuous and great career—that calumny, and envy, and hatred, and violence, should hasten the good man's death, and then rage and blaspheme about his grave? Should we call *this* glorification among men? Then how could it be so in the case of the Son of God, if there be not a hidden purpose running on to its grand fulfilment in vicarious suffering, and atoning death, and glorious resurrection?

But there is more here than mere words. There is the actual mysterious suffering that the words describe. It is not that the Saviour stands afar off, and contemplates what is coming—a spectator, so to say, of His own passion before it comes. It *is* come. He is in it now. "*Now* is my soul troubled." We read these words, my brethren, in calmness; but, as spoken by Him, they are words which reveal a present and heart-searching agony. It is Gethsemane already. It is the very cross. He is being crucified. He is struggling with the world's sin, and offering Himself in atonement to God. The corn of wheat is dying in the ground. "Now is my soul troubled, and what shall I say." This deep cry of trouble and solicitude is sent up to the Father. Man has no power in the case. It is lifted away beyond human things. Father, save me from this hour!" By some interpreters these words are put interrogatively—as thus: "Shall I say this? Shall I say, save me from this hour?" "No, I cannot; because for this cause I came unto this hour." That rendering is perfectly legitimate. But I am persuaded that the deeper meaning is the true one.

He is in the passion *now*. The horror of great darkness is falling upon Him. That strange experience, death, which even He has never tasted, is coming near, and with it a great world of gloom, and fear, and anguish, of which it is but the symbol; and He prays to be delivered, "Save me from this hour!" I can see no objection to the belief that there may be here some natural fear of death—the shrinking of the flesh and the spirit from that dread dismissal—and, yet more, the fear of the death *within* the death—the desertion, the loneliness, the suffering inseparable from the great redemptive act in which the sin of the world is taken away, and earth and heaven reconciled. The prayer is thus literal and real. "*Save me.*" So great is the struggle! So profoundly does it touch the very springs of endurance and life within Him! But equally real and from the heart is what immediately follows. "No, it cannot be. There can be no deliverance for Me now—that shall not leave undone what I have come to do. The work would all fail if I were delivered. For this cause came I unto this hour. Welcome trouble, darkness, sorrow unto death! Father, glorify Thy name." The prayer thus perfected, heaven answers. The Father Himself speaks—not by the voice of the thunder, not by the word of an angel, but by His own voice—" I have both glorified it, and will glorify it again." Thus assured and strengthened, He breaks into a strain of confidence and triumph, He sees the Prince of this world cast out. He sees the cross, not as the symbol of shame and pain, but as the centre of a world-wide and unending influence, and He cries, "I, if I be lifted up from the earth, *will draw all men unto me!*" "This He said, signifying what death He should die."

Such, as we believe, is our Lord's own teaching concerning His death. Such, too, His very suffering while realising it. And there is no explanation of all this that is sufficient or even intelligible, except that which is so dear to all Christian hearts—that He "died for our sins according to the Scriptures;" that He was raised again; and that it "behoved Him thus to suffer and to enter into His glory." And His glory has been increasingly manifest ever since His death. From the Resurrection day until this day it has never waned; it has never ceased to grow. The corn of wheat that died has produced much fruit—fruit, in actual numbers rescued from sin and death—fruit in the characters these have borne, in the good works they have done, in the destruction of evil principles and the advancement of good ones in the world, and in the whole progress of Christian civilisation—fruit also which we cannot reckon here, of victories in death and triumphant entrances into heaven—and in the dauntless and unconquerable hope this day living in the heart of the Church, that all the world will be drawn at length to the Cross.

We read in this passage another great meaning, only second, and in some aspects *not* second, to the former one. It has often been said, and truly, that we can have no share with Christ in His atoning work, that we can simply be recipients of its benefits. Systematic theology makes a great gulf between Christ our Passover and Christ our Pattern. But it is very remarkable how often and how very closely these are united. Here, while explaining the peculiar significance of His own death, He cannot wait until the explanation is complete, but touches at once the deep unity of His people's life with His own. He says, in effect, even while the agony is coming upon Him: "*This* is what every man, in his human measure, ought to be. This life I am living, this death I am dying, this glory I am winning, is the life that every true man ought to live, is the death he must die, is the glory he must purpose to win." "He that loveth his life shall lose it; and he that hateth his life in this world shall keep it unto life eternal." That is the principle of a true human life, exemplified supremely in Christ Himself, yet very really in every one of His people. "If any man serve me"—what must he expect? Easy work and ample wage? No strain, no difficulty, no sorrow? Flower, and song, and zephyr, balmy days, and mellow nights, and paths of peace leading on to the eternal blessedness? No. "If any man serve me, *let him follow me*." "Let him follow me in this path of utter self-sacrifice. Let him suffer as I now suffer. Let him die as I am now dying. Let him go with me, not only in profession and name, but in soul-sincerity, 'not counting his life dear to him,' and where I am there shall also my servant be."

Life out of Death.

Such are the terms of the Christian service. Such is its inward character. It is never less than a sacrifice; it is never less than a death—a sacrifice of self, of the lower, meaner self, that the nobler self may spring from its ashes; a death of the whole selfish life—"the old man"—that "the new man" may have birth and growth. Our Lord lays down this principle again and again; it is insisted on with the utmost plainness, so that there may be no mistake about it.

Do you see that young man, the very type and pattern in many respects of what a young man ought to be, leaving the Master's presence in sorrow? He will not be crucified. He will not die. Do you see that scribe walking close behind Christ, and then venturing to speak. "Master, I will follow thee whithersoever thou goest." A noble resolution, if he really meant it and knew what it meant. But, at any rate, he shall know now the whole case, and then follow or forsake as he will. "The foxes have holes, and the birds of the air have nests, but the Son of Man hath not where to lay his head." Harder yet. Here is one who must not go even to his father's funeral when he is needed to preach the kingdom of God; and one who, quite resolved now, is hasting home to say farewell, when he is told that that farewell even must not be said, but that if he puts hand to the Gospel plough, he must hold it fast, and look the way the plough is going, and draw the furrow straight, or be judged not fit for the kingdom of God. Something exceptional there may have been in some of these cases. But our Lord declares with solemn reiteration that no one can be His disciple who does not take up His cross, and no one who is not willing to give up all for His sake. No suffering, no glory! No narrow way, no large and wealthy place! No dying with and for Christ unto sin and self and the world and time, then no joyful living with Him in the pure land of light.

Let us apply this rule of Christian living, *each to himself*, to his own spirit and his own life, with unsparing faithfulness.

It is Easter morning. The Christian world is bright to-day. The Church is full of song. The very air has the pulsing of resurrection in it. But what and where am I? Am I in the risen life? Am I risen with Christ? Or have I never died to sin and self, and the life that now is? Ah, then—what is Easter Sunday to me? It is a gate through which I have never passed. It is a song I have never learned to sing. It is the call of a Master whom I do not follow. It is a feast sacred to a company in which my name is not enrolled. Let me now repent. Let me now take up the cross. Let me now die to sin. Let me now begin to live anew—and the tomb will open, and morning will break, and it will be Easter Day indeed! And if we are already disciples, not the less, but all the more, let us apply the test. Let us deny ourselves day by day, and bear our cross, and accept our baptisms, and drink of our Master's cup, and live the consecrated life, and "follow" to the end.

Then further, while thus severely judging ourselves, let us look around us with a believing charity and a confident expectation of finding many who are following the Master. A superficial view of this subject and of human character might lead one to say : "If this be Christianity then there are no Christians." Say not so. It is true, alas! that many wear the Christian name who have no right to it, and who have yet to get the first idea of what it is to follow Christ. It is also true that many sincere Christians are very defective and very inconsistent. But it is also true that there are many of a purer and nobler stock. There are those who make the service of Christ the business of their life—the one thing they do. There are many who live simple, consecrated lives, all out of sight. A wife and mother for long years lives for husband and children, and for Christ in them, and no one knows her in the world outside. The house is filled with her loving spirit and her unselfish service, and not until the Master calls her away—her work on earth finished, her place in heaven prepared—do those who have been most near and dear to her fully know how like Christ she was, and how faithfully she followed Him. And this is but one instance amongst very many which we shall find if we look for them. If Christ were to come and call His true servants to stand out to view, the number would be larger than we think, far greater than in our moments of despondency we fear. It would be the old story over again. The seven thousand who have not bowed the knee to this Baal-world, and who have not sacrificed their noblest selves to time and sense, would arise at the call, and stand up with the light of heaven on their faces.

Finally, let us look higher still, to heaven itself, for our Lord says, "Where I am, there shall also my servant be." If the suffering, then the glory—the glory as soon as the suffering is over—"Absent from the body, present with the Lord." Death is but the gracious fulfilment to His people of the Saviour's promise. It is His coming again to receive them to Himself; and if we saw this thing as it truly is, we should chant a victory-song over them when they leave us, instead of mourning for them with sighs and tears. Let us at least so live ourselves, in the power of the Saviour's resurrection and in faithful loyalty to His service, that, when we die, we may be able to sing our own victor-song, as we leave the death-shades behind us, and go up among the white robes and the green palms, to wait, amid happy multitudes, until the harvest of the earth is ripe, and the triumphs of the Cross are all won.

VII.

Straightway.

"And straightway he preached Christ in the synagogues, that he is the Son of God."—ACTS ix. 20.

PROMPTLY and without delay Paul began to preach. He was a man whose heart would be always telling him that he must influence men, that he must preach *something*. Now the matter is settled; he must preach Christ, and he begins to do it "*straightway*." Like David, he "made haste and delayed not" to keep this commandment. This quality of *promptitude*, standing where it does in the Apostle's life—at the beginning of the new course, and for the carrying out of the new convictions—has much instruction for us.

There are many beginnings in the world which stand alone, or which shine out in mocking contrast to all that comes after. Many a rosy morning becomes a cloudy noon, precursor of a stormy night! Many a man who starts in life well, swerves and wavers as he goes on. In civil society and in mercantile life you hear the question, "How is he standing?" although the first start may have been good and full of promise. The divine life has to our eyes the same uncertainties about it. You cannot absolutely predicate ultimate results. God can do this, but such knowledge is not ours. However bright and clear the change, however favourable the conditions and auspices, we cannot say in any one case, "Here is everlasting salvation achieved." We have to wait for proof, for the fruits the years will bring, for patient continuance to the end. Yet in some beginnings we can see conditions and causes which, continued, have led from strength to strength, and at last to a prosperous and triumphant issue. One of these, very prominent in the history of St. Paul, is this quality of promptitude.

Promptitude is a pre-requisite and essential element of success. A beginning, we have said, is only a beginning, and yet much depends on how it is made. Some beginnings are like the spring on the mountain-side, gushing into life and flowing clearly; some are like waters from a mossy soil, trickling, oozing, so little visible and so uncertain, that you cannot tell where they begin. But here is a vigorous, clear beginning; here is the saliency of a new life. "Straightway he preached Christ in the synagogue, that He is the Son of God." Apparently Paul did this from the impulse of his own mind, under the influence of the Spirit of God. As soon as he saw his duty he did it. What wilt Thou have me to do? had been his prayer. "*Do this*," is the answer. "Preach Christ. You know me now, who I am, what I have been to you. You have persecuted—now preach;" and he did so "straightway." In giving the history of this very time, Paul himself tells us in the Epistle to the Galatians that he did not ask counsel of men; "but," says he, "when it pleased God, who separated me from my mother's womb, and called me by His grace, to reveal His Son in me, that I might preach Him among the heathen, immediately I conferred not with flesh and blood." If he had so conferred, if he had taken advice from friends or fellow-Christians, or from those who were apostles before him—Peter, James, or John at Jerusalem—it is almost certain that his whole course would have been different. Some would have said: "Stay awhile; keep in quietness until the memory of your career as persecutor has somewhat died away." Others would have said: "Be cautious. Do not commit yourself thus early. You may repent it in a while if you do. Your present convictions may be only transient. What seems a deep life-purpose may be no more than a passing emotion. It can do no harm to wait." Suppose he had sent or gone to Jerusalem to consult with the apostles, what would Peter have said? He who said to the Master, "Not so, Lord," would have been quite as ready to say "*Not so*" to the servant. Not Peter alone, but probably all the apostles, would have advised caution: "Come up hither, and wait on us awhile, and make proof of your apostleship; let your faith be stronger. Do not begin to preach yet, especially not in Damascus." In short, there is not the least likelihood that a consultation with flesh and blood would have put into Paul's history that one word which stands so conspicuously at the beginning of it, "*straightway*."

It was very important that that word should be

there, representative of the quality of promptitude which it expresses. That promptitude saved him from many difficulties which else would have beset his course. It raised his conversion above suspicion. It opened his way. It confirmed his faith. It enlarged his knowledge. It gave him an advantage against any who might be his enemies. It put him in possession of the ground. It made retreat more difficult. It made him a fit example for all who are beginning the Christian course to the end of time. That word will be needed so long as there are beginnings in the Christian life. The first sign of a rectified condition will always be the prayer, "What wilt Thou have me to do?" The next will be to do it "straightway."

The thing to be done will, of course, be different in different cases. Comparatively few are required to devote their lives to the preaching of the Gospel. But every one who receives it must live according to its laws, must breathe its spirit, and must seek its extension. In a sense every one who receives the Gospel must preach it. There will be *something* to be done, which is as much in relation to the past life and present circumstances of that individual, as preaching Christ in the synagogues of Damascus was in relation to the character and career of Saul of Tarsus. Nothing less than preaching would have sufficed for him—open, fearless, earnest preaching of Christ—because he had been open, fearless, and earnest in striving against Christ. He felt that he must undo and unsay all that, in so far as he could, and that it could only be undone and unsaid by as much openness and publicity on the right side as formerly he had shown on the wrong. Any one now, speaking or writing against the Christian cause, on coming to a better mind would require to do just as the apostle did, to stand out and say or write, "I am for Christ now," and to do this promptly with no delay. There are some who favour the doctrine of reserve in regard to religious feeling and conviction. It is thought to be right that a man—even one who assumes the position of a literary teacher, who is accustomed to think and to express his thoughts—should keep comparative silence through his whole life on the question of personal religion. He may have reverence, and godly fear, and the love of Christ, and the faith of His Gospel, and yet never give full and frank expression to these. It is said that such things ought to be felt rather than expressed. That is not the teaching of the Bible. "We believe and therefore speak." "We cannot but speak the things which we have seen and heard." "I said I will not make mention of him nor speak any more in his name. But his word was in mine heart as a burning fire shut up in my bones, and I was weary with forbearing, and I could not stay." "Ye shall be witnesses"—not *silent* witnesses surely— "unto me, both in Jerusalem and in all Judea, and in Samaria, and unto the uttermost part of the earth." Such was the original law, and there is no reason to believe that it has ever been changed. Why is religion *now* to be only a thing of reserve? Why are the men who can speak best on such a subject to speak least?

Why are those who are always writing, never to write the thing they consider truest (supposing them to be Christians), never to speak out the things that are holier, dearer, more important than all else in their esteem? Because some others say too much must they say nothing? Does one extreme not only cause, but justify and require the opposite? Because thoughtless people sometimes talk not wisely and not well on religion, must thoughtful people seal their tongues in silence and keep all dark till the day of death? Let there be no expression of what is not believed and not felt. But if the scales have fallen; if the light has come; if a spiritual baptism has filled and purified and freshened the soul; if there is an open path heavenward, surely there ought not to be a life-long silence, or even a habit of stopping suddenly, in the expression of religious truth or emotion. A far nobler habit is that of which we have the example in him who "*straightway*" made known his faith, and preached the Saviour who had found him.

If this principle be true, it is applicable all down the scale; not to great men only, but to every man. Each man ought, in his own measure and in his own way, to do the like. For a quiet man to speak in conversation, is as much as for a public man to write. For one man to offer prayer in a house, would be more than for another to preach in a pulpit. Or with some, a change of habit and life may be the most expressive thing they can say or do. The question as to the form which the duty of the new state shall take is a question which one can never settle for another. But the principle is this—that there is to every one *something* to be done, by look, or speech, or action, or habit—or all of these together—to be done for Christ as soon as you believe in Him; and that that thing ought to be done without delay. "Straightway" do what thy hand findeth to do! It may be less or more. It may be in public or in private. It may be a thing or a course that may be commented on by others, or that will be passed over in silence. These are minor matters. The principle is that when the light comes it is to be followed. When the sense of duty is felt, it is as sacred to the soul as the voice of God. It *is* the voice of God—it is heard only to be obeyed.

"*Straightway!*" And your new consciousness will become bright and clear, as it never will do by abstinence and repression. Doubts gather around the inactive mind, over the slumbering reluctant will, as mists and exhalations above the stagnant pool. Work in spite of them; work through them on to duty—and they are gone, or only linger, thin and luminous, like vapours that are vanishing away.

"*Straightway!*" And the outer difficulties which gather like the inner doubts, will, like them, be dispersed, and you will see them no more; or, better still, seeing them, you will not fear nor regard them, but go on your unswerving way. He who begins on the yielding system, is very likely ere long to give up the whole strife, for these outward difficulties that hinder the soul's first alacrity will hinder it more and more.

There are some animals which will not molest you if you face them, but they will follow you if you flee. We might almost fancy that the circumstantial difficulties that beset beginners especially in the Christian life have a kind of brute instinct in them to attack the fearful and the wavering, while just as certainly they will dissolve and flee before the face of alacrity and determination. *Be* driven with the wind and tossed—like the helpless wave, and the wind will drive and toss you, the four winds will make you their sport. But trim your sails for progress, and hold on your course by chart and compass, and the winds will blow but to help you, and the tides will lift you on to the haven where you would be.

"*Straightway!*" And you will give to your soul one of the first and most indispensable conditions of growth. Children would sicken and die if they were kept in a state of inactivity. A man might be born a Samson, but if he never used his muscles, if he never went out and shook himself, any Delilah could bind him, any Philistine could take him captive.

"*Straightway!*" And you will lay the first stones in the great edifice of habit. We are in a large measure the creatures of habit. Does that make us less noble? Would it be better if we were all impulse and emotion? No. It is no small part of our greatness that we can build our life into strength as well as beauty by the stones of habit. Every year may be a pillar; every day, or even every duty, may be a stone of the living house. A man may thus build what he himself cannot easily destroy. He may build himself up into safety. He may build himself up to heaven. This is the true tower with the heaven-reaching top, the tower of a man's life, and on the very first stones of that tower you see written the word "Straightway."

"*Straightway!*" And you will end no small part of what may be called the lesser miseries of life. For, indeed, not a little of that misery is the result of duty undone—a word unspoken, an action postponed, a visit unmade, a letter unwritten, a sacrifice declined—how do such things as these shadow our days sometimes! How do they secretly drink up the joy of life! We can never have a retrospect perfectly clear, even for a day; there is always something to dim or stain it, something to make us thankful with the old thankfulness for the open fountain. But this word "straightway" put into our life will make that misery as little as it can well be. It will put a man in the way of clear, good, happy living. It will fill him more perhaps than any other attainment with the joy of the Lord, which is strength.

"*Straightway!*" And the enemies of our true life and of the Gospel of Christ are taken at advantage. All their tactics are foiled, their plans are broken, their prophecies of evil are set at nought—by the simple yet sublime plan of going, without hesitation, right on to duty or endeavour. Try to be wiser than they in worldly wisdom, more politic, more cunning, and you will have no success—you will fall like Israel before the Syrians when she had forsaken God. But be simple, true, and *quick* in the duty of the time, and they will fall back and away from before you as though you rode on the chariot of the clouds, with wheels of whirlwind and arrows of flame.

"*Straightway!*" And timorous friends—the discouraged, the weak, the halting—receive, as it were, a new inspiration. Spiritual strength goes from one to another like electricity; and a soul in prompt action necessarily gives it out, charges other souls with the celestial fire, until they too glow and burn with love to Christ. We shall never know on earth how much of spiritual power passes thus from one to another. Sometimes simple *presence* in a place will communicate the strength that is needed; sometimes in this way even the strong in Christ Jesus, in their hours of weakness, receive inspiration from far simpler and weaker men than themselves. Long after this time, after many years of exhausting toil, Paul was going to Rome, a weary prisoner, and some of the Christians there, hearing of his approach, came to meet him. The very sight of their faces was reviving. "When Paul saw them he thanked God and took courage." How much more must the strong inspire the weak, the discouraged, the wavering! When young men begin to preach the Gospel, as Saul did in Damascus, from a principle of simple loyal obedience to Christ and a very real desire to bless men—not for display, not for a livelihood, but for the Saviour and for souls—the effect is sometimes wonderful. I have seen strong men vanquished willingly by the stripling thus, and wise men taught, and old men looking up with wonder and thankfulness at the young face. But such power of Christian constraint may be possessed and used by those who are not called to preach. Only do, say, give, suffer—at the word of Christ, and in living consecration to Him—and the greatest and most beneficient force that can issue from one human spirit to another will go forth from yours.

Finally, let us remember that this word is not alone for the beginning, although it is most appropriate and significant then, but for the whole of the Christian course. We might go along this glorious life of Paul and find the word everywhere in it, or the thing, if not the word; binding and holding all together like a golden thread; or breaking out now and again as a sunflash; or like a river which, however it may wind, will never rest till it rolls into the great and wide sea. "One thing I do." "What I do that I will do." "Whereunto I also labour, striving according to His working, which worketh in me mightily." "I will very gladly spend and be spent for you." Then at last, as if mounting the chariot of triumph when the battle is won, "I have fought a good fight, I have kept the faith, henceforth there is laid up for me a crown of righteousness."

The result is great, but the mode of reaching it is very simple. It is only to put this word at the beginning, and to hold by it all through the course and on to the end, *so* we shall reach at last the prize of our high calling in Christ Jesus.

VIII.

Girding on the Harness.

"Let not him that girdeth on his harness boast himself as he that putteth it off."—1 KINGS xx. 11.

THESE are spirited words for Ahab, who certainly was the weakest of all the kings of Israel, although his weakness was compensated in an evil balance by the tigress-like spirit and quality of his wife Jezebel.

On this occasion Ben-hadad, the great monarch of Syria, is besieging Samaria, the capital of the kingdom of Israel. Thirty-two kings are with Ben-hadad. They are called kings by courtesy, each, perhaps, monarch of a single city; but they represent a great deal of power, and they command a good many men in the aggregate. Ben-hadad, therefore, has the rough justification of strength for the insolent message he sends in to the timid monarch of the besieged city. "Thus saith Bed-hadad, Thy silver and thy gold are mine; thy wives also and thy children, the goodliest, are mine." And—blush for thy king, Samaria!—there came back immediately the craven message: "My lord, O king, according to thy saying, I am thine, and all that I have."

Girding on the Harness.

"This boasting prospers well," thinks Ben-hadad; "I will boast yet more, and threaten more insolently! Go back to the King of Israel, and tell him that his abject submission is not enough, for I will send my servants to-morrow to search the house and the houses of his servants, and they shall fetch every pleasant thing away."

Ahab consults now with his elders and his people (perhaps it might have been as well if he had done that at first; the kingliest king must always be the stronger and the more kingly, if he be supported by the convictions of his people), and the result of the consultation is a just, temperate, yet firm message of resistance: "My first engagement I will stand to, I will hold myself bound to homage and tribute; your proposal now cannot be entertained. This thing I may not do."

Then Ben-hadad breaks forth into wild, perhaps drunken rage, and sends back a message threatening to beat Samaria into dust, and to carry it all away— all the dust of mountain-throned Samaria hardly sufficing for a handful to each of the soldiers of his army and the people of his camp.

And then comes back the message, as wise as it is spirited: "Tell him" (no more of "My lord, O king" now!)—"Tell him, let not him that girdeth on his harness boast himself as he that putteth it off"—a message which, although it probably did little good to Ben-hadad, has warned and counselled and helped a great many people since.

The figure is a military one. We can easily fancy a soldier, young and inexperienced, who has never been in a battle, girding on his armour to go to the field, where he will encounter not only brave enemies, but all the dire chances of war; and how unbecoming and ominous would it be if such a stripling should begin to boast and to talk of the great feats of arms he meant to do! But here is another, who has been in many a battle, and is now returning home more or less victorious, from his last campaign. He has some scars of the conflict in his flesh; he is weary with marching; his armour is heavy and bears many a dint; but he has borne himself well; he has fought bravely, and he may be excused—not for boasting in an evil sense of the term—but he may be excused if, on throwing off his harness, he speaks with some pride and joy of hard-fought and well-won fields, and of the conquered and captive foe.

First of all, this text, with its historic connections, may well admonish us, generally, *as to the justice and rectitude of our plans.* It may give us with effect this plain teaching: that we ought to undertake nothing on our own responsibility which we cannot justify and defend. This great Syrian king is engaged in a wrong thing. He has no right to be here at the gates of Samaria—no more right than a man would have to thunder at his neighbour's door, and demand his neighbour's property. A nation is like a house; and great kings, with their armies, have been, in too many instances, really nothing better than gigantic housebreakers. It *may* sometimes, for a wider good, be right to subdue a nation by force, and to annex it or absorb it. But this is not to be done simply at the prompting of ambition or tyrannical self-will. Reason sufficient must be given for it; and the accomplishment of the purpose should, if possible, be peaceful, not violent. Palestine was little among the kingdoms, especially small by contrast, as it lay between the two great empires of Egypt and Assyria. But her right to live separately was God-given, and, indeed, was amply made out on the lower human grounds. An old author says, commenting on this passage, "Thus a great dog worrieth a less, only because he is bigger and stronger;" this however, is hardly just to the great dog, which very seldom, in point of fact, does worry the less without considerable provocation. Would that great kings and great nations had always the magnanimity of the great animals!

The point for us as individuals is—that rectitude should lie at the basis of all our express undertakings. There are many things in which we must act, but with greatly qualified and modified responsibility; and some of the finest questions in our moral life, and the most difficult of clear settlement, arise in connection with joint action. The servant is not the keeper of the master's conscience, although, of course, he is bound to keep his own, and never do what would be *to him* a wrong thing. The single member of a company, or government, or society, cannot be expected to charge himself with more than his own share of the joint responsibility, and must yield to the will of the majority for the accomplishment of common ends, or must withdraw. If each individual will must rule in everything, there could be no joint action. But all this makes it the more needful that in those matters in which our responsibility is sole, the things which we ourselves expressly initiate, control, or conduct, *rightness* should be the foundation and the prevailing element. We ought to be able to say concerning our schemes, plans, or endeavours: "This thing is the fruit of my thought, and I can justify it. This thing I have initiated, and I mean, if God will, to finish it, for it is right. This is the fulfilment of my heart's desire, and I am thankful for it." Live so, and you will not ever be in Ben-hadad's evil case.

But now, supposing a thing to be right in itself, so far as the individual can judge—a thing not only justifiable in his esteem, but well worth proposing and doing—in what spirit should such a work be undertaken? Surely in *a spirit of modesty, and self-distrust, and fear.* "Let not him that girdeth on his harness boast as he that putteth it off."

If at all times it be right and becoming in us to clothe ourselves with humility, surely that robe is particularly seemly at the beginning of our undertakings! We are dependent creatures, and when we are beginning what will require from us a great amount of strength, it is meet that we should look towards the Fountain-head of all the strengths. We are frail creatures. We may not be able to carry the harness very far which we are buckling on proudly enough to-day. Many a soldier sinks on the march long before he has reached the field of battle. Yes, the mere "*harness*" of life is heavy to many a one. It is not always an easy matter to keep going on even from day to day—watching and waiting, and working by turns! Up at the hour, after a restful or a sleepless night! Ready at call during all the day! Decisive in judgment at the opportune moment! Patient amid disappointment or delays! And then to be ready to-morrow—and to-morrow—to go through the same strain of service!

How few people who propose to do anything worth doing find life a holiday. The yoke of life in itself is *not* easy; the burden of life is not light. Therefore let him who is taking the yoke of a serious purpose, and lifting the burden of resolve, remember that these may perhaps not be carried very far, that the personal strength may give way. And if the strength holds out, still let him not boast. "The race is not to the swift, nor the battle to the strong, nor riches to men of understanding." "Time and chance happeneth to all men." Life is full of cross-currents, and cross-roads, and cross-purposes; the unexpected is often that which comes. The looked-for is that which is delayed; and the right thing is broken to pieces; and the wrong thing holds on its way! How many busy hands are there concerned about things which will affect the thing about which *you* are concerned! How many watchful eyes! How many masterful wills to guide them! Individual plans must be modified, must be wrecked sometimes, by the surge and swell of the general forces of life.

Surely then, one who is beginning anything, in view of all this uncertainty and mutation, ought to be ruled by modesty and self-distrust. He that only girdeth on the harness should not boast!

But this kind of reflection may easily be pushed too far, so as to paralyse the very nerves of action in a man, and hinder him, in fact, from ever girding on harness at all. Looking too much on the chances and uncertainties of life, one may come to the conclusion—and especially if he be of an unambitious, or indolent, or selfish habit—"Well, it hardly seems worth while to gird on the harness at all in anything that we can help. If all things happen alike to all—if chance is mistress of practical life—if capricious elements may control, direct, or thwart the purposes we form, and the plans we seek to effectuate—then we had better do nothing, or as little as we may—just enough to get quietly and not ignobly through. To sail right over the sea of life and battle with the storms may be a good thing to those who desire it—to those who are fitted for it. But if one can go coasting to the same destination, always taking the harbours and sheltered places when the storms arise, that will be better. At least, it will be better for us." No, no; this will not do. This is to restrict and degrade life, or at least to keep it from rising; and it has been made to rise. Gird on "the harness." Have *something* on hand worth doing; it is not to be believed that you can find nothing calling for and justifying your exertion. If it is not more, it will be less; and less may be done with so much zest and vigour, that it will seem more, and will really *be* more. There is no real want of agreement between a vigorous decision in action, and a modest humility in spirit. Indeed, we may say that they almost necessitate each other. He who does what his hand finds to do with the greatest promptitude and energy, will probably be the person who, taking an intelligent survey of this human life—its chances and possibilities—holds himself ready for what men call failure at particular points; for disappointment here and there in his plans; and possibly even for defeat. He is putting on the harness, and putting it on with a will; but he is not going to boast as though he were putting it off.

Let us ask now if it be possible for any one to come to this modest, self-distrustful, resigned, and yet resolute state of mind about temporal things, about worldly chances, and fortunes, and family cares, who does not look at all *beyond* these things, and above them, to a higher world of duty and faith? No, it is not possible. Unless we have regard to the higher things we cannot walk steadily among the lower.

Vessels larger and smaller are every day leaving England for east and west, north and south. Would you say to the captain of one of these: "Now, you must attend to your own business. Do not trouble yourself with things too high for you—with magnetic poles, and heavenly bodies—look simply to your ship and get her quick to port?" Yes, but how could he, without chart or compass, or sight of sun or star? The higher always rules the lower; the most stupid, mechanical people in the world cannot do the commonest work, without trusting, although perhaps quite unconsciously and ignorantly, to the great certainties of the heavens, to the things which are stable as the throne of God.

This relation of the unseen world of faith, and the silent secret forces of heaven to every human life, is fully acknowledged and accepted only when that life takes its highest form, and becomes life in Christ. Of all beginnings this is the most intensely interesting. How can it but be so, when indeed it embraces everything? It is the true beginning of life, and of all that life contains. When I begin to live unto God, if I make that resolution and act upon it at a particular time, I begin from that moment to do everything differently. Life is grander, larger, more awful, and yet it is also more tender and more beautiful. It is full of holy meanings now, and rich opportunities, and means of progress and of service. It is an ascending pathway towards the eternal hills and the eternal city which they surround. It is departure more and more from hell beneath. It is struggle with all obstacles, and with every enemy by the way. It is perpetual conflict with self. It is reverence to truth, obedience to duty, love to God, and love to man. It is fidelity to Christ, and undying gratitude to Him. It is an irrevocable vow to be true, and pure, and loving, and good; and in order to all this, it is an engagement to seek promised grace, by which alone all this can be attained.

O what an enterprise have we here! Shall sinful flesh dare so much? Shall mortal man aim to grasp an immortal crown? Yes, yes, it may be done. Put on the harness. "Fight the good fight of faith." "Lay hold of eternal life,"—not merely as an intellectual exercise, but by laying hold of Him who *is* the Life, and who, because He lives, will make you live also. Feel that you are indeed the chief of sinners, and by that very feeling, if it be sincere, God will raise you to safety and saintliness. Feel that you *may* fail in your great purpose; nay, that you *must* fail unless your poor human strength is corroborated and upheld by the energies of God, and that very feeling will be your eternal shield of safety. Gird on the armour so,—humbly, self-distrustfully, yet bravely and resolvedly,—and you will put it off only when you slip off this mortal coil, to be proclaimed more than conqueror through Him who loved you and gave Himself for you. Amen.

IX.

Nicodemus—the Lesson by Night.

"Jesus answered and said unto him, Verily, verily, I say unto thee, Except a man be born again, he cannot see the kingdom of God."—JOHN iii. 3.

IT would seem on this occasion, when our Lord was in Jerusalem at the feast, that he wrought many miracles. We read in the previous chapter, that "many believed in his name when they saw the miracles which he did." Nicodemus had evidently seen some of these miracles. He had no doubt of their reality, and no doubt that He who wrought them came from God; but he was not yet convinced that Christ was the Messiah, and he came seeking light on this all-important question. He came "by night," for the purpose of avoiding as much as possible the suspicions and hostile action of his associates in the Sanhedrim. Nicodemus seems to have been a very cautious man—" prudent in matters "—with a large admixture of timidity and modesty in his character. He loved truth, but he feared ridicule. He was most anxious to be taught, yet sensitively afraid of being committed by the teaching to any new practical course of life. There is every reason to believe that he *did* commit himself more and more to Christ in newness of life; but, in so far as we have traces or glimpses of his history in the gospels up to the time of the resurrection of Christ, he shows the same timid, shrinking temper which now brought him to Jesus under cover of darkness. The resurrection, being the seal and crown of all our Lord's earthly work, and the signal for the coming of the illuminating and strengthening Spirit, had a wonderful effect on the disciples generally, and it may have been the occasion of the complete confirmation of Nicodemus in the faith of Christ. Meantime, we see him amid his first anxieties, his mind dimly opening to perceptions altogether new, his heart unconsciously seeking the portion which it ultimately found.

"By night," somewhere in Jerusalem—in some quiet humble house, with few listeners, probably none but the apostle who tells the story—our Saviour gave to Nicodemus, to this inquiring, shrinking spirit, the high and mystic teachings of this passage.

Hints of thought and brief explanations are all that can be attempted on a subject so large.

The first thing to be observed, as we read the discourse just as it lies before us, is the clear deliverance, by implication at least, on the doctrine of *the complete depravity of human nature*. For where, morally and religiously, did Nicodemus stand? His position is a very interesting one. It might be thought that he had not very much to do to be among the disciples of Christ. He seems to have been a man naturally amiable, of a high moral character, a man conscientiously discharging his religious duties according to his lights, and who might have said to Christ, as another once did, "What lack I yet?" It is to this man, with his morality and unblemished life, with his position as a teacher of the only true religion that was in the world at the time, and not to some dark sin-defiled creature who had trampled on all law, that the Saviour says, "You are all wrong. You need to be put altogether right. You are wrong especially, in your inward being, in your very heart; and *so* wrong that no efforts from without will do for effectual recovery; you 'must be born again;' you must be radically changed, and that by a power which comes directly from God."

Here we have all that is properly understood by the phrase *human depravity;* it could hardly be asserted more strongly, and that it is asserted by implication only, places it if possible, in a still clearer light. Taken in connection with the closing verses of the previous chapter, it becomes more striking. "He needed not that any should testify of man, for He knew what was in man." And *this* is in man! So much of evil, of sinful bias and inclination, sinful principle, affection, and habit; that he must be recreated, born again, if he is to escape and live.

The next and corresponding truth is *the radical character of the religion of Christ.*

In order to meet this great need, that religion goes to the root of everything within us, and, touching and transforming all, "creates us anew in Christ Jesus." It is true that it has been disputed whether this passage has reference to universal humanity. Even some evangelical interpreters hold the opinion that our Lord, in speaking to Nicodemus, regards him merely as representative of *the Jews*, and that what He means by the new birth is this—that the Jewish people needed a great change in their opinions and feelings concerning the Messiah. They needed to lay aside the prejudices and prepossessions which led them to expect an earthly deliverer, in order that they might adopt truer views concerning His spiritual kingdom. We may almost say that the statement of the theory is its refutation. The spirit of the passage is universal and unlimited; the very terms of it embrace the race, "Except *a man* be born again." "Except *a man* be born of water and of the spirit, he cannot enter into the kingdom of God." And the "kingdom of God" can mean nothing less than the whole gracious economy which Christ came to open and constitute, not for the Jews alone, but for the whole human family. The very terms of the passage proclaim this fundamental radical change as the only gospel for men, as men, without distinction or exception.

We are led thus to another thought—the *inexorable character* of this requirement.

It is a law of the kingdom of Christ, and it stands

at the entrance to that kingdom, never to be disannulled. "Ye must be born again." "Except a man be born again he cannot see the kingdom of God." Like the rocks which sometimes guard the entrance to a safe and spacious harbour, these words stand. A ship must enter *here*, or turn back to the wide ocean, with no haven or home. "*Ye must be born again.*" There is no way of going into the kingdom but this. Of course this does not apply to a man *unless* he is going in. If any one is quite contented to stay without; if he is well pleased to sail up and down amid storm and calm, thinking that the end of his voyage is well enough attained without making for a port; rounding the world for ever, or at least until a grave shall open by land or sea, and end his travel in the waves or in the dust; if any man deliberately takes that view of his own life, then this law does not touch him. But if he desires to "see the kingdom of God," and to enter in, he "must be born again." That law will not bend, it will not break, it will not stand out of the way. It is inexorable.

A man comes, strong in life's integrities, who has never consciously done an act of injustice, never violated the code of honour, whose word is as good as his bond, and he says, "I want to enter into the kingdom of God." He sees the gate open, but the law shines out above it. "Ye must be born again." Another comes radiant with social charities, in whose tongue is the law of kindness, and from whose hands drop continually its precious gifts; whose heart has been a thousand times melted to pity in scenes of distress, and he too desires to enter. Again the gate opens, for it is shut to none—all who turn away from it, turn from an open gate—but again the words stand revealed, "Ye must be born again." Yet another comes who is not only just and generous, but religious according to his own ideas. He sometimes reads his Bible, he professes to accept its teachings, and he more or less attends on the services of religion. On him also, as he would enter, the law flashes out like lightning from heaven. "Ye must be born again,"—you as much as the others. Not integrity, honour, kindness, not the charities of life, nor religious observances, beautiful and good as all these are, so far as they go, —not any of these, nor all of them combined, constitute fitness for this kingdom of God. These virtues, however deep they may seem to go in a man's life, *do not go far enough*, and they leave untouched its centre and essence. The question may be asked, "Can a man be more than just?" No. But he can have the principle of justice so raised and rectified that it shall apply to divine as well as to human relations, to God as well as to man. "Can a man be more than loving and tender, according to the measure of his susceptibility?" No. But he can love Christ and all men for Christ's sake, and then his charities will be quite other and higher. "Can a man do wrong in attending to religious ordinances?" No. But only by accepting Christ's grace of regeneration can he worship God in spirit and in truth.

If God had not given us any revelation of Himself, if He had not spoken to us and made us acquainted with the relationship which we hold to Him, the case would have been different. But as it stands now, although such knowledge is forced upon no man, and although it is quite possible for a man so to warp his reason and darken his spiritual sight that he shall not see and acknowledge the revelation, yet *the fact* that it is given remains. At the root of all virtue, and behind all human claims, there is the claim of God on the love and worship of the creatures He has made. A just man who "robs God!" The angels surely wonder at the solecism. A tender-hearted man who has no love for Jesus Christ! There must be a central hardness beneath all his tenderness. A religious man who expects to get into the kingdom of God by virtue of outward observances! He utterly mistakes its nature. It is a spiritual kingdom, and all its subjects must be spiritual men, born anew by the spirit of God.

Although this law is itself radical and inexorable, *there is nothing uniform or unchangeable as to times and modes of its fulfilment.*
In these there may be, and indeed there is, endless variety. As it is well not to fall short of the teaching of Scripture, it is also well not to go beyond it. And there is a constant tendency to do this—to be, so to say, more scriptural than the Scriptures. In this matter of regeneration or conversion, nothing can be firmer and clearer than the law, nothing wider and more unlimited

than the mode. It may be thus or thus: by love or fear, with great difficulty or with marvellous ease, slowly or quickly, unconsciously almost, or with agonies and birth-throes of the soul. It is one and the same process, but it is accomplished in many different ways. Here men have always been apt to intrude into God's sole province, and to lay down certain modes and systems which He does not acknowledge. Men have reasoned, that because conversion in certain well-known instances was effected in a particular way, it must always be in that way, or in some way like that. The Philippian jailer was converted in an agony of concern and fear, and therefore some are apt to think that there can be no gracious work in a man's soul unless it be shaken with a kind of moral earthquake. And it is so in some instances, but we have no intimation in the New Testament that this experience is to be the sole type for all others. It will be instructive to many, but there will be many more to whom it will have little or no adaptation. Paul was converted by shining light and by the Master's voice; and, therefore, there has been a craving for sudden arrests and extraordinary sensations, and a clear transition in some short period of time out of the darkness into the light. But we are not told that Paul's conversion is to be the type or model of other conversions. He never so speaks of it himself, although he makes frequent and touching references to it in his Epistles. In writing to Timothy (1 Tim. i. 13) he says, "I was before a blasphemer, and a persecutor, and injurious;" and he draws the inference that the grace of

Christ, so "abundant" to him, is available for all, but he does not say or infer that it will come to all in a similar manner.

On the other hand, John Bunyan and some saints of his time were long in spiritual fear and trouble, much and heavily exercised with terrors of the law, and wrath of God, and burdens of sin, and alternating hope and fear; getting gleams of light to-day and covered with clouds of darkness to-morrow; and so working on wearily to the daylight of assured peace and joy. Therefore some have regarded with considerable suspicion all modes of transition which are gentle and easy, as if these could not conduct fully and surely into the kingdom of God. And others, seeing that divine laws in nature act smoothly, incline to think that the fullest conversion is that which is gradual, like the springing of the seed-corn, the growing of the tree, or the dawning of the morning light. Perhaps, if we are to have *any* typical form of this great change, this last is the most perfect, and it is the one which will probably displace all others in the end. It is the form which is most largely seen in Christian families and in Christian congregations. But the truth is that no one of these varying forms is to be considered as a model for us. The only model we have by which to frame and inspire our life is Jesus Christ, who was never converted, "who did no sin, neither was guile found in His mouth." To Him we are to conform. We are to grow up into Him in all things. But we may do this in many ways. There are certain acts of the mind

Nicodemus—the Lesson by Night.

which are common to all believers in coming to Christ, and in which there will be substantial agreement and unity. And yet, circumstantially, there are ten thousand ways of coming. The thing itself is the same in each case, and the law regarding its necessity is inexorable. But in the modes of its accomplishment there is as much difference as there is in human faces or histories.

If this fact is realised, it ought to suggest some very serious thoughts. It is a sublime and solemn thing to stand so alone, where none ever stood before, and where none will ever stand again. No man since the world began has had your individuality, your circumstances, your history. You are treading your immortal way *alone*, and of the people there are none with you. No doubt there are large bands of fellow-travellers near, and a great cloud of witnesses, but on your individual way there no footmarks but your own. We are so related that we can mightily help each other. We are so isolated that each is saved alone. And the experience of each has something in it which does not belong to the experience of any other. Your conversion to God may be in any way that He has appointed, and that is suitable to the circumstances of your life and the state of your mind. But remember, it must be *your* conversion. This liberty as to mode is not a loophole of retreat, it is a serious and affecting call to a deeper consideration. You must say to yourself: "It is *I* who must think. It is I who must feel. It is I who must turn and come to God through Jesus Christ. When the thoughts and fears, the doubts and struggles, of other men, the living or the dead, are thrown over to me (in kindness by those who would help me); when it is said to me, 'Take these and wear them and you will get through more easily,' I may be obliged to answer, 'They do not fit—some of them not at all; none of them perfectly.' I cannot doubt exactly the doubts of another mind; I cannot weep the tears that have streamed from other eyes; I cannot catch the *very* flame of love which has burned in another heart. I am alone! Every onward step I take is as if on a surface of untrodden snow. I must be the more careful to have Divine companionship, to turn to God indeed."

This great change is very blessed.—Great happiness will accrue to a man when it is accomplished, and when he is living the new life in Christ. It is, indeed, a most blessed thing that such a change is possible, still more that it is realised in actual fact, that it occurs in cases around us, that God thus comes to dwell with man, that His spirit touches and transforms human spirits, that men become "new creatures in Christ Jesus." These are great and good things. We have used the word "*must*" very often here, because it stands strongly in the passage, but now let us put another in its stead, and read "Ye *may* be born again." Does not that give us a new and more luminous aspect of the case? Why should we look upon the new birth only as a stern necessity? Why not regard it as a glorious privilege? For so indeed it is. It is by far the most beneficent change that takes place under the sun. It is the seed of all virtue, the starting-point of an endless progress, the first outburst of the living water "springing up into everlasting life." It is described as "seeing" or "entering" into a kingdom, the great kingdom of which God is the King. It begins on earth as a kingdom of "righteousness and peace and joy in the Holy Ghost." That alone might well be enough, but it opens into other worlds and stretches far away into a vast infinity. Death is only a gate in it, and the Lord of the kingdom holds the key. Sorrow is but a cloud on its sky, and He who is "light" will melt it all away. This kingdom has "thrones" on which conquerors shall sit, and "cities" which faithful souls shall rule, and wide realms for happy multitudes, and "many mansions" for the children of God. There is rest there for the weary, and work for the strong, and knowledge for open minds, and love for regenerated hearts. To be "born again" is to enter into that kingdom, and is that a matter for sorrow and reluctance? Is that a thing to which we must always apply an inexorable *must*? Ought we not rather to write over its gates a bright and joyful "*may*"? *I may* come in to receive all this. I may be a citizen and a subject here, and go no more out for ever.

Or take that other and more central figure of the passage, "being born again." Surely the very ingenuity of unbelief can make nothing dark or sorrowful out of that! If we are born, then, we have parental care, and God is father and mother to all His people; and His hand will lead us, and His stores will be opened to us, and we shall wear His image. Chastisement will be a proof of love and a mark of sonship, and the great inheritance will be ours, we shall be "heirs of God and joint heirs with Christ." And I may be born to all that! There is no doctrine like this in all the world, and, as a fact, it wins the notice of the heavenly hosts. "*Born again!*" Philosophy tells me that I must *think again* and be wiser; and I think and think—until my brain is giddy and the universe seems to darken, and God is still far away. Morality tells me that I must *act again*, and be more virtuous and more sincere; and I whip my conscience and nerve my will and try to bring up all my powers to the sacred task. But I make little way, or if I seem to make way for a little time, it is strangely lost again. Philanthropy tells me that I must *feel again* with quicker sympathy and open deeper fountains of benevolence and tears. But in that I fail, I cannot make myself feel; in the very presence of suffering I can be cold, and sometimes I am in no little danger of having a hardened heart. Priesthood or priestcraft tells me that I must *pray again* the old sacred prayers that have been sounding in the church so long; that I must confess, and worship, and linger about sacred places, and wrap myself all round with sacred things, and go to the kingdom full clad in a panoply of forms which will resist the arrows of the enemy. Yes; but, oh! the burden of it! I am weary and heavy-laden with it all; and my heart yearns and longs for a place and a Presence where I can throw it aside—leaving sacrament and ceremony, and even Sabbath and church behind—while I enter into rest. Then Jesus speaks, and tells me that I "*must be born again.*" Ah, that is it! If *that* can be, then I may yet be well! That is gospel to me! My heart leaps up at the sound, and my tongue begins to sing. Now I see some light in the darkness, some gleamings of glory through the mist. I now have hope, for—although I am a poor prisoner far in the inner prison of sin, where philosophy can flash no light and morality give no strength, and all the world can bring no deliverance—there is an angel at the door beckoning me to come, and my chains are falling off, and I will arise straightway and go forth into the liberty that is won for me. *I may be born again!* Then I can throw off the old slough of sin ; I can have the root of bitterness taken all away. In one word, and dropping all figure, I can now live my proper life. It is for this I was made. For this cause was I born, and to this end came I into the world that I might be born again, that the image of God might shine in me once more.

May we not say (as the Queen of Sheba said to King Solomon) to Him who is greater than Solomon, when we see His kingdom, and the meat of His table, and the sitting of His servants, and the attendance of His ministers and their apparel, and the ascent by which they are all going up to the house of the Lord in the heavens : " It was a true report that we heard in our own land. Howbeit we believed not the words until we came and our own eyes had seen it; and behold, the half was not told us. Happy are Thy men, and happy are Thy servants which stand continually before Thee!" Yes, and these servants rise up and tell us that they are blessed; that their life in Christ, while it is the noblest, is by far the sweetest they have ever known, and that the Christian service, although it calls to earnest toil and strife, is yet a land of rest and liberty.

Come, Holy Spirit, Author of this divine life, brood in all our hearts, create us anew in Christ Jesus. Blow like the wind through our secret soul; and, although we may not trace Thy coming or Thy going, may we feel Thy presence and be sealed by Thee unto the day of redemption!

X.

Come with Us.

"And Moses said unto Hobab, the son of Raguel the Midianite, Moses' father-in-law, We are journeying unto the place of which the Lord said, I will give it you : come thou with us, and we will do thee good : for the Lord hath spoken good concerning Israel."— NUMBERS x. 29.

(For the New Year.)

IT is a long time since these two men thus talked together in the wilderness, and yet how fresh their words are and how full of instruction! Hobab is brother-in-law to Moses. His father Jethro had returned, after visiting Moses, to his own land. Whether Hobab was with him on that occasion, and stayed behind till now, or whether he came afterwards, making a visit to his brother-in-law and the wonderful people he was leading through the desert, does not appear. At any rate he is here now, and this is their conversation. Moses asks him to go with them through the wilderness to the land of promise, and supports the request by the assurance that they would do him good if he went. The meaning is that they would give him a share in the best of their own fortunes, and that these fortunes were not uncertain but sure. Hobab thinks of kindred and home, and says in reply to Moses: "Nay, I will not go; but I will depart to mine own land, and to my kindred." Then Moses entreats, and makes appeal to another and a nobler principle of his nature, and says, in effect: "If you will not come with us for the good we can do to you, come with us for the good you can do to us. We are to encamp in the wilderness where we are strangers, but where you are comparatively at home. Be to us instead of eyes. You know all the ways of the wilderness,—the camping-places, the springs, the oases, the plots of pasture that lie up among the mountains or buried out of sight in the valleys. The cloud will show us where to rest, but we still need 'eyes' to look about us in the resting-place and discover what is there."

Here, as always, there is beautiful union of the natural with the supernatural. Divine providence and human care and energy are joined together. The cloud of God moves, and the eyes and feet of men are busy, and the will of God and the safety of man are wrought out as the result. What Hobab decided to do we are not told here, but there are pretty strong reasons for thinking that Moses prevailed and that he went with them. Be that as it may, the words are very appropriate as the expression of the desire and prayer of the true Israel towards those who are about them, related to them by natural ties, by neighbourhood, or by religious association in worship; who are about them and yet not going with them; lingering, hesitating, uncertain, drawn by the world, and sometimes, when Israel is moving on and away, setting face in another direction: "Come thou with us and we will do thee good, for the Lord hath spoken good concerning Israel."

"Come thou with us." Whither? Israel was going quite through the wilderness into Canaan, the land of promise. Israel of the spirit is going through earth and time to heaven. When the Church says "Come thou with us" to any who are hesitating and undecided, her face is heavenwards, her movement is in that way; she holds in her hand the roll of promise, the map of "the better country, even the heavenly," and sees her own title to possession written there as with the finger of God. She is not lured onwards by the dreams of natural enthusiasm, or by the flickering lights of philosophy, or by the dim hopes which arise in the human breast of something better and nobler to come, by God's goodness, out of all this wrack and storm of disappointment, sorrow, and change. These things are good in their own place and measure, but the Church has a word of promise from God, a promise clear and firm about another life, a perfect state, "a better country, an heavenly." To that country her steps are all directed; into that country she is moving her ranks, as regularly as the morning dawns, as quietly as the night darkens. With the rolling of the years, with the numbering of the weeks, and even with the striking of the hours, she throws her wearied travellers into eternal rest and safety. We see the part of the company that is bright, and strong, and active, but there is always a more illustrious part of it, which we do not see, away somewhat in the distance before us and passing in silence, through sickness, and by the dim ways of death, into the good land of immortal life and glory. And this procession goes on, and will go on, until time shall be no longer: and still, as the mystic company moves, and the eyes of others watch her, and the feet of others are heard not far from the line of her march, she holds out to them the hand of earnest welcome, and with looks and tones of entreaty says, "Come with us, and we will do you good."

Now, observe that it is not open to any one to say in reply, "We shall not go with you, but we are going all the same. We take another road through the wilderness, and we shall meet you yonder." In one sense that is true. In another sense it is not true, and is even full of danger. Of course, it is true that men are going to heaven in every kind of earthly garb; in all countries; with all degrees of knowledge, from that of the mere child to that of the sage; in every variety of outward form and usage; but depend upon it there is some root principle common to them all, there is some essential thing held in the faith, and in the heart of every heavenward pilgrim on the earth. There *is* one way marked by each traveller's foot; men may not rise up dogmatically and authoritatively to define it to each other and to the world; but the true-hearted feel it; the traveller knows, clearly or dimly, that he is on the living way. There is a repentance that needeth not to be repented of; there is a saving faith; there is a holy purifying love; there is a filial spirit in the bosom of every home-going child; there is a conscience, and a moral discipline, and an effort, and an aim, what we may call a "spirit of life in Christ Jesus" making free from "law of sin and death," which are common to all who are in the way.

This is the wilderness journey in which we ask your company when we say "Come with us." It is a journey of faith, self-denial, discipline, and honour; it is a certain moral course which, by Christ Jesus, we take through life; it is a grand moral object and end after which we strive in all this wilderness way and work. And this is really the essential thing; it is not of much use to feed our fancy with realistic pictures of heaven; they must always come far below the sublime and glorious thing which they try to represent, and, when pushed to any figurative excess, they even do harm. They sensualise as well as sublimate the future life. They make heaven only a larger and more comfortable earth. I do not say that there may not be truth here also. There is a new earth lying sleeping under the mask of this old world, and, if we were all in full newness of life, perhaps we might be able to slip off the mask and gaze upon the hidden beauty. There is a new heaven hanging in the sky above our heads, and some day it may shine down through the murky vapours, like the very smile of God.

Let it be so. Still the way to heaven here or heaven beyond, is the wilderness way where God's people walk, and it is really of far more importance to be on that way, led by spirit and truth, if not by cloud and fire, than to have any particular views of what is to come after it is trodden to the end. We can well afford to postpone any further definitising of our conceptions of heaven, locally and sentiently considered, if only we throw all our strength into the moral preparations for it, plant our feet firmly in the way that leads to it, and get our eyes ready for the vision when it comes. We shall soon be at the Jordan. Death, the revealer, will soon be here. What will he reveal when he comes? That depends on where we now are, on what we are aiming at, and hoping, and striving to be. And there is no time for divided purposes, for lingering delays, "Come with us,"—quickly come, lest you should be down to the dark river long before you think; lest your eternal home, the place you are going to, should flash out upon you, and lest it should be, to your surprise and grief, a very different home from that which you are idly hoping to reach.

"*Come with us and we will do you good.*"—It is good to be with the good. A thousand nameless gifts and precious influences are reciprocated, given and regiven, and enhanced, as they circulate among the faithful. "We will do thee good" is no vain boast; it is the everyday experience of the saints of God in fellowship, of the soldiers of God in conflict, of the sons of God on the way through the wilderness to their home. To be with a person in spirit-friendship is to get, in a measure, what he has in him to give away, be it good or evil, glory or disgrace. You must be changed in a degree into the same image, whatever that image may be. The effluence of his life will flow into yours, and of yours into his. The sublimest action of this principle is when the disciple is with the Master, giving nothing, but receiving all, and then men take knowledge of him that he has been with Jesus. But it is really the action substantially, of the same principle when the company of His followers, standing well together in their fellowship, and going step by step in their march, are able thus to promise to all whom they invite, "we will do you good."

It is good to be with the good. It is good to be aiming after goodness. The Christian recompense begins as soon as the Christian endeavour begins. To try is to succeed; not, it may be, in the objective thing aimed at, but certainly in the subjective state promised by the aim. Now, there is no place in the world where endeavour is so sincere and high as in the Christian Church, no place so good as within her ranks. Her laws of labour, her views of men, her sense of God, her moral spirit, her inextinguishable hopes, her calmness, her patience, her prayers;—where else find you the like? Where else, therefore, have you any semblance of the opportunity that she affords of working out your own best ideal of life, and reaching, when life here is over, the best and purest issues?

Come with us, if not for the good you will get, *then for the good you will do.* You shall be to us for eyes, if it shall turn out that you can see more clearly and further than we. You shall come in with your organic faculty unimpaired and use it to the utmost; with your natural tastes and tendencies that are sinless

K

undepreciated; with your points of natural superiority to be acknowledged and used. You shall be eyes to us, to see what you only can see; and tongue, if you will, to tell the seeing for the good of all: and I think this, that if there be one spark of nobleness untarnished left in you, you cannot resist such an appeal. It is not to your selfishness; it is not for your own salvation; it is for the guidance and the good of God's struggling people; it is for the salvation of your fellowmen who may become God's struggling people through your means. There lives no man who has not something characteristic and peculiar to himself by the full development and expression of which he can benefit his fellow-creatures as no other but himself exactly can do. That idea can become fully real only in the Church of God. In many a man it lies dark, and grows darker still as life goes on in selfish striving, and then dies with him and goes to shameful oblivion. For it is a shame to take out of this world a great power of working for it and saving it that has never been used; even to hold such a power in reserve in such a time as this is a sin. "Curse ye Meroz, said the angel of the Lord; curse ye bitterly the inhabitants thereof; because they came not to the help of the Lord, to the help of the Lord against the mighty."

Such, then, is the invitation of the Church to those about her, at her gates, in her ways; to those growing up in Christian families; to those meeting her at special points, as here, in the wilderness. "Come with us." That invitation is given to some who have long

been near her march, without quite being in it; to
some who have really been going with her, almost step
by step, invisibly and underhand; to some whose time
of decision has only just come. In her name I speak,
as expressing her message and her earnestness. Your
Moses, for the time—I speak to you, Hobab, brother,
sister, friend, neighbour, asking you if you will not
come? I invite you to come with all the generosity of
the Church's love, with all the tenderness of her fears
on your behalf. By the good we can do you; by the
good you can do us; by the struggles and achievements
of the pilgrimage; by the glories of the land to which
we are going, I ask your company, I ask your heart!
See we are near a great projecting rock, that comes out
from the spur of the mountain: it is dark below but
crowned with flame! We shall round that rock soon,
and then have another reach of the journey before us.
Would you not like to be in the company when they file
round the rock, and look up the valley of another
year? Let it be to you as Horeb, the Mount of God.
"I cannot pass that rock alone; I must have company;
I must have the best; I confess with my mouth the
Lord Jesus; I cast in my lot here with the chosen
people; and step by step with them, I will try to walk
to heaven."

XI.

The Parable of the Trees.

"The trees went forth on a time to anoint a king over them."—
JUDGES ix. 8, 15.

(*To Young Men.*)

THIS parable contains lessons adapted for nearly all times and places. A few words, however, will be necessary to explain the historical connection and circumstances. Go back with me, then, to the time of the Judges, more than 1200 years before Christ. The wise, brave-hearted Gideon is dead. After rendering great services to his country and people, he died in a good old age, and was buried in his father's sepulchre in Ophrah. He left many sons, for, according to the Eastern custom of kings and great men, he had many wives. He had one son, who in time became notorious, by a concubine (a lawful wife but a secondary one) whose children could not inherit. The name of this concubine's son was Abimelech—"*my father a king.*" It is said that his father gave him this name; but there is shrewd reason to suspect that he gave it at the mother's prompting. She seems to have belonged to a good family in Shechem, and one which possessed considerable local influence. She was probably a woman of some ambition,

The Parable of the Trees. 133

who gave her son his name with a purpose, and contrived to make its meaning stir early in the boy's heart. From less to more it came to this, that he had himself proclaimed king in Shechem. His father, a far worthier, kinglier man, when the crown was offered to him, rejected it both for himself and for his children. This bold man of blood grasped at it greedily; and that he might wear it in peace, unmolested by any lawful claimant, he caused Gideon's seventy sons, his own brothers, to be put to death. They were slain "upon one stone" at Ophrah, the native city of the family. Horrible as this seems, it has often been the state policy of Eastern countries; the ascent of one brother to the throne being the death-knell of all the rest.

Now, Abimelech reigns without a rival—without a brother left. Yes; there is *one*. The youngest of all, Jotham, by some means has escaped, and cannot be found. But he is not of much consequence. "Let him alone. Hasten the preparations for the inauguration and enthronement of Abimelech."

All the men of Shechem and all the house of Millo are gathered together for this purpose by the plain of the pillar, in the deep valley, as some think, between the two famous mounts, Ebal and Gerizim. The festival is at its height, when lo! an apparition appears on the mount of blessings. The lost Jotham suddenly stands out on the brow of the hill, his form seen against the sky. His name passes from mouth to mouth, until the whole great company is aware of his presence. There is silence for some moments, and then Jotham speaks; or rather, as we might more truly say, he *cries* to them. Like the old Hebrew prophets, like most Eastern men, he has great power of voice. In stentorian accents he rolls his speech over the great multitude gathered below, and he holds them there in listening silence until he has spoken every word he means to utter. They—a great people. He—one man. But the speech itself is the wonderful thing in the circumstances. It is not a plea for his own ambition, for he seems to have none. It is not a summons to war. It is a parable, delivered with calmness and courage; and it is full of wise lessons and of moral instruction, which comes home to the men and the circumstances of our own time as if it had been uttered yesterday. Let us hear it.

"The trees went forth on a time to anoint a king over them; and they said to the olive-tree, 'Reign thou over us?'"

"But the olive-tree said unto them, 'Should I leave my fatness, wherewith by me they honour God and man, and go to be promoted over the trees?'" So begins the arboreal conversation. Here we have "tongues in trees" long before Shakespeare thought of them—the whole vegetable world, the upper classes, and some of the lower too, vocal with wisdom—old trees teaching young men of all coming time.

It is worthy of notice that the teaching takes the form of Parable. It is an allegory, a drama, a novel, if you will. A little tale is here constructed by the power of imagination, for the sake of the interest that it will excite, and for the lessons that may be put into it. Things which themselves, however beautiful, neither speak, nor move, nor act, are represented to us in speech and action, in order that the power of pictorial effect and vivid representation may carry farther into the mind, and more deeply impress upon it, the truths which the parable embodies, and which, in their abstract and didactic forms, would be apt to pass with small attention. This parable of Jotham is, it is supposed, the very oldest in existence. We reach here, in a literary sense, almost to the source of fictitious writing. Not, of course, to its real beginning, for to say that this is the oldest parable in human records, is not to say that it is the first parable that ever was uttered or even written. It is much too perfect for that. Indeed, we know that the parabolical style—pleasant and welcome in all latitudes—is native to the East. Orientals have always made quick interpretation of the symbolism of nature. They have always made the inferior creatures speak and act like men and women. Jotham was understood at once. His hearers caught his meaning quickly; and he was so sure of this, that he had no sooner spoken his parable, than, like a man wise as well as bold, he took to his heels, and never put bridle on his swiftness until he was at Beer.

Our Lord royally used the parable as a means of instruction. The world will never forget His shepherd leaving the ninety-and-nine sheep in the wilderness to go after the one that had gone astray; his good Samaritan on the way to Jericho, seated on his own beast; the virgins—sleeping, waking, trimming their lamps in haste—while the cry rang sudden through the midnight darkness, "Behold the bridegroom cometh." The woman, humble mistress of some cottage-home, losing the silver piece; seeking in vain for it in the deepening twilight, then lighting the candle and peering everywhere; then grasping the broom and sweeping out all the neglected corners; and then, having found her piece, calling friends and neighbours together to share in her thrifty joy. And the kings with their kingdoms; and the servants with their talents; the figtree planted in the vineyard; the leaven hid in the meal; these and many more have given the highest sanction to the fictitious principle in literature, by the actual use and application of it by Jesus Christ in a great number of instances. True, these instances are simple, drawn from real life, full of human feeling and of the constant experiences of men; and in these respects are a contrast to many works of fiction of later date, but the fictitious principle is involved in them all. Our Lord told instructive tales, which all His hearers knew to be imaginary. He told them not in idle moments—for of these He had none—not to while away an hour, for His life was so short for what He had to do, that He was pressed and straitened every day. He told these tales long after he was accepted by His followers as a divine Teacher; when multitudes of people waited on His words; when He was expressly imparting religious instruction to them; even when His death was near.

It is a question sometimes put to religious teachers, "Do you object to works of fiction?" For myself I can answer at once. "I do not." If I did I should condemn perhaps all the peoples that have ever lived, simple and cultured alike. In the snow-hut of the Laplanders, in the warm wooden house of the Norse peasant, in the sunny islands of the Southern sea, and all through the burning East, genius has in this way expressed itself, and men have been pleased and improved by its ministries. I listen to blind Homer weaving his webs of fact and fiction so perfectly that no man can draw a thread from them without spoiling the piece; to Sir Walter Scott; to the poor prisoner of Bedford jail, telling to all coming generations his story of the pilgrimage to the heavenly city; and to many besides these, with gratitude and reverence. But question me further. Ask me if I object to much of the sensational literature of the day, and I answer, I do; with every fibre of my manhood, with heart, and soul, and strength, and mind, I object to it; not because it is fictitious, but because of the evil in more or less degree which it contains, and because it is sorry nourishment for human minds or hearts. I do not object to the stage in itself, or because it is a place where men represent historic or imaginary characters—possibly it might be made pure and elevating in its influence—I am forced to object to it because of the doubtful plays that are sometimes acted, and because as a fact, bad persons and bad things have always gathered round the whole institution. The scenes and delineations in such books or plays are often untrue to the realities of life; or if true, are only exceptional, and ought not to be given as if they were of the common staple of human experiences. Nor does it follow that evil things, although they did transpire, are to be multiplied each by ten thousand copies, or represented to thousands on the stage, and so offered as intellectual and moral food to the quick senses of the young. To be "*true to nature*" is their very condemnation. It is the very reason why we should strive, by casting them into oblivion, that they shall never be true to life or nature again.

The Scriptural fictions have all a clear and sound moral purpose. They are intended to instruct, to inform, to warn, to encourage. They commend some virtue. They condemn some vice. They make truth beautiful. They reveal the higher way, the nobler part. They enshrine the love of God. They shed the light of hope down into the sphere of misery. But they cast no dark shadows, make no evil suggestions, keep no horrible mysteries darkening around us, surprise us with no awful crimes. They help and do not hinder, and they have helped myriads to live the consecrated life, to fight the good fight of faith, and to lay hold of eternal life.

To return to Jotham's parable. "*The trees went forth on a time to anoint a king over them.*" There must have been a good deal of talk among them before it came to that, much wagging of arboreous tongues, twittering of leaf, and groaning of branch. They did

The Parable of the Trees.

not need a king. The beginnings of kingship are frowned upon in the Scriptures. When it actually did begin this is the account and the history of it. "I gave thee a king in mine anger." For Israel to seek a king was to reject the Lord. But it would be wrong to conclude from this, as some of the commonwealth men did, that there is any condemnation of the monarchic principle of government in the word of God; just as it would be wrong to say, as the Royalists and Jacobins did, that in the fact of the divine appointment of the first king, there is a divine sanction given exclusively to that principle. The scriptural teaching is that civil governments, "the powers *that be*," are ordained of God. Men make them, or they see them made by circumstances, and God sanctions them if they have the elements of real government in them; if they recognise justice, act by law, and promote order. The Scriptural principle seems to be that any government is better than no government at all. If a government works well in the main, and is capable of improvement in those points in which it does not work so well, it ought to be honoured, loyally amended, never intemperately broken down.

But the procession has started. We must follow and make part of it, if we want to see and hear.

Now there is a halt before an olive-tree. And they said to the olive-tree, "reign thou over us." A splendid offer, to be the anointed king over the whole vegetable world! We listen to hear the reply, couched in the deprecating cautious phraseology usual in such cases.

No such answer is given; but a clear distinct refusal of the proffered honour.

Before we listen to the answer, let us look for a moment at the olive-tree. It has a great many excellent qualities and uses. The wood is very hard in the grain and very heavy. Insects cannot easily pierce it. When cut, it is of a fair colour, it is beautifully veined, and takes a fine polish. Its smell is pleasant. Its berries can be eaten with bread. Above all, the oil of the olive-tree has in every age and country had great value; no vegetable oil is equal to it; it can be applied to a great variety of household uses, and it is the foundation or vehicle of all the more celebrated perfumes. The olive-tree can live a long time; some have thought that a few of the very trees which grew in Gethsemane on the night of our Saviour's passion are yet left—about 2000 years old. Now this, the most useful tree that grows, receives in our story the first offer of the crown. Let us hear the answer. "Should I leave my fatness, wherewith by me they honour God and man, and go to be promoted over the trees?" "*By me they honour God.*" My oil lights the lamps for the tabernacle; prepares the priests for the services; is mixed with the cakes of fine flour; goes into the incense which fills the house. "*By me they honour man.*" No priest officiates without my unction. No king reigns until I have crowned him with my anointing. No prophet speaks with authority until I have bedewed his brow. What could I wish or have of real honour more than is already mine? And must I leave all this rich usefulness for promotion over the trees? Must I tear up my roots from the kindly soil where I have had my home for a thousand years, and cease to receive the secret but willing ministries of the earth, and close up the channels along which they have come? Must I shake the hard grain of my body by locomotion, and have my leaves withered in a triumphal progress, and see my berries grow scant and shrivelled, and produce no more oil for God or man, and all this that I may be a king?

Wise olive-tree! Keep thy roots where they have struck and spread! Build up in concentric rings, as the years come and go, the hard pile of the serviceable wood! Store the secret fragrance! Distil the precious oil for many uses! Give men the annual harvest and God the continual glory of thy growing!

Can we miss the lesson? *Usefulness is better than honour.* Of course some discrimination is necessary in its application. The prospect and hope of promotion is a legitimate and wholesome incitement to exertion, especially to youthful exertion. A young man who acts on the principle of contenting himself with whatever comes, if only it be tolerable; who never strives to surmount disadvantages, and to improve, as much as may be, the general conditions of his life, will probably never reach the olive-tree state at all. Usefulness, if it be of the higher kind, is attained through long growing and long striving. But when it is attained, when there is a normal regulated usefulness flowing steadily out of a man's life; when he bears his fruit every year, month, week, and day; when his leaf is green, although it may not be very splendid; when he feels the wholesome waters both of nature and grace about his roots; when he serves God and man where he is and by what he is, the offer of promotion ought to carry with it some very strong and clear enforcements to induce him to think of acceptance. Real usefulness is far preferable to honour. If the honour is to come as an appendage to still higher usefulness—well. A man may take it so. In that case he cares not, or but in a secondary degree, for the honour, and covets chiefly the greater usefulness. He acts then in the spirit of Pope's couplet:

> "Honour and fame from no condition rise,
> Act well your part, there all the honour lies."

If he is acting in that spirit, and called with that calling, then—smooth and open his way. Let him go up higher. Attend him with your benedictions as he goes! But if he is going away from the better parts of his life, from homely fellowships and associations, from copartnery in labours with and for others, from opportunities of giving and praying and working, away into he knows not what, some so-called higher kinglier life; where other airs will blow about him, and other lights will shine, and whence he will *look down* on his present place and circumstances; and occasionally, perhaps, in a mood of condescension, *come* down again for a little among his old friends, but never with the old kindly humble heart; then you cannot hinder him; but pity him as he goes by, and pray for him, for it is but too likely that you will see his face no more! It will be *another* man whom you will see growing up somewhere away on the social heights. Another man, who will come down and look at you, wearing *his* face, and grasp your hand with his, once a year or so, but not your old olive-tree friend, with whose shadow, fruit, and fragrance you have often been refreshed.

This temptation of honour over usefulness is one of constant action in our modern life, especially in cities. We see it appearing in the silent arrangements of the districts of a city. The west end for the aristocracy and for the monied men who are not satisfied with money, but who want to buy rank with it, and place and power. The east end for the workers and the poor. The attraction is strong and constant, and the number of persons is perhaps comparatively small who lightly esteem the empty honour and mere district promotion, and regard usefulness as nobler and better. If we yield to the law of fashion we shall be carried, if not into great perils, possibly into diminished usefulness, and all perils may lie in that. All perils do lie in that for English society at present. We have been drifting off for a long time into separate sections called "*classes.*" The movement is not new, but the increase of wealth during the last forty years has made it more extensive and more visible. Men do not ask themselves now where they can live and grow most to the advantage of the city, the state, the kingdom of Christ, or their fellowmen ; but where it is most honourable or most pleasant to live. And so we see the process—thoughtful cultivated men moving away from the ignorant; wealthy men from the poor; men of rank from the masses; the privileged few from the toiling millions. There can be no salvation for this country until we have some coming together of these severed classes, some cordial mingling of interests and feelings which have been too much held apart. The organic wholeness of the social state requires continual and trustful interchange of common elements among its parts, no one part saying to any other, "I have no need of thee." Meantime, if some olive-trees flourish in poor soil, in some of the world's arid wastes, so much the better. They are olive-trees still, and their generous benefits are more welcome there than if they grew in a garden or adorned only the richer landscapes of life. Having received their answer from the olive, the trees go on to another. Which shall it be? We may well suppose the leaders of the movement, talking a little anxiously as they pass along, and deciding to descend one grade in the scale, in order to make sure of the success of the next application.

Here is *a fig-tree* by the wayside. It belongs to an old and most respectable family. It traces its pedigree up to Eden. It leads a useful life, and yet it has much less to give up and leave than the olive. "Agreed. We are unanimous for the fig-tree. Come thou and reign over us. Thou hast really very little to hinder; it will be all advantage to thee." But no! The fig-tree has not much, but it has something substantial and good. It has beautiful leaves of deep shining green, and better still—for the fig-tree makes no mention of its leaves—it has figs which carry in them a wonderful sweetness when they are fully ripe. At anyrate, the fig-tree, satisfied with what it has, and is, and fearing that change, even with kindly honour, will not be on the whole an advantage, says, "Should I forsake my sweetness and my good fruit, and go to be promoted over the trees?"

"Wise fig-tree! Keep thy roots also in the earth where they were planted, and glory in thy 'good fruit,' rather than in any circumstances, or surroundings, or offers, or prospects! For this trees and men have been created, that they should bring forth fruit. Stand meekly in thy place, clothed in thy leafy mantle, under which thy fruit may ripen! Thou art not seen from afar; but those who come to thee, travellers along the dusty way, workers from the hot fields, will find thee cool and sweet. Thou art in thine own place and office, and thou hast the sense to know it, and to abide in the same, to thine own comfort, and to the praise of God."

Sweetness is the one quality which the fig-tree felt that it possessed. "*My sweetness,*" quoth the fig-tree, "if I lose that, I lose all." There is in some human souls a sweetness which imparts a kind of fig-tree flavour to the whole life. You often see this sweetness in children; not so often in those of riper years; for care, and toil, and sorrow, and ambition, and success, these things are apt to draw out the sweetness from character and to make some well-conditioned spirits sour. But some escape, and grow on in sweetness, and the relish of their life is good. Sometimes this sweetness comes out into the face. Now and then you see a face in the crowd or in quieter ways, that it calms you to look at. You think "this woman or this man has escaped, at least the bitterness of human sorrow, and has gotten a rich inheritance of sweetness from God." But often the quality exists when it finds little expression in the countenance. It finds outlet in tones, in little touches of tenderness amid the rough things of life, in guileless winning ways; and it is very precious. When you meet one who possesses this gift moving about among rough ways and persons—touching other spirits which have perhaps been soured a little, or hardened by labour, or suffering, or disappointment, with his own emollient quality— consider that you see something far more than merely pleasant, something of exceeding value to the world, of which we ought to be very careful, and for which we ought to give God thanks, as a traveller for a well, as a hungry man for rest and food.

"Then said the trees *unto the vine*, Come thou and reign over us." Surely there will be no refusal now! The vine cannot stand alone, it needs to be propped. It will leap at the offer of a throne, up which to climb and on which to hang its nodding clusters. "What is the vine-tree more than any tree?" says the prophet Ezekiel, "or than a branch which is among the trees of the forest?" He means that it is a good deal less than many other trees in some respects. No ship can have a mast from the vine; no door can have lintel or sidepiece; no hole in the room can receive a pin from it, on which a vessel may be hung with safety. It can only do one thing: it can bear clusters of grapes. Ah! but that one thing is of force and value enough to keep the vine steady under temptation. "Should I leave my wine, which cheereth God and man, and go to be promoted over the trees?" In the olden time, in a figure, God was cheered by the wine when it was poured upon the sacrifices which He was graciously pleased to accept. God is "cheered" by the wine still, when it is used in the Sacrament, or when it is given to the poor in sickness, or to him that is ready to perish, or to the weak, or the weary, in wise moderation. But it is not possible to doubt that if more than half the wine that is consumed were literally poured out on altars, and burnt in sacrifice, it would "cheer"—that is, it would please—God far more than in most uses to which it is actually put. That it should *all* be so destroyed I cannot bring myself to think of as an advantage ultimately. This vine would reprove me if I were to say so; for, in stating its case, it mentions not its clusters of grapes but the cheering "wine" which these clusters produce.

As there are some human lives with sweetness in them as their main element, so there are some with this brighter, racier quality which "cheers" and animates the spirits of others. There are some who seem to distil the wine of life unconsciously out of their very being; they cannot help it. For them to live is to be bright and bracing to others. To meet them and talk with them is to quaff the *elixir vitæ*, is to drink joy and courage out of invisible cups, is to see gleams of sunshine breaking through the darkest day, and Jacob's ladder slanting up to heaven out of loneliness and sorrow. It is sometimes nothing less than a public misfortune when such men are assuaged and made sad; when they are loaded with heavy duties or promoted to great honours.

Certainly, whatever cheerfulness God has given us in personal possession, we ought to keep and use as a precious inheritance for others as well as for ourselves. Life has shadow enough, dolour enough, hardness and difficulty enough! If we have in gift any of that bright gentle penetrative power by which workers and sufferers about us may be "cheered," it is a power to be cherished and used to the utmost. *Be a vine* if you can be nothing more; it is a great deal to be! Distil and distribute the wine of life. Let men buy it of you without money and without price; and when their need is the sorest give them fullest measure, and of purest quality, so that looking up to you through their tears, they may say, "Thou hast kept the good wine until now!"

Now, at length, we go to the coronation. The trees have found a king. "Then said all the trees *unto the bramble*, Come thou and reign over us." *Accepted as soon as offered!* The bramble needs no time for deliberation. It may have gone rapidly through some kind

The Parable of the Trees. 149

of low crawling reflection upon itself and its circumstances; but there is no sign of even this much. It accepts the crown at once. Look at the bramble or spiky thorn of Palestine with its long straggling branches. It has no "fatness" to leave, like the olive-tree; no "sweetness," like the fig-tree; no clusters, like the vine. It casts no shadow, like the oak. It has nothing but sharp, piercing spikes, and of these it has abundance; every branch is full of them—and yet hear how the mean creature speaks!

"If in truth ye anoint me king over you"—as if it were the most natural thing in the world that they should—as if it were looking back upon its past life as one who remembered a long and beneficent career—as if it were thinking of its ripe baskets of fruit, and of the weary pilgrims it had sheltered. "If in truth ye anoint *me* king!" Think of it, in presence of them all! The cedar, nodding his dark plumes; the oak, with castled strength of stem and branch; the beech, in its sylvan beauty; the palm-tree, with its cylindrical stem and feathery leaves, and bounteous burden of dates; "and the fir-tree and the pine-tree and the box together;" and those that have declined the honour—to all these it says, "*Come and put your trust in my shadow!*" The unbounded impudence of this address is remarkable, and would be amusing if it were not connected with peril to the whole arboreous kingdom. This peril the bramble knows, and has the art to hold it out in audacious menace. "If not, think of it well. You have gone too far to go back, you are now in my power; and that the noblest among you shall feel the first, in case of the least show of opposition." "If not, then I can pierce; I can make bleeding hands and thorny crowns; and, in the last resort, *I can burn.*" "Let fire come out of the bramble and devour the cedars of Lebanon!" It has literally been so many a time in the history of this country—in the martyr fires kindled for those of whom the world was not worthy—and in every other country, in Church and in State alike. The best cannot but suffer when the worst have rule. Indeed, the whole state must suffer and be put in peril, unless it is ruled by men of honesty and uprightness.

It is, alas! too little susceptible of doubt that society, in all its sections, is yet full of bramble-men, who are striving for every sort of personal elevation and advantage. If they would "strive lawfully," it were well; but they strive with cut and thrust, and spiky force, with every mean and mischievous appliance—by chicanery in trade, by duplicity in politics, by watching at the doors and hanging on the skirts of the great in social life. When an offer is made, or when an opportunity arises for any kind of promotion, they never deliberate, never think tenderly of the place where they have been growing, or apprehensively of that towards which they are striving. They are ready—they will go! They will cut their way through. They will wear any robes, any tinsel crowns; and as they go to win them, let other men beware! Their spikes are long—they will not scruple to lacerate, to pierce—to take reputations, albeit unstained—to take fortunes, hard won by honest toil, and

The Parable of the Trees. 151

intended for mourning wife and fatherless children; even to pass on over broken hearts.

Do not call this description uncharitable and exaggerated. These men are the product of an age like ours—full of high pressure, and mercantile struggle and competition for the prizes of wealth or social standing. I want you to see these men and know them, wherever they are—in Parliament, on the Exchange, in the City, at the Bar, in social life—in order that, seeing them as they are, you may estimate them truly, and come what may, never yourself be one of them. By the picture in this parable I want to help you to scorn the principles they act upon; and to despise the honours and advantages they win! I want to purge your mind of the least tincture of envy of them, as they go pushing and thrusting along the social road. I want to make you conscious of the greatness of your own being, of the glory of your life in Christ, that when you see them at their highest, shining in such poor lustre as can be carried by creatures so mean, you may be able to say—strong in your own integrity, satisfied with your life of quiet usefulness—and knowing that, by God's grace, you stand on a moral elevation far above them: "As for me I am content. 'Godliness with contentment is great gain.' And as for them, they are but bramble-men, after all! Honour! It is mine; if I bear the yoke of Christ, and carry His burden; if I am living as He would have me live; ruling my life by Christian law, aiming at Christian ends, animated by Christian love. Thus I have promotion all the day.

Honour is my shadow and cannot leave me. I reign with Christ; I rule my circumstances; I rule myself; I am a labourer with Him for the harvest that shall be gathered when the year of this world's life is over.

> "I live for those who love,
>   For those who know Him true;
> For the heaven that smiles above,
>   And waits my coming too;
> For the cause that lacks assistance,
> For the wrongs that need resistance,
> For the future in the distance,
>   For the good that I can do!"

XII.

To live is Christ.

"For to me to live is Christ."—PHILLIPIANS i. 21.

THE rendering is literally, "*To me life is Christ*," which makes the meaning more comprehensive and more intense. Life altogether, everywhere, always, is neither more nor less than this. This is the grand formula which will express better than any other all its force and meaning; which will cover all its history and development; "To me life is Christ." At present we can take but parts and aspects of a meaning so vast.

"*Life*."—The word has wide application. The blade of grass lives, the tree, the limpet, the worm—they all live. The beast and bird, man—and God—live. So that the most diverse kinds of life are comprehended in the general term. But there is a life proper to each thing and creature. In the lower forms life is simple— the conditions of it are provided—the process of it is easy. The great Life-giver opens his hand, and each creature is filled with good. But, as we ascend in the scale, life becomes more complex, more full of parts, relations, adjustments, laws. It becomes more difficult, and therefore more noble. For that is the noblest thing which encounters and surmounts possibilities of failure and disaster; or suffering from them, yet retrieves itself or is retrieved.

The life of man has so suffered, and has been so retrieved. Almost without the Bible a reflective person might conclude that some terrible far-reaching accident had happened to human nature. If you see every tree in a wood scorched and smitten, even the evergreens shrinking and withering, you cannot but imagine that some fiery heat or some bitter cold has gone to the heart of all that vegetable life. So when you see men everywhere—retaining something of the lofty stature that becomes them, and having on them some of the greenness of wholesome growing, and yet smitten and maimed, and withering here and there, and not one shining evergreen among them all—what can you infer but that some withdrawal of heaven, or some furious blast from hell has touched this human forest, these trees of God which ought to be all full of sap? Is it not true that men generally see an excellence they do not reach, recognise a higher virtue than they practise, aim at more than they achieve? Is it not true that now and again one and another is seized with a sense of blame, with a conviction of personal guiltiness in this matter? What is this but the fall, the practical daily fall, of human nature. It does not grow well. It does not grow as it ought to grow. And what is the religion of Christ, rather what is the *redemption* of Christ, but the retrieval of this loss and the rise of human nature in Him? You who are in Him "*live*," yet not you, but He lives in you.

All this is assumed—it lies beneath this text, or in it, and must be true of every one who can use it as the motto of his life. "For me to live is Christ" seems to express an infinite indebtedness, the sense of a benefit received which exceeds all expression and all appreciation. No man could confer a benefit on fellow-man so great as to put him under the law of this text. Say you are poor, and some one dowers you with wealth. Say you are maligned, and some one magnanimously defends you, shows your righteousness, and routs your enemies. Say you fall into the sea and that you are drowning, when some strong swimmer perils his own life in bringing you safe to land. Not in any of these cases, or in any supposable case of help or deliverance that man could give, would you be bound to fall down at the feet of your deliverer and say, "You have won all. You have won me for ever. My life is all yours." But this is what a man says at the feet of Christ. He makes acknowledgment that his life is won back to him in the deepest, furthest sense; and that it has been won at such cost, with such love, and for such ends, as make it for evermore the property of the Winner. "For me to live is Christ." Until we achieve *this* meaning in our experience; until we yield to Christ a personal consecration that knows no reserve, and thinks of no limit, we shall not be able to reach any other true meaning that the text may contain. But reaching this—standing by the Cross, and beholding there our sin at once condemned and expiated; our nobleness preserved; our future all in blossom; our very heaven coming on; then we can discern some of the many meanings which lie wrapt up in these few words, "For me—life is Christ."

This Canon rules the thought.—The intellectual life is His. All the thinking a man goes through, all the philosophy he may excogitate, must come under this law of Christ-life. Be it well understood, however, that this is not to impair intellectual freedom. There is a rigorous narrow way of conceiving this thing which we ought to avoid. There is a kind of religious talk one often hears, or reads if it be written, which seems to imply that Christ has revealed *all* truth—that a man has nothing to seek for, nothing to expect, anywhere else than in the pages of the Bible. This is simply not true, and to believe it and act accordingly is in this respect, at least, to get hindrance and not help from the revelation of God. This is to make Christ not "the way," but the stumbling block; not "the truth," but the holder of the rusty key of forbidden knowledge; not "the life," but the Lord and Patron of a certain amount of religious information, beyond which any inquiring spirit must travel at its peril. It cannot be proclaimed too clearly that Christianity leaves man, we might truly say, indeed, wins for man his entire intellectual liberty. He may expatiate on any field, making fresh discoveries at every step. He may arrange his knowledge and conduct his thinking as seems to him best. He may adopt this system or that; and *some* system he must of necessity adopt, for no man can think consecutively without a system. He may thus go forth inquiring and seeking, in the certainty that he will find; for the hidden treasures are more than those yet found. Gold dust is scattered through all the intellectual world, and those who dig will find. Gems of rarest lustre lie in darkness, waiting to flash in the light of the seeker's lamp. But here is the point; something is found already, which will never be lost; something is revealed, never to be withdrawn. Christianity is a positive something which, to every one that receives it, takes firm abiding place at the centre of his life, and puts itself of necessity, and immediately, into regulating, vitalising relation with all his intellectual findings. No one point of knowledge, great or small, can be the same to him whose "life is Christ," which it would be if that were not true. From this vantage ground he not only can put all his acquired knowledge into right relation, but he can detect specious fallacies and stigmatise errors, and choose the right method and way, and still keep the Cross at the centre of all. Christ does not reveal *all* truth in the Gospel; but he reveals very clearly the highest truths, and those stand like mountains around the whole intellectual world, so that a Christian is never out of the view of some of them, be he where he will. Here, for example, stands a stupendous fact rooted deep in Earth, crowned with snow and cloud; yonder a dim outline of ridge stretching far away; there are plenty of discoveries to be made up among these mountains, and over the plains they water, and along the rivers they feed; but while the Earth abideth, they themselves can never be moved from their place; and he who has recognised them as landmarks for his guidance, can never believe in a geography, and certainly can never himself construct a map that leaves them out. Something *is* revealed—God manifest in the flesh—the Father in the Son. Love from eternity, a law of right through the universe, dark things working to bright ends. You may pluck stars from the firmament with your puny hand, or, literally, plunge the Alps in the ocean sooner than move these things from their place. But, if you are in Christ, you are so far from wishing their destruction or denial that, in fact, amid all your intellectual activities you refresh your powers by gazing at them, and direct your labours, and shape your ends with them in sight—" For to you life is Christ."

We have been considering life as thought. Now take it as sentiment; and again this canon will cover it to a Christian—" *To me life is Christ.*" Sentiment is thought. But it is something more; it is thought with aroma in it; thought with beauty on it; with a certain nameless delicate interest, which flits and changes, lightens and darkens, from day to day. There is a well-understood odious sense of the word sentiment, or "sentimentalism," as it is sometimes called, with which we are familiar enough. The better sense of

To live is Christ.

the word, which is the true one, is apt to escape us. We speak now not of the shallow and profitless counterfeit, but of the true, delicate, beautiful thing. No life is complete without it, and perhaps, in fact, no life is entirely destitute of it. Some lives seem to be, but often that is because we ourselves are too rough, and hard, and blind, to see the thing where it really is. Much tenderness sometimes lies hidden under a rough and boisterous exterior, and little gleams of heavenliest light escape, and go flickering among hard and stony things. The cactus is about the roughest plant that grows : its flower is one of the most beautiful. The oak is not pensive, and slender, and symmetrical: it is a gnarled, self-willed, unobliging tree; and yet how exquisite are the acorns it produces, and how soft the shadow it casts over the field! Do not judge the man by his prickles, by his twists, by his hard knots of selfishness; but catch him if you can in his flower-state, and watch to see how trustfully the child will come within the shadow of his strength. Every man has sentiment. There is a delicate something which plays about every life; and the winter is coming, indeed, when that something departs. That is an awful passage of Scripture in the centre of which stands the phrase, "Who being past feeling." God preserve us all from that!

But how? How shall we keep the poetry in our life? How shall we dignify the struggle for daily bread? How shall we manage to shed through the rough framework of things a tender halo, and live in this world as in God's garden still, although many a thorn and many a thistle grow in it, and the workers are weary and the mourners weep? How? I know but one way. There is a name which you can keep in your heart, and talk of or whisper in your journey through the days, and that will do it. "For me life is Christ." "If I can think of Him, and be true to Him, and keep Him at the centre of my life—that will be beauty, and tenderness, and true light of heaven wherever I am upon the earth." Sweet hallowed name that can turn life into poetry, that can turn any individual's life into a poem! with here and there no doubt a rough stanza and halting lines, yet a true poem; in its darkest parts, full of sweet and high suggestions, full of the beginnings of nobler things, and in the purer, clearer parts, full of the glory that is to be revealed.

I know but this one way. You may read poetry; you may satiate your imagination with voracious meals of light literature; you may gaze at paintings by the hour; you may have the key that admits you to society, or the courage to stalk in without a key; you may associate often and naturally with refined intellectual people, who carry the lights of sentiment in themselves, and are always shedding them out—all this will not put you really and effectually in possession of the true ideal of your own life. To get that you must go to Him who keeps it for you, who shows you what it is in the beauty of His own life, and who especially reveals *this* secret which neither poet nor painter ever knew until they learned it of Him—namely, that all the beauty and tenderness and glory of this human life that will last, spring from a cross, and are so seen to spring from it, that those who have most of these stand nearest to that cross, and say with clearest voice, "God forbid that we should glory, save in the cross of the Lord Jesus Christ, by which the world is crucified unto us and we unto the world."

Again, take *life as force*—active moral force—and the text covers it all. By force I mean all that a man does, the effect he produces by living, his endeavours, his gifts, his labours; or thus—his thought and sentiment expressed, with winter clothing on, and implements of labour in hand, thought speaking itself into a benefit, sentiment glowing into a worthy deed.

A life without much force may be pure and good, but it never can be what a life so much needs to be in this world—beneficent—without that quality. The abstract original force that is in a man, may go this way or that way, as his disposition is, as his intention directs it. It may shine like daylight, or smite like lightning. It may distil like dew, or go roaring like a flood along its channel. It may devastate nations and lay hundreds of thousands of the strongest men in bloody graves, as did that of Napoleon Bonaparte; or it may open prison doors over a continent for the visits and services of that heavenly Charity, who had long stood weeping by these doors without being able to find entrance, as did that of the gentle but indomitable John Howard. To constitute a good human moral force we need far more than mere energy, self-will, or determination. We need a right aim or ends to be striven for. We need right motives to inspire the striving, and we need the use of wise and right means. When the aim is true, and the motive is pure, and the means are wise and right, then you have that grand thing, the full and proper force of a human life. Now if you leave Jesus Christ out of your life, you cannot have any one of these perfectly. This thing and that, this person and the other, may seem to fill His place for a little while. It will only be in seeming, it will only be for a time. Strength will be wasted, defeat will come; and that splendid quality of life-force which once lay in such potential magnitude in the breast—all shattered now to dust by successive disappointments—only feebleness and misery are left to brood over the scene. "Be strong in the Lord, and in the power of His might." Let motive, and means, and aim, and end, be all formed on His life and teaching, and all tried and purified and strengthened at His cross, and then you are as strong as God means you to be; you preserve the strength He gives you, and you turn it all into force, as gentle as that of vegetation, and as beneficent. Your light will shine before men, not like flashing lamp or blazing bonfire, but like the sweet light of common day, and others, seeing your good works, will glorify your Father which is in heaven.

Finally, take life as *hope, aspiration, destiny;* as an

unquenchable impulse towards the future; as an instructive yearning towards immortality.

What *is* life if it be not this much? A shadow of a shadow, an echo of an echo, a poor fevered flickering thing, whose momentary joys and sorrows will soon be all stifled in the silent grave. Without an assured future, no present of any kind can be worth a hearty or passionate interest. In a dismal, hopeless sense (the very opposite of that meant by the sacred writer) we may then indeed "weep as though we wept not, and buy as though we possessed not, and use or abuse this world as the mood may come to us, for 'the fashion of it passeth away.'"

The question is a simple one. Have we an assured future without Jesus Christ? By what authority other than His are we certified that we shall live at all after the breath is out, and this clay house has gone to its kindred clay? Still more, who tells us and gives proof that we shall live in joy? Is there, in literature, any heaven but the heaven of which He is Lord and Light? What immortal life has ever been sketched in poetic vision, or drawn in firm lines by philosophic thought, or discovered by scientific eye piercing through the film of sentient things? All is darkness, or only so much struggling light as to make the darkness visible. All is silence, or silence broken only by subterranean thunders and ghostly stirrings. Surely here with emphasis we may say, "For us to live is Christ." We live in Him, and "because He lives we shall live also." He liveth and was dead, and is alive for evermore.

"Fear not." He has the keys of death and Hades now, and death is to His followers but an hour of sleep, and the grave but the place of warrior's rest, until the morning trumpet shall sound, to gather the hosts for battle no more, but for triumphal entrance into the regal city, whose builder and maker is God.

Thou Lord of life and King of immortality, what do we owe Thee for bringing these to light? And what can we do better or nobler through all our mortal days, than press on in spirit and purpose that we may be with Thee where Thou art, and behold Thy glory, and humbly enter into Thy joy? Come, mourner, wipe thy tears! thou art not far from the land whence sorrow and sighing flee away. Pilgrim! revive thee and press on a little longer, when thy tireless feet shall be on mountains of myrrh and hills of frankincense, while the balm of immortal health shall be in all the air.

But now, *is it Christ for you to live?* Is your life Christ? What a descent one has to make from that life which, in some of its forms, we have been endeavouring to describe, to reach the actual life that many a one is living. The alteration one has to make in the phraseology to make it applicable is perfectly frightful. "For me life is—*money*—the getting and the keeping and the spending, and the greedy passion for it—until my soul is all stained with the filth of the lucre it loves."

To me life is—*sentient pleasure*—which I seek even by day, and still more by night, feeding my hungry soul, if it will be fed, with lamps and flowers and songs and jests and gay moving spectacles and feasts, and all vanities of vanity fair, to produce, if it may be, a satisfied stillness of all the senses, like that of the fed ox in the stall.

To me life is—*ambition,* which moves me to climb, to sacrifice everything to get on and up in this world. Not that I so much value the intrinsic worth of the elevation as I enjoy the spectacle of those who are left beneath and behind.

To me life is—*indifference, emptiness.* I take it as it comes. I care not how soon it is over. These are the kind of answers that would have to be made by one and another to the question: "What is your life?" And do you not see that the answer of the text, if you could give it, would be infinitely nobler and better? O will you not live? Why will you die, and die, and die again through your days, until one day there may come that death from which resurrection is not? You, too, have a hidden life if you will but claim it and live it. Yes, we may truly say a life hid with Christ in God. For there is not one among us all, whose very soul is not dear to Him, whose life He will not redeem by blood of atonement and water of sanctity and spirit of power, with eternal redemption. He came to this world and is always coming, and has come again now, that we all may have life, and that we may have it more abundantly. "He that hath the Son hath life, and he that hath not the Son shall not see life, but the wrath of God abideth on Him."

XIII.

The Blade, the Ear, the full Corn.

"First the blade, then the ear, then the full corn in the ear."—
MARK iv. 28.

"THE kingdom of God" is the Gospel in its practical power, whether in the heart of the individual or in the social community. Our Lord, in this parable, gives a graphic and clear description of the origin and progress of religion, showing especially that, while human labour comes in and plays a large part in the *instrumental* efficiency of the work, the ultimate effect is wholly independent of man's industry and care. The figure in the parable brings out this truth in a way not to be mistaken. Man must sow and man must reap, but all that comes between is beyond his power, and even out of his sight.

We take the order of our Lord's thought :—

The seed in the ground.—The kingdom of God, or religion in the heart, *is secret in its beginnings.*

This is suggested by the parable. A man casts seed

into the ground, and then leaves it to Nature—that is, to God. He does not wait in the field to watch and help the beginnings of germination. He goes and "sleeps and rises, night and day," lives as usual, makes no difference in his life because he has sown the seed. And if he were to try to discover or help the actual beginnings of life it would be in vain. If the sower were to penetrate down to the seed and work in the soil at the time of germination with purpose of help, it would be nothing but an act of hindrance. Life is too silent a thing to admit any human disturbance, too secret to be found out, too sacred to be touched. And when its proper conditions are provided, it is wholly independent of the person who has provided them. The sower may be far away, the grain will still grow. He may even be dead, the grain he sowed will grow none the less.

Such is the silence and secrecy of the divine life in the heart. We have the truth of God as seed. Compared with natural or scientific truth (which yet we would not disparage) it may well be called, as in one of the Psalms, " precious seed," and the sowers of it may well go forth "weeping"—*i.e.* with intensity of will, with all their sensibilities stirred to the sowing of it; and yet let them know—it is well for us all to know—that a sower can only sow. He cannot decompose the grain. He cannot vitalise the inward germ. He must leave the seed with God. Attempts are made, sometimes, in times of religious revival and excitement, to force the living process, and even to have essential power and action in it; to make it begin at certain times and in certain ways; but the success of these efforts is but small. Very often the result of such intrusive violence is simply this, that Nature is made to look like grace for a little while, only to sink back into Nature again. We are only *sowers*. We "cast the seed into the ground," we "sleep and rise night and day." We go about our customary avocations and know nothing for certain of what has become of the seed for a time. By and by we shall know by the appearing of the blade above the soil, by the growing and by the ripening; but at first we know nothing. It is very solemn for a sower to think of this, to think that the work is taken altogether out of his hand at a certain period and conducted in mysterious and impenetrable silence. We know not "the way of the Spirit;" we know not His modes, His times, His comings in and goings out. He is as viewless as the wind to which He is likened. He is silent as the footfall of time. When the "God of peace" works His work in the soul, we hear no noise, we see no process, we are left standing far outside; we can but pray that the quickening touch may issue in immortal life.

The Blade.—Not only is there secrecy at the beginning, but even after life is begun *the manifestations of it are very slender and even dubious.*

Life must appear in some way, else we cannot apprehend it. We know life, not in its very substance, but only in its attributes and fruits. The first appearance of life is therefore a time of great interest; we

The Blade, the Ear, the full Corn.

watch it as the farmer watches the blade when it first shows above the soil. It does not then look at all like the corn it ultimately becomes. "*First the blade.*" Take it when it is just visible above the soil—tender, pale, hardly green as yet—and compare that with the treasures of the threshing floor. What a difference! and how wonderful it seems that those should come from that! Not only is the first appearance small and slender, but to the unskilled eye it is very dubious and uncertain. Looking at the blade in its first stage of life, you could not tell whether it is destined to die or to live. It looks so tremulous, so sensitive, so utterly unfit to meet the frosty night and the rainy day. Even when it is green and a little strong, quite formed into "the blade," it does not declare itself to every eye to be corn indeed. If you saw it growing among blades of grass you might not know the difference. It is not every one who could certainly say, "This is corn, and this is grass;" although you know it practically when you see it in the corn-field where plough and harrow have been.

Even so! The springing of the precious seed of divine truth out of the secret soul into the visible life, is known at first often by manifestations very slender and sensitive. The begun life is so feeble that you can hardly say "It is there." A flush on the cheek or a gleam of the eye betokens some unusual inward feeling. Something is done, or something is left undone, and that is all! A Bible is kept in the room, and sometimes read in the morning or the evening. A new walk is taken that a certain person may be met, or missed. A letter has a sentence or two with the slightest touch of a new tone in it. Or there is some other faint suggestion of a change of mind and view. And if one should come with a high standard and a strict measuring line he might, of course, say, "Is that all?" Do you expect *that* to endure the conflicts and tests of life, and overcome its difficulties? Do you look for golden harvest out of only that?" So little and so feeble is the new life at first. Take a young Christian just beginning to call God "Father," and a ripened spirit ready for heaven; how unlike in some respects they are! How much love to God there is in the one, how little in the other! How heavenly the temper of the one, while of the other all that can be said is just that a wandering breeze has touched it, and that there is a little trembling like the shaking of a leaf when the south wind is rising. And yet that young, tender, trembling soul will grow in grace, and will be at last as ripe and mellow and ready for the garner as the other.

We have said that corn may look like grass at first; and grass is a very good thing, although it is not corn. There are natural virtues that look as if they were the virtues of grace, and these are good of their kind and in their measure, even when we cannot determine to which class they belong. Sometimes this condition of practical uncertainty continues for a considerable time. There is nothing to difference some persons from the better class of men who, however amiable, are without God. The differentia or characteristics of true spiritual

The Blade, the Ear, the full Corn. 171

life have not yet come clearly out, and these may remain long hidden in the sheath, like the undeveloped ear of corn in cold or dark weather. So that here again human agents are at fault. Sower, weeder, and watcher are all powerless—not only powerless to help in the development at this particular stage, but ignorant whether there really is anything to develop. There is an eye that looks on every blade of corn and of grass in all the world, and knows the secrets of each as it grows. But we—although we are "growing together until the harvest"—drawing our life-nourishment from the same field, and drinking in the same air and dew and light—we do not know each other always, nor ever perfectly. We are obliged to stand off from each other and wait—in hope and prayer—for God's revealing day. And He has arranged that that day shall come, soon or late. According to His plan, if the life be prolonged it comes in this world.

"*Then the Ear.*"—God's day of revelation.

Every one knows corn in the ear—all dubiety is over when we look on the ear of corn. In the spike that holds the grain, as in a protective loving embrace, we know, although we do not see it, that the corn is enfolded. And when the spike expands with the force of vegetation, and the seeds of corn appear, no one can deny or doubt their existence. So there is a revealing or declaring time in the spiritual life. The sheath must be broken; the early restrictions and envelopments must be thrown aside; the resiliency, the retirement, the fluttering and the fear of the early time must come to an end, and there must be decision, and profession, and an outwardness of fruit as well as an inwardness of life.

Now, as this stage is reached, not by living a certain number of years, but by thought, feeling, prayer, purpose, the question may be asked of those who have not reached it, of all who are in the earlier state, that of the "blade," "Is not the earing-time come?" Is not God saying to you, "First the blade—that is past with you;" *now* "the ear?" *Now* name the name of Christ. *Now* begin family worship. *Now* say, in the exigencies of life, in which you have been used to hide your faith, as if not perhaps quite sure of it yourself, "I am a Christian." Life, hidden beyond the proper time of manifestation, will die. The corn in the ear cannot be preserved; it must grow on, or perish. So is the kingdom of God in the heart. It rises or sinks continually. In the motion of a great wheel the workmen are sometimes protected by a mechanical contrivance which prevents the backward revolution. There is a preservation of all the accumulated force, and an application of it towards the ultimate end. They may even leave it for days—it will keep its place. But there is no moral or spiritual machinery to prevent the backward movement of the human spirit. Downwards it tends as soon as the upward movement is stayed. Therefore we have such exhortations as these—"Grow in grace." "Work out your own salvation." "Whatsoever thine hand findeth to do, do it with thy might."

"*The full corn in the Ear.*"—The work of grace perfected.

As the result of the growing comes the ripening, or what is here called "the full corn in the ear." It is the signal for the harvest-man to come and put in the sickle, because the harvest is ripe. It is ripe, and must be gathered into the garner. Now man's suspended agency in the natural corn-field begins again. The husbandman threw the seed into his field and left it, while he went about his other work. At harvest time he comes again. God has done the work in his absence. "The earth bringeth forth fruit of herself;" needs no help from man; could only receive hindrance from him in the living process of germination and growth. How little there is of man! How much of God! Man throws the seed into the ground, as one might throw a handful of pebbles into the sea; and months afterwards he comes, and carries away, by reaping and harvesting, thirty-fold or sixty-fold. He throws in one and carries away thirty, as it were direct from the hand of God. It is God who has been working during all these silent months. He never leaves the field. Down beneath the red mould He has His laboratory. He kindles there ten thousand invisible fires. He carries on and completes in unreckonable instances that process of transmutation which is the most wonderful that takes place beneath the sun. He opens in every field ten thousand times ten thousand fountains of life, and out of these living fountains spring the visible forms, blade, and sheath, and ear, and ripened corn. And after God has been thus working, then again comes the man, with his baskets, with his empty garners, and God fills them.

Now the chief lesson—the very teaching of the parable—is this: that the human agency is no more in proportion and degree, within the "kingdom of God," than it is in the field of corn. "*So* is the kingdom of God." The spiritual life is as much and as constantly under God's care as, in the natural world, is the field of growing corn. Indeed, we may say the spiritual life has more of His care. For, while man has the sowing and the reaping in the natural field, in the spiritual field he has the sowing but *not* the reaping. "The angels are the reapers." Souls ripened for heaven are not reaped by men on the earth. It is not they who gather in to the heavenly mansions. They see the shocks of corn ripe in their season removed, but they see not the faces of the reapers. They only see the vanishing of the sheaves and the gradual emptying of the field. The full joy of harvest is not for us until we cease from all our sowing and watching, and are ourselves reaped and garnered in heaven.

The practical uses of the great truth taught in the Parable are such as these.

It teaches us a lesson of *Diligence*. We can only sow, therefore *let* us sow. The reasoning of our natural indolence would be, "Because we can do so little, and because that little is only instrumental and does not hold an *essential* function in the life process, therefore we need not be very anxious about the doing of it." It is very well worth our notice that, on the contrary, the Bible, in some well-known passages, makes our feebleness and our ignorance of results *the very reasons* for our increased diligence. "In the morning sow thy seed, and in the evening withhold not thine hand." *Sow*, because without sowing there can be no harvest. Some one must throw in the seed; you or another! Man, or angel, or God! *Sow*, because if *this* fails *that* may prosper; or if that fails this may succeed; or they may both flourish and give the more reward. *Sow*, beside all waters, and you will be "blessed." *Sow*, because the wing of night is falling over the field, and soon you will stumble in the darkness and have to leave it. *Sow*, because *as* you sow you will reap. After all, there is in God's plan a sure connection between the human sowing and the divine reaping.

A lesson of *Reverence*.

What wonders are being wrought very near to us in silence! The Spirit of God is striving with human spirits! Convincing them of sin; opening the blind eyes, and leading the prisoners out of the prison-house, and cleansing sinners in the fountain of a Saviour's grace. God is near to us, burning corruption in unseen fires, building of living souls temples for his praise. He is working a work that shall endure when the heavens and the earth shall have passed away.

And all this great work of God is connected with

the words we speak, with the actions we do, and with the prayers we offer. The seed drops from our hands, and the eternal Spirit takes it into *His* care and vitalises it for ever. At any place and at any time that great transaction may be going on, and it makes this earth sublime as we think of it. Shall we not say with Jacob, "How dreadful is this place! This is none other than the house of God, this is the gate of heaven." And to us, as to Moses, may not the words be spoken, "Put off thy shoes from off thy feet, for the place whereon thou standest is holy ground."

A lesson of *Abstinence*.

Having sown the seed, leave it with God. Think—"It has passed now from my care into a more sacred department, and into far higher hands. With Him let me leave it." Many a one stirs the seed and spoils the growing. "The things of God knoweth no man, but the Spirit of God." There is a time to keep silence. Let a man learn to hold his peace even from good; to possess his soul in patience; to still his heart, and even stay his busy hand in the presence of the sovereign worker. Let him "*stand still* and see the salvation of God."

Finally, a lesson of *Trust*.

There is a time for everything lawful; but there is no time for despair or even despondency. At the very darkest hour you can never know that God is not even then working. His care embraces and encircles all your little cares. "If ye being evil" care to sow, will not He much more care to make the seed spring? He is bringing to full ear the great harvest of righteousness and peace in this world, and in all worlds; yet that little seed-plot of yours, watched and wept over, perhaps for long weary years, will not be forgotten in the great plan of His providence. Only give Him absolute and unmeasured trust, and the happy hour will come—sooner, it may be, than you dare to hope—when you shall have the joy of harvest.

XIV.

The Resurrection of Christ Historic.

"And with great power gave the Apostles witness of the resurrection of the Lord Jesus."—ACTS iv. 33.

(*Easter Sunday.*)

THE resurrection of Christ is the most important event in all history. It expresses in itself the whole Gospel of God to man. The first preachers of the Gospel preached it as "the Resurrection." When a new apostle was elected it was that he might be "a witness" with the rest of the resurrection. The cynical philosophers and more frivolous people of Athens mocked when Paul preached this doctrine to them, but it is certain that there and everywhere the apostle preached it; that it was the very centre of his teaching; that he considered bound up with it the sum and substance of the Gospel. We can easily understand the reason of this. For this fact is the demonstration of all the other vital things in the Gospel that went before it. Jesus was declared in His resurrection to be the Son of God with power. He *was* the Son of God all along; but the glory of Sonship was much eclipsed in this poor mortal life. And if He had passed away in death, and never reappeared, it would have been impossible to persuade the world that an Almighty Saviour had died for its redemption. In His resurrection God publicly owned Him in the face of earth and heaven, and testified to all things vital in His life and mission, to the sinlessness of His character, to the divine truth of His teaching, and to the sufficiency of His atonement. "He was delivered for our offences, and raised again for our justification." The curse of the law mysteriously darkened over Him in His death and lay heavy on His grave, but was melted away in the light of His resurrection. And while this fact is the demonstration of all that went before, it is also the pledge and promise of all that is yet to come. It opens the gate of a future life; it brings life and immortality to light; it is the pattern and the assurance of our own resurrection; the Church rose again in Christ, and each individual member of it has power and privilege to say, "Because He lives, I shall live also!"

With truth, therefore, this fact is put in the Scriptures, and in systems of theological thought constructed from them, as the key-stone of the arch of Christianity. Take it away, and the whole system crumbles to pieces—nothing is then left to us but shadows of failure and ashes of disappointment. Our preaching is vain; your faith is vain; we are yet in our sins; we have no more hope in Christ for this life, or for any other. "We are of all men most miserable." All depends on this, which we have assumed to be, and which the Scriptures expressly teach us to be, the most important single fact in all history.

Such a fact, from its very importance, requires the very strongest confirmation, and confirmation of a strictly historical kind. The resurrection of Christ is a fact in history, it must be proved by historical evidence, and the evidence must be strong and clear if we are to found upon it a strong and clear faith; that it is so we shall now endeavour to show. It is in these days well worth while to spend a little time in showing *how strong* is the plain historic proof of the resurrection of Christ.

As to the fact itself. *It is a fact quite capable of proof.* There is no difficulty in imagining it to have occurred. There are no invincible laws against it. There are no natural principles or instincts of the human mind which reject it. All that can be averred is that it is not in the line of our usual experiences; but it is not a thing, in its nature, which any one would be unable to believe, if it were only substantiated by proper and sufficient evidence.

Now arises the question, What *is* sufficient evidence? What are the laws of evidence among men, in common things, which would affect the present case? By English law, *one* witness is sufficient to testify even to an important fact in a case, if the jury are willing to accept his testimony; and they do so always, although he is the sole witness to the particular point, when his testimony is corroborated by other witnesses in other things which lie close upon the point. In Scotland the law demands *two* witnesses. Indeed, it may be said that all human laws assume that the testimony of two witnesses, when that testimony is unchallenged and when it is confirmed by collateral evidence, is enough. A court can rule anything on that evidence. Such a conviction is produced of the truth in the case, by the testimony of two, that human life will be taken away on the strength of such evidence. This is not to say that *any* two men would be believed in anything they might choose to say. They must be, in the first place, honest men, upright and worthy of belief. Then they must be able to show that they had adequate and ample opportunity for ascertaining or observing the thing to which they give testimony, that they were the dupes of no illusion, and that they were in full possession of their faculties.

A judge or jury will ask concerning a witness in any important case : " Is he a sane man, of sound mind and ordinary discretion ? Is he an honest man, sure, or at least likely, to speak the truth as far as he knows it ? Had he the means of thoroughly or truly knowing the thing about which he is going to give evidence ? Is he free from any possible imputation of selfish or personal interest in rendering his testimony ? Is his testimony uncontradicted ? Is it confirmed in any of its points by that of another witness ?" Such questions answered in the affirmative, the case is clear: the human mind is so constituted that it *must* receive such testimony. If it were not so, human society would be no longer possible; no important case could be decided in any court of law; in fact, no law could be administered at all.

Now, the historic fact of the resurrection of Christ, on which hangs all the Gospel, must be substantiated, if at all, in the same way and according to the same principles of evidence which command belief in other spheres of human experience. Let us see, briefly, how the matter stands in these respects.

First. *How many witnesses are there to this fact of the resurrection?* One? Two? Three?—After all we have said of the ordinary laws of evidence, that might have been testimony much too feeble on which to hang so stupendous and unparalleled a fact. But the truth is that we have multitudinous and overwhelming testimony. Let us briefly trace it up to its beginning; for there was a moment when there was but one witness. On that memorable morning the first to see the risen Lord was Mary; then her companions, the other women, shared the privilege with her. Then John and Peter saw Him. Later in the day He met the two disciples on the way to Emmaus. In the evening He appeared to the brethren as they sat at meat; and again, a week later, to them in presence of Thomas. He came to the Apostolic company by the lake; on the mountain more than five hundred brethren at once saw Him; and then—not to speak of other interviews, of which we have only hints, and of others which in all probability took place, but of which we

The Resurrection of Christ Historic. 183

have no record—He led the little company of His followers to the top of Olivet, when He went away. It is probable that six or seven hundred people, at least, saw Christ after He was risen (some think nearly a thousand), and knew Him to be the Jesus of Nazareth with whom they had been more or less acquainted. True, we have not a separate testimony in writing from every one who saw Him. Writing in those days was not an easy matter. But this we have, which to my mind is most significant and convincing: we have the testimony, clear and strong, of the central men, the Apostles, and some of their fellow-believers. We have the testimony of the four Evangelists and of James, Peter, and Paul—to what? Not only to what they themselves saw and heard, on which they speak distinctly, but to the fact that a great many others saw and heard with them; and there is no denial from any of these.

Here, for instance, is a letter which Paul writes to the Corinthian Church, which he must have known very well would not be kept a secret, but would be circulated far and wide; and he asserts in it that Christ was seen after His resurrection by more than five hundred men, most of whom, he says, were then alive; and yet there is no contradiction of the statement from any quarter. Could any man—above all a man like the Apostle Paul—make an assertion like that on mere idle hearsay, without certain knowledge of the fact? He must, in that case, have felt that he would be liable to be confronted with a hundred questions, and that his whole character and life-work would be ruined unless he could answer them satisfactorily. Corinth itself was full of objectors, and some of them would have been nothing loth to undermine his authority. They would have said—"Five hundred persons saw Him at once! When? Where? In what circumstances? Who were they? Name them. Who among them remain? who have died?" And if he could not have answered such questions—I do not say exhaustively and down to every minute particular, but by information sufficient to satisfy reasonable and honest inquiry, his whole testimony would have fallen to the ground, and this Epistle would not have been worth the parchment on which it was written. The casual observation, dropped as it was incidentally, "Some have fallen asleep," indicates that he knew many of the persons referred to, and that, had it been necessary, he could have given further details respecting them. Enough has been said to show, that although we cannot fix on any precise number of witnesses to the resurrection, yet that the number must have been very large. In the Epistles and also in the Gospels there are references to these outside witnesses, and there is no contemporaneous contradiction of these statements.

To return to the central and chief witnesses, the Apostles and their companions, we ask—"*Who are they? What character do they bear? Are they honest men?*" The answer to these questions needs to be but brief. Let any one read the Gospels and see what kind of men the writers are. True, and honest, and simple-hearted are they, if ever such men were in the world. Scepticism does not now fling against them the old rude charge of knavery and dishonesty. "They were enthusiasts," it is said; or "they were too simple," or "they were in some way self-deceived;" but "at least they were honest." So far well.

Next, *as to their soundness of mind*. Where is there any sign of weakness or of hallucination in these Gospels, or in the Epistles, from first to last? There is nothing artistic, nothing elaborate, nothing strained; but an unadorned, almost, we might say, a passionless simplicity. They seem almost *too* calm, too little carried away by their theme. It is impossible to conceive evidence more perfectly given. They were simple men, and most of them unlettered; not given naturally, and not able by any literary culture, to give much expression to their own emotions. They *were the subjects* of profound emotion; but they knew very well that the world could have no great interest in learning the state of their feelings, and that what they had to do was to tell faithfully and truly the great facts which had excited such feelings in their breasts. We repeat that no evidence could be more perfectly given.

As to *their opportunities for ascertaining the truth* in the matter to which they testified, these have already been mentioned incidentally. They saw their risen Lord many times: in the evening, in the morning, in the afternoon. They saw Him in many places: near the sepulchre, in the city, in the quiet room, on the way, on the sea shore, on the mountain. They heard Him speak; they talked with Him; they touched Him; they saw Him eat; they felt His breath; they saw Him ascend to heaven.

But had they not something to gain by this history ? Consciously or unconsciously was there not some sinister end, some personal advantage that lured and drew them on, and by the attainment of which they rewarded themselves for all their labours? It is not difficult to ascertain what they *did* gain by their testimony, and what, as reasonable and observant men, they must have expected to gain by faithfully maintaining it: they gained disrepute, persecution, spoiling of goods, " houses and lands" passing away from them as the price of their faithfulness. They gained bonds and martyrdom; and they *never* gained earthly comfort, or social standing, or money, or any other thing the world counts good and dear, by their testimony. The noblest chapter, perhaps, in all history is that which narrates the simple constancy, the faithful diligence, the unconquerable courage, with which the first preachers of the Gospel—the first witnesses of the resurrection—went on with their work, and went through with it, sealing it with their blood. We may reason this way and that about the resurrection of Christ; but *they* believed it in life and death. If they did not believe it, their course of action makes them the greatest madmen the world has ever seen.

Remember, further, how *their testimony was received, how undoubtingly it was accepted by men of their own generation.* It has been said that eighteen centuries is a long time across which to verify import-

The Resurrection of Christ Historic. 187

ant historic truth; that it grows dim with distance, that it is hard to grasp and hold. But, in fact, it *was* grasped and held by those to whom it was near, who could judge of its truth as we judge of the occurrences of our own time, and who could not be deceived. Remember the wonderful effects this belief produced: peace and love and joy in individual hearts, and new societies and new nations in the world; and it has gone on from age to age producing the same results; at this hour Christendom, with all the light and love and tenderness it contains, is the fruit of the faith that there is a risen Christ; and the purest and the gentlest and the noblest spirits on earth to-day believe the most simply and entirely in the resurrection and its enfolded truths —think of all this, and of the other reasons adduced, and say if it be not legitimate to declare that the resurrection of Christ is the best authenticated fact in the history of the world.

Eighty years before the resurrection of Christ, Julius Cæsar, with two Roman legions, landed on the coast of Kent. Who thinks of doubting that? There is not a sceptic in the island. I suppose, if eternal salvation depended on believing that Julius Cæsar was once in this country, there is not a sane Englishman alive who would fail of heaven; and yet the actual historic proof of this is far less complete, cogent, convincing, than is the proof that Christ died and rose and revived, that He might be Lord both of the dead and of the living. Men believe without any doubt or difficulty in the Sabine farm of Horace, where his friends quaffed the Falernian wine. We believe that Virgil died on a journey, and that he lies buried, at his own request, at the second milestone from Naples on the Puteolan way. We believe in the plough of Cincinnatus, and in the poison-cup of Socrates; but all kinds of conscientious scruples and honest doubts, which must be treated with great tenderness and delicacy, arise in some minds when they are asked to believe in the resurrection and ascension of the Lord Jesus Christ. We feel inclined to say of such, everything in its own place. We would not break any bruised reed, or quench any smoking flax, or fail in any point of encouragement to those who are troubled or distressed; but if any one will not take the trouble to inquire into and examine the evidence for the resurrection, and yet will complain that he is unable to believe it, sympathy with such a person may be unfaithfulness to truth, and a slight even upon rationality, because he asks for comfort while rejecting light. Let men be honest and earnest in this great matter, let them use their utmost endeavours to find the very truth, and *then* let them ask for sympathy if their faith is not so clear as they could wish; no true heart will withhold it, and God, who "knoweth our frame" and who "is of tender mercy," will guide the meek in judgment and will lead them in His way.

Christ's true people do more than simply give historical credence to His resurrection. To you it is the Gospel. The words of Christ are by it sealed and made luminous for ever. Let them "dwell in you richly." The sacrifice of Christ has its eternal efficacy proclaimed by this illustrious fact. Be sure the forgiveness is yours. Christ is risen; then we too rise. What! believe in a risen Christ and myself be in a grave of sin? No; I burst the cerements; I come as out of a rock prison; I hail the morning light; I rise with Christ into newness of life! Old things have passed away, and all things have become new.

Nor is this all; for the resurrection of Christ is the gate of life immortal. He "hath abolished death"— changed him from a king of terrors into a mere melting shade. The grave is no longer a bed of corruption, but a seed-plot of life eternal. "This corruptible shall put on incorruption, and this mortal shall put on immortality." The members must be with the head. There could be no heaven to Christ without His Church; no eternal joy for Him if His ransomed lay low and far away in earthly graves, storms beating on them, and winter lowering dark over them, and death holding an eternal mastery. For them, as for Him, must the song yet ring through the heavens, "Lift up your heads, O ye gates, and be ye lift up ye everlasting doors!" that all who follow the King of Glory, to the last and least, may enter in.

In the faith of these things, and that our faith may be the stronger, we celebrate to-day our great Christian festival, and in prayer and song and holy Gospel, we do virtually what they do actually in some of the villages of Germany, as, meeting each other on Easter morning, they whisper as they pass, "*The Lord is risen indeed!*"

XV.

The Way wherein we should go.

"Cause me to know the way wherein I should walk."—
Psalm cxliii. 8.

THIS is one of the most pathetically earnest of the Psalms of David. It has no joy in it. But it has in great strength the elements and experiences out of which joy and deliverance spring. As we look upon the suppliant humbling himself in conscious sinfulness, imploring divine mercy and forgiveness, lamenting his desolation and solitude, sadly recalling former days which were happier than these, recognising the presence of enemies and adversities, stretching forth his hands to the unseen God, and thirsting after Him as a thirsty land—we feel that in no long time deliverance must come; that this "weeping will endure but for a night, and that joy will come in the morning."

The text may be said to comprise every other prayer. If God gives His servant "to know the way wherein he should walk," and strength to walk in it, peace, and order, and liberty, and joy, will soon come.

The Way wherein we should go.

What do we need but this—knowledge of the way wherein we should walk, and daily divine aids to walk in it—to make us possessors of the same blessings?

The subject may shape itself to our thought in this form:
> *Life a daily difficulty.*
> *Christian life a daily deliverance.*

Difficulty.—Life is difficult. It is difficult every day; on some days, and at some times, unusually so; taking it in its ordinary conditions and character, it was so to David, and it is so now to us, if we are trying to live as he did. Here we may be reminded of some Scriptural declarations which go apparently in the opposite direction; and, if we go by the letter only, it is easy enough, on this or on any subject, to get one Scripture to modify another. We have all heard of the "plain path," of the "easy yoke," of the "light burden," of the "ways" which are "pleasantness and peace." There is, however, no contradiction in fact. This way which David asks so earnestly that he may be taught *to know* is a "way of pleasantness" when it is found, it is easy enough to one who is briskly walking in it. But is it found thus, once for all, in the case of all the good? Do not answer by any theory; answer by the result of your own experience. Have *you* so found it? In one sense, perhaps, you can say "Yes," if you have found God. There are certain things found by a believing man never to be lost. They come up freshly and in unquestioned reality day by day. But not to say that many Christians feel their hold of some, even of these things at times uncertain, are there not many things closely connected with them, regarding which we have only changing and precarious perceptions? Are there not continual circumstances and trials and duties of ordinary life, which, in one way or another, make life a continual difficulty? These Scriptural figures, which are so beautiful and so helpful, are, in some ways, misleading; they are misleading when we misread them, when we make them mean more or less or other than the intended Divine sense. Ah! if life were indeed like a path through green fields, which no one can miss! Or like the shortest road from one part of a great city to another! But *our* "*way*" is very different. Everything is included in the expression; our way is our life—and our very life has never been lived until now. Abraham lived and found a way, and that helps me to find mine. But mine is not his. Elijah lived and made a path of fire through life, which became bright illumination and glory at the last. But my way is often dark enough, and will certainly never run me up into a chariot of fire. There are footmarks of our forefathers on the track, but sometimes the difficulty is to find them; or when found, to decide whether their steps were right, or if right, whether therefore we ought mechanically to follow in our very different circumstances. Think of the number of things that are to be believed, that are to be renounced, that are to be examined, that are to be distinguished in themselves and from other things, that are to be tentatively dealt with, that are to be done, that are to be left undone, that are to be waited for, that are to be suffered. All these are included in the "way wherein we should walk."

Take some of them in succession.

Opinions and beliefs.—There can be no living way for a man that does not involve these. A man is more than a growing tree, or a grazing animal. Even those who speak slightingly of opinions, and lay stress rather on what they call spirit, and instinct, and practical action, when they rigorously analyse their own thought in this matter, or when they have it analysed for them, are obliged to confess that in one form or another, separated from other things, or solvent in them, opinion and belief must be comprehended in spirit, even in instinct, in a measure, and certainly in practical action. But how hard it is now to form opinions and settle beliefs! Harder perhaps than it has ever been before. And this— not only because we have more than the common amount of scepticism in the world—but because (as I verily believe) men are in some ways more sincere and more earnest than they have ever been before. They cannot so easily subscribe creeds, composed of many, and some of them hard enough propositions. They cannot so easily repeat on a Sunday morning in their devotions what, if true, dooms an overwhelming proportion of the human race to "perish everlastingly." We are quite now into the solvent time. The grand truths and the great persons, I believe, yet stand out as clearly and as impressively as ever before; but the human definitions and descriptions of them are sharing a very different fate. We may like this state of things, or we may dislike it; but that it exists through the whole sphere of intellectual religion no one can deny, and it makes our individual "way" difficult and cloudy.

Some, indeed, insist on having the matter settled by one decisive word. "*We must take the Bible, and the Christian doctrines, and the Church*, or else we are infidels." And to such persons, if any teaching at all can be given, it would be this: "By all means take that side in the case, and keep it. But answer first the further question. How can you *be sure* you are taking it, in this unintelligent and uninquiring mood, in this unworthy state of timidity and fear?"

Hold by the Bible? but it must be intelligently, and with some idea of what it is, and wherein its real authority lies—*i.e.* in the *truth* it brings to us from God; in that, and not in anything that may be asserted or formulated out of it by men. Hold by the Bible? but surely not by the spurious texts in it. Hold by the Bible? but take some pains to understand what it contains. If you think closely you will allow that its doctrines—*i.e.* its teachings, must in one sense always be open questions. They must be so, since, in fact, it it is *only in this way* that the Bible can remain our property and our treasure. On the other supposition it has been taken quite out of our hands long ago. It has been examined for us, and the substance of it accurately and infallibly ascertained (although all this has been done by fallible men), so that now our duty is not so much to read, and study, and pray over, and understand *the Book*, as to accept the findings of others. No! This will not do. There is no easy way of it. It is a simple but a stern alternative. Either there is some external authority that has settled for us what is Bible, what is Gospel; or we are thrown absolutely upon private judgment. *Our own* private judgment—not Luther's, or Calvin's, or Knox's, or that of the compilers of the thirty-nine articles, or of the Assembly of Westminster Divines—but our own. Our private judgment may be a poor thing as compared with the judgment of such men; but, poor as it is, it assumes a judicial competence, even if it only elects to take the law from their lips. And it is bound to examine their opinions—if for no other reason, at least for this: that there are opposite opinions, as learned, as devout, as sincerely urged as theirs, and if we choose the one and reject the other, we must do it for some intelligible reasons; and these reasons, when stated, will be found to cover the whole field of the controversy, and will show that we are, in fact, judging the whole case. There is no easy way of it, we repeat, and God never meant that there should be. He meant us all to be watchers, waiters, askers, seekers, diggers, finders! Each saying for himself, "Make *me* to know the way wherein I should go, for I lift my soul to Thee."

Of course it is distressing to have things which seemed to stand so firmly, and to have been so accurately and fully ascertained, called into question, or even strongly denied. But the mere fact that they are thus called in question, and that they are denied *for reasons given*, leave us no choice in our course. Alleged reasons must be examined, opinions frankly stated must have consideration. And what although I have to give up some particular phrase or statement? To go to the central thing of all: are we to say that God has been defined and described as fully as the world needs for all future ages? God is far more and far better than all men's descriptions of Him, and than all their conceptions. We shall be gainers, not losers, by the changes that are coming. "Though the vision tarry, wait for it." It will come in due time—a vision of clearness, and truth, and beauty—such as the world has never seen, and the exclamation will then be, " Lo! this is our God, we have waited for Him, and He will save us."

On the other hand, we cannot *continue* in the attitude of waiting for our own personal opinions and beliefs, in so far as we have the means of forming them. We are bound to form them, and the point is that there is *very great difficulty* in forming some of them, or in keeping them when we have them. And yet to this difficult and solemn task we are bound by everything which makes us Christians, by everything which makes us men. But it may be said, " What are we to do? Are you not making the case more than difficult, almost hopeless? If we are not to trust in ourselves,—if we are not to trust in our fathers, or in any human opinions,—are we not then doomed to perpetual vacillation and uncertainty? Are you not sending us over to that numerous enough company which practically holds that to ascertain truth to any great extent is altogether impossible, and declares that all we can do is to examine, inquire, and wait?"

That company of people is one of the last I should wish to increase, although we ought not to forget that true and noble spirits are in it. We ought, however, also to remember that they are not in it as their home, but only in passage to assured findings and firmer ground. And there is no need to belong to it at all. From this hour any one of us, if we will, may be of "them that believe to the saving of the soul." How? *By bringing the whole case fully and earnestly before God.* "Cause me to know the way wherein I should walk, for I lift my soul unto Thee." There, and there only, you have the whole case; the meeting, and, in a measure, the settling of the difficulty. If you choose to add a number of other things which seem to you helpful or accessory to that—so be it; viewed practically it is not worth while to raise any argument on such a point, although there is a danger that these minor things shall be put out of their proper place, and hinder rather than help the coming to God. But if we come really to Him, we have solved the difficulty, we have come into the new and living way, and God will make that way more and more plain before our face; whereas if we abide among the exterior things—examining, considering, comparing, putting this opinion against that, and working the whole matter simply as a high intellectual problem, without ever making the last and highest appeal—we have no certainty of a good and true issue.

The religious world of to-day is dividing itself into two camps or companies; those who believe in authority—authority more or less formulated, more or less despotically expressed; and those who, gladly recognising the authority of truth, which, of course, will be largely found in the whole course of Christian history, yet seek for themselves, and find its supreme and pure source in God. "This is life eternal, *to know Him*," in personal knowledge; to bring our spirits into direct and individual contact with the Father of spirits. We talk of ritualism in the language of alarm, as well we may, but we too often regard it as some extreme and unreasonable thing. It is, in truth, diffused, far-reaching, and universal. It touches and weakens our faith. It keeps us from God. Some of the first men in England are ritualists, and they live noble, devout lives, and some of them very ably defend the substance of the Christian truth. God forbid that we should meet error in blind uncharitableness! But they do believe in sacramental grace. They do tell us that the way is not open, or that we may not come into it, alone and without human direction and aid; or that if we so come, and make known our need in the great Presence, we shall be sent back to get part at least of the answer to our prayer, through human intermediacy, and through some of the channels of a human priesthood.

We, on the contrary, found everything on a declaration like that of this text. Each one stands out alone.

Each one comes alone to his God (Oh, how reverently and humbly should we come!) and says, "Cause me to know the way wherein I should walk." And that is intellectual and moral salvation. No final darkness can settle on such a soul. No perdition can come to it. "God is light," and to come to Him is to come into light. It may not be clear light at first: the brightest summer day has a dawning; but it will be light "more and more unto the perfect day." When you come back to these intellectual difficulties which abound in this age as perhaps they never abounded before, you may perchance find them difficulties still. There are still problems you cannot solve, dark things you cannot see, mixed things you cannot analyse, shadows of uncertainty you cannot melt, broken things you cannot piece together, and things wanting which you cannot, of course, number. But the source of truth has been reached in God. The living Truth has been touched. In so coming you have taken your place with "the meek," whom "He will guide in judgment. He will guide you with His counsel, and afterwards receive you to glory."

Conduct.—In respect of conduct also we find life to be a scene of constant difficulty. There are still, no doubt, simple, harmonious, peaceful lives upon the earth, gliding quietly on like meadow streams. Where you have a placid—not to say a sluggish temperament—easy circumstances, pleasant neighbours, an unchanging lot, what can you have but a gentle, peaceful life? The conduct of the day might almost be said to cast a mould, or deepen it, into which the conduct of the next day is to flow. There is no difficulty, or, at least, none that cannot be easily overcome. But this is now quite the exceptional life, especially in cities. Every morning that dawns awakens great numbers of men to new cares and anxieties, to new duties and difficulties. Even those who know the way they should go, so far as it consists of beliefs, convictions, principles, find it still in their practice to be a way of continual difficulty. It is easy to say "*Act on principle.*" Of course, we must act on principle, but on what principle? What is the right principle for the case? Or what is the proper combination of principles? And how are they to apply? It will sometimes be that all is dark as to what is about to happen in the immediate future, and yet action must be taken at a certain time ; and, in order to be well taken, preparation must be made for it now. And that darkness perhaps cannot be made any less by our intellectual activities, or by our moral impatience. We may knock at the doors of the future with all our importunity, but they will not open a moment before the time. What can we do? *We can pray.* We can use this text, and get the benefits it carries, "Cause me to know the way wherein I should go, for I lift my soul to Thee."

Or the case is exceedingly perplexed and intricate. It lies all open before us. There is nothing more to reveal, and yet we cannot understand it. Our way, "the way wherein we should go," lies right through the heart of those perplexed and ravelled things, and our

The Way wherein we should go. 201

"going" is sure to alter them somewhat, perhaps much. What shall be the ruling principle of our action? Shall we go quickly or slowly? And shall prudence or firmness have the reins? Who can tell us? And in this pause, what can we do? We can ask Him who knows the way that is all unknown to us to "cause us to know it," so that, as we tread it step by step, and make it thus our actual way, it may prove to be indeed the way of righteousness and peace.

Or the case, in its two sides, is perfectly balanced. There is nothing to choose between them. We may cast the weight of our action on this side or on that with equally good conscience. And yet, out of the choice we make, a very different class of results will spring; and other things will come in then, and issues never contemplated as possible will arise. So that there is a right side, a "way in which we should go," even when no human wisdom could give any sufficient reason why the one side should be taken rather than the other. How shall we find it? *How*, but by coming to Him who knows all ways that human feet are to tread. He has his eye on that best way, that perfect way, that Christ-like way, which my feet ought to mark, and if I come to Him to ask about it, it may be that, while I am yet speaking, the light of revelation will illumine it, the finger of Providence will point to it, and the voice that has directed so many pilgrims will say to me also, "This is the way, walk ye in it."

But one may say, "Who is God?" and where is He? I see Him very dimly, sometimes I even seem to doubt

His very existence; how can I go to one who is hardly clear to my own mind as a Personality? I meet you on that lowest ground: for you must, as a rational being, admit the *possibility* of the existence of God. I go with you to that dim Possibility, to that flickering uncertainty which dwells in the recesses of your heart, and which perhaps you have never yet taken honest means to certify and evidence to your faith; and I counsel you still to go there—to that shadowy dimness which represents all you believe of God, and lift up your soul to Him. All our highest conceptions must come so infinitely short of the truth regarding Him, that a conception, even so dim and doubtful as yours, may be the starting-point for a journey to fuller light and clearer vision.

The solution of all difficulty, be it what it may, is to "lift up the soul to God." He is the infinite, the all-perfect One. He is the sum of righteousness, and to come to Him is to say that we desire to act righteously. God is the fountain of wisdom, and we thus put ourselves into the divine light and are no longer wise in our own conceit. God is love. All tenderness, all patience have their home in Him; and in coming to Him we escape from our narrowness and factiousness, our strife, our envy, our ill-will. God is the Almighty —the ever-active One—"working hitherto" in height and depth; and to rise to Him is to come close to the Almighty strength, and to be drawn by it out of our indolence (which is sometimes the cause of our difficulty) into the movements of order and obedience. God is the God of peace, and to lift up the soul to Him is to rise out of storm into calm—is to leave the self-made troubles of life beneath us, while we mount up on eagle's wings into His eternal and illimitable tranquillity.

Call in the inattentive powers! Wake up the slumbering affections! Let thy being rise up, in undivided wholeness, to the Fountain whence it sprang, to the End whither it ought to be always tending!—and the problem of your life is solved, and the difficulty of it is vanquished: vanquished at least, as one feels his journey to be, when, after toil and pain, he stands at last on the hill-top and sees home and rest in sight.

XVI.

On Christian Giving.

"Give."—LUKE vi. 38.

THE first word to be said on this subject—and one which must come before the word which we are specially to consider—is "*Get*." It is a strange word to say in a great city, but if we think of it first, it may perhaps help us to understand our subject and open the way to the statement of the case.

Get, gather. Fill the basket and the store. Increase in riches. Lay up for yourselves treasures. "The hand of the diligent maketh rich," and it is good to be rich, when the rich man has a wealthy lordly soul. True—excess of getting becomes one of the greatest of sins, and one of the greatest of perils. But excessive acquisitiveness will never be cured by stigmatising or opposing, nor even by neglecting, the original organic principle in our nature from which it proceeds. That principle is implanted there by the hand of God, and therefore we may be absolutely certain that it is good, and that it is put there for good ends. What modification or what sublimation of it there may be in a sinless world one cannot tell; evidently in this world it is right and necessary that (in a Christian sense and in Christian measure) every man should look to himself. If a man does not look to himself, and seek to "provide things honest" for his earthly life, other men must look to him; and if all, or even any considerable number of people, were to act on the principle of leaving others to care for their temporal well-being, society itself would soon be impossible; we should all need caring for, and there would be none to care for us.

The desire of possessing is one of the springs of many a noble character, and of many a noble career. It is one of the root-principles of the manifold and wonderful activity, and enterprise, and resource of our industrial life. That principle builds our cities, wings our ships, extends our empire over all the world. It is not far from the heart of our literature, it works in every process of legislation, it is one of the animating principles of all that we understand by progress and civilisation. There is a great majestic wheel of progress rolling onwards (for the wheels of Providence never roll back), but look within and you will see ten thousand little wheels, ten thousand times ten thousand busy men, and the central spring of every little wheel is this, that each man is striving to possess. A great part of Christian virtue and goodness consists in harmonising this principle with others; but without it nothing could be done. We know that the perfect social goodness for the world is this—that a man "shall love his neighbour as himself," but if he neglects himself, his love for his neighbour will hardly be worth the having. Do you say, "Ah! but the noblest men in the world have been self-forgetful as to outward and present things?" No—not so. Who more self-forgetful than Paul, and yet who more resolute in the maintenance of a spirit of personal independence! "Ye know," he says,—holding forth, as some think, his hands while speaking—hands dark, browned, stiffened with honest toil—"Ye know that these hands have ministered unto my necessities, and to them that were with me. I have showed you all things, how that *so labouring* ye ought to support the weak, and to remember the words of the Lord Jesus, how he said, it is more blessed to give than to receive."

Now, it is generally supposed that it is hardly necessary in Christian or social teaching to tell men to gather and get. It is thought rather to be only needful to limit, check, and keep the principle within bounds. But is this so? Are there not many persons who naturally are of a very careless and prodigal disposition? Such persons have the easy benevolence of impulse; but they have none of the finer and nobler benevolence of principle. They never make a business of getting, and when they do get by chance, they allow what has come to them to flow away again as by another chance. Are there not many, too, who are naturally very indolent? Like Issachar, they "see that rest is good," and they take it plentifully. When they think or dream rather than think, of the ways of

On Christian Giving.

activity in this work-a-day world, they always see in their dream the lion that keeps the way. Then there are the young: the whole rising race (most happily, as we cannot but think) needs more or less instruction on this subject. Avarice is not the vice of youth. It would indeed be terrible to see the puckered look of the miser on a young face, and to feel the grip of greed in a young hand. Pleasure and prodigality, rather, are the tempters of the young. So to them, especially, this word is appropriate—"*Get.*" Begin to gather. Lay by you in store a little, as soon as you possibly can. Let your expenditure always be clearly within your income. However little your income may be at first, let it be always more than you spend. It is good to get moral power by resisting the temptations of the actual time and life season. *Your* strongest temptations in relation to money and means will probably be to put on a certain style, some show, or appearance, which are not strictly justified if it takes all you have to put them on. It is very natural for you to paint the future with the colours of imagination, which in youth are rosy and bright; but it will be a good and wholesome exercise to keep sternly to facts in this matter; giving imagination full wing, if you like, in other things less close upon your actual life. Bind yourself severely and manfully to the present facts of your circumstances. Say: "Here am I—in this city where I dwell—in this year of grace. I am not going to be self-deceived. I am not going to take for gospel these inward whisperings of vanity and hope, 'You have nothing to fear, you are a rising young man, you are shrewd and capable! Live according to your merits, and your means will soon correspond to them.'" Let your answer be : "I will do nothing of the kind. I will live according to my means, and trust God that whatever powers I have will not be lost to me or to the world. I have so much, no more. I must spend only so much, and no more. And out of the little I have I must contrive to save something, however little it may be, to be the nucleus of a growing store, for the uses of my future life, and for the service and glory of my God."

And now comes the second word.

"*Give.*" Begin to give as soon as you begin to get. That, and only that, will prevent the danger of a growing covetousness. We are all very much under the influence of habit, purely as such. Of course, we are liable to the inroads of evil principles and affections; we are liable to imbibe the love of evil things for their own sake, or for the sake of the passing pleasure of them; but we are also liable to be drawn towards them, and by degrees fixed in them, by habit even more than by first affection. Many a man becomes a drunkard by not watching habit. Many a man becomes a practical miser by habit. He is not in pure nature a miserly man, but he builds his soul up, and round and round with circles of habit. It cannot grow; it cannot breathe; it can hardly live. Habit has been called "a second nature." An amendment of this apothegm

On Christian Giving.

might be that habit is not a second, but a *first* nature; that it *is* nature. Habit is nature acting and growing, taking fixed and enduring form. Habit is *I myself*, becoming what probably I shall be through life, and, perhaps, for evermore. How important, therefore, that in the growing time, in youth and earlier manhood, the form should be good, that the robe I am weaving for my spirit to wear through life and death should be of the right texture, and should have in it some colourings of celestial beauty that will never fade. *Not to give* is to fall into a habit which it will be difficult to overcome. Not to give is to neglect to form a habit which it will be hard to attain. It is very well known to those who are acquainted with the religious world, that there is a very great difference in professing Christians in regard to this matter of giving; and that the difference is not always explained by a reference to their respective circumstances, and by saying that the man who gives is rich and he who withholds is poor. It is not always so. It is sometimes very far from being so. Sometimes the rich man is niggard, sometimes the poor man is liberal, and that not because they are not both Christians, but just because one of them has been untrained in this special grace of liberality. And, therefore, it is well and wise to begin to give as soon as we begin to gather. As soon as the store begins to swell, however small it be, the hand of love ought to be searching it and taking from it, not all that comes, but some portion regularly for presentation to the gracious Giver. As soon as the well begins to rise, one or more streams ought to be drawn from it for the watering and refreshing of some thirsty places. There is very great danger in separating by any long distance the beginning of giving from the beginning of getting. "Honour the Lord with thy substance, and with the *first fruits* of all thine increase."

How significant and picturesque in its beauty was the presentation of the first fruits in the old Hebrew times! The basket laden with the ripe clusters. The owner's confession as he presented it to the priest. The setting of it before the altar. The articulate speech of the offerer before the Lord, ending with the renewed solemn presentation words: "And now, behold, I have brought the first fruits of the land which Thou, O Lord, hast given me!" All that must have been very beautiful and instructive, and it embodies an eternal principle. It sets forth God's unchanging claim to the *first*, as well as to the best of all we have. Giving late in life and after long withholding, (there is very little of such giving at all) is as though a Jew had come up to the temple with his basket filled with the fruits of years long gone by—all the bloom and fragrance gone from them long ago—old grapes, old figs, old sheaves of withered corn; what were such a basket put beside the offering of the man, who with odours of summer all about him, comes straight from the fig-tree, the vineyard, or the yellow corn field?

Farther, *the giving should be in some proportion to the income.*—I do not presume to fix the proportion with arithmetical exactness. There are insuperable difficulties in the way of fixing or naming any numerical proportions for Christian liberality. It is true that some will take advantage of this difficulty to give little or nothing at all. Professing to be shocked by the idea of love measured out by number, and weight, and mathematical precision, they express their own in a perfectly vague manner, which defies all calculation. But we should never be able to reach such persons in any way by any rules, however despotic or scriptural they might be; and it would not be according to scriptural authority to fix any one precise proportion for all persons, and for all circumstances,—*e.g.*, for some a tenth would be too little; for some it would be too much; enough at one time of life and in certain circumstances—too little or too much at another time and in other circumstances. Besides, it is impossible to draw any exact line of distinction between one kind of giving and another. A Christian feels that in giving to relatives, to friends, to social human objects, he is truly giving to God.

But, while abstaining from naming any definite and fixed proportion in giving, we the more insist on the *principle* of a fair and just proportion, and on the consequent duty of the individual to turn the principle into practice, and to find out for himself how much his own proportion ought to be. Another may not come to him and claim certain sums, but he may claim them of himself—he must, if his judgment and conscience tell him they are due. `Another may not write out for him any precise figures, but he himself may write a tenth, or a seventh, or a half, if it is right; or if he shrink from fixing any exact proportion, as some natures do, he can at least come so near to it that his givings will be practically regulated by it.

Now this proportion will never be reached, or, at any rate, will hardly for any long time be continued, except in connection with another principle of far deeper hold and wider sway—*the principle that what is left is given too*—that all we have belongs to God—that we ourselves are not our own. This principle penetrates to the very centre of our being, and sweeps round the widest circumference of our life. It touches our life at every point, and fills it through all its successive acts and days. It makes the giving of the parts that are sent away natural and easy—not strained, mechanical, and difficult. It makes the holding of the portion that remains a simple trust, never for a moment an absolute possession. The formal Pharisaical giving will take from the stock the amount that is considered to be discreet—to appease conscience, to keep God quiet, as it were, or perhaps even with some secret hope of an early repayment with interest by His Providence. In true Christian giving the gift is representative of all that is left. So much *there*, and so much *here*! That which I give, gone in the very act out of the region of my personal responsibility, to flow away like the ripples on the water, or the sounds in the air, God alone knoweth whither; this which I retain, to be kept as talents in my stewardship, traded with, watched, held in trust for God. Thus what is left is given too. No man, in fact, can give willingly anything to God, however small—no, not so much as the widow's mite—if he puts the grip of a selfish holding on what remains. The Christian claim never stays short of "the uttermost." We are saved to the uttermost, and to the uttermost we must show that we are saved, by writing the name of our redeeming Lord on everything we have, and holding Him as proprietor of all.

The time is coming when "Holiness unto the Lord" shall be upon the bells of the horses; and when even "the pots in the Lord's house"—the plainest, poorest, commonest things of life—"shall be like the bowls before the altar," sacred, consecrated things. Coming? That time is come if we will. Christian people have an immense power of improving on the sentiment of that old hopeful song which speaks of "a good time coming." With them the "good time" has come. A man who wills it so may look round on all that is in his house—on his furniture, pictures, jewels; on all he holds in goods, stock, money; on the fields where his cattle graze; on the ocean where his ships sail—and see the mystic awful inscription everywhere, "To the Lord," "To the Lord." And if he could look upon himself, if in some celestial glass he could see himself as he is—a sinner forgiven, a child reclaimed from wandering, and going home to the Father's House—he would see written on his own brow, "You are not your own; you are bought with a price;

therefore glorify God in your body and in your spirit, which are God's." It is becoming more and more evident that the religion of Christ is such that we cannot touch the spirit and essence of it by anything less than wholeness of consecration. Parts, fragments, or selected pieces, these will do no longer. But when we give the whole—ourselves, our endowments, our possessions—then the giving of each part in fit time and place cannot be less than a blessedness and a joy.

And it is also true that we shall never understand really what Christian giving is *until we get beyond and above what is called " the duty " of it* (although that is good to begin with) to this higher ground, where only the *blessedness* of it will be felt, and where we shall hear very clearly the Master's words, standing as we shall do in His nearer presence, "It is more blessed to give than to receive." That is a universal truth, applicable not to money alone, but to the whole of life's experiences. It has stood on the inspired page from the beginning, and yet it is still to too many a hidden thing; only one here and there goes quite to heart of the open secret. When all Christian people begin to be penetrated and possessed with this knowledge, it will be like the outburst of spring after a dreary winter, with the glory of summer and the wealth of autumn beyond.

Thought. It is very pleasant to receive quickening thoughts. New, fresh thoughts are among the best gifts of the Father of lights to men. A man may well feel richer and happier when they come to him. But there is yet one happier thing, and that is (godlike) to give these thoughts again, not cautiously and carefully, as men sometimes exhibit precious things for a moment—opening the casket and unveiling the sanctuary in a kind of dread—but with unsparing and unfearing liberality, setting them out in the bright light in which they came. And lo! the light is brighter now than ever before. Probably never since the world was made did God's luminous thought-gifts pass and repass from heart to heart in His great human family as they do now.

So of sympathy. It is a blessed thing to receive it in time of need, when weak or weary, or sick or sorrowful, or dying. Only in some such time can men know how much there is in the grasp of a hand, in the sound of a voice, in the sight of a friendly countenance, in a word or two of prayer, or even in silent waiting, while pain racks the body and sorrow melts the soul. It is a blessed thing to receive sympathy in such times. But it is yet more blessed, if God wills it so, to be the helpers than the helped, to be the comforters than the comforted, to comfort others who are in any trouble, with the same comfort wherewith we ourselves are comforted of God.

The same is true of life itself. It is a blessed thing to live and to receive life from the living God in fresh gift every day. It is good to see the green awakening earth and the overarching sky. It is good to hear the song of the bird, and the whisper of the breeze, and the prattle of the children, and all the sounds of human love. It is good to smell the rose, the violet, the honeysuckle, as we pass on our way. It is well to touch the velvet texture of the blossom on the mossy sward, or even the hard unyielding rock. It is good to taste with wholesome relish the food that sustains us. Is it not well to have these five gateways of knowledge and channels of delight always open, and to know that they are but channels and instruments and ministers, waiting in continual service on the nobler powers within? To discern, to judge, to remember, to hope, to fear, to love, to rejoice. What wealth there is in our being! What a song should we sing to the God of our life! Is it not a great thing thus to become aware of an unlimited universe around us, and conscious of inner faculties and spiritual affinities and possibilities, by which we are related to truth, to eternity, to God?

But there comes a time in the history of every true man (happy he to whom it comes in early life) when all the joy of receiving, even from God, is mingled for a while with an awful fear and a bitter sorrow—a time when the process of receiving seems even to be suspended for a little, while a higher possibility dawns upon the spirit and a nobler duty comes into view—the possibility, the joy of *giving* life, self, to God for ever! And when the possibility becomes in his consciousness the actuality, when the duty becomes the achievement, a man comes to himself, he enters on his manhood, he

On Christian Giving. 217

begins to live in sympathy with the ever-loving and ever-giving God.

And may I speak of a time when again *he must give*—himself and his whole earthly life up into the hand of God. That time may come to a young man soon after the consecrating day. He may be required to give up his whole life in one last gift: its sweet early memories, its bright gleams of promise, and various culture, and blossoming hopes, and dear attachments—all to God. Or the home-call may come after many long years of happy giving life; after the sowing and the reaping of many a season, after the work of many a busy day and the sleep of many a restful night; when the snows of age and the honours of virtue meet to crown the old man's head; but come when it may—to him who lives the unselfish giving life it will come with a joy unspeakable and full of glory. For to give life all away thus is, in fact, only ourselves to go that we may receive it again elsewhere—in a happier world, in fuller measures, in floods of clearer light, in waves of higher rapture, and, I am sure, for some still more glorious service somewhere in the universe of God.

> "Out of itself, into itself;
> All that we see and know
> Swings like a mighty pendulum
> Or an endless ebb and flow.
>
> "But over it all and beyond it all,
> As the sun is beyond the sea,
> I can but think there is something else,
> For which all this must be.

"Out of themselves, into themselves,
　　The rivers of being and love,
　Mingle and flow through the world below,
　　And all the worlds above.

"And God, like an all-including globe,
　　Self-poised, unincluded, free,
　Holds all that was, and all that is,
　　And all that ever shall be.

"Not *He*, but in Him, is the universe,
　　And His life is the life of all,
　And on His bosom of infinite love,
　　For Life and Love I fall."

XVII.

Divine Expulsions.

"As an eagle stirreth up her nest, fluttereth over her young, spreadeth abroad her wings, taketh them, beareth them on her wings: so the Lord alone did lead him, and there was no strange god with him."—DEUT. xxxii. 11, 12.

WE know that God does not hesitate to speak as a man, using freely the language, the passions, the affections of men, to express His own divine sentiments and emotions. But it is also true, and more remarkable, that He impersonates the inferior creatures, and by means of the habits and qualities of the animals, high and low, expresses to us His will, His judgments, and the fulness of His grace.

"I will be unto them as a lion; as a leopard by the way will I observe them. I will meet them as a bear bereaved of her whelps."

He hovers over men as the dove. He would gather them into shelter and safety as a hen gathers her chickens under her wing; and here He makes the king of birds, on its lofty eyrie, speak to men of His omnipotent protection and watchful care.

There is no need to describe the nature and habits

of the eagle. Even children know what a royal creature of the air it is. And they know its habits and ways; how it builds on the high rocks of the mountains, and on inaccessible cliffs of the sea, partly because it loves the elevation, the mountain air, and the nearness to the sun, but chiefly to have its young ones in safety, beyond the arrow of the fowler and the huntsman's foot. There, in the rude nest, they are brought forth, and fed with such morsels as the parent eagles can find in the country round. Lambs, hares, even infants, it is said, have been carried away as food for the eaglets, although, happily for our sensibilities, the stories of the little children in the eagle's nest generally end by their being rescued and brought home. And there the young eagles are taught to fly by the example of the parent birds, are stirred up in the nest, caught and carried on their wings, and ultimately pushed or dropped into the air, and sent out into life for themselves.

Such is the brooding and watchful care of God over His people. Such His design and aim for them; even that they may fulfil the laws of their nature, and, as it were, use free wing, and fly far and high in the open heaven of His grace. God bare Israel out of Egypt and through the desert "on eagles' wings," and He is always so dealing with His own people.

There are various thoughts suggested by this passage:—

Divine Incitements.

The stirring up of the nest. Yes, *the nest.* For what

Divine Expulsions. 221

the birds do the men do. This world is all alive with nest-building. Men seek comfort, satisfaction, and rest in outward things. In a scene where all is flowing they try to make fixity. In things, which in themselves are superficial and evanescent, they try to find substance. Circumstances must be conquered in order to be used; must be brought into a certain arrangement, and fixed there. A man says to himself: "I must have so many things! And I must have them here! And I must have them so! And they must be so compacted, and built, and woven together, that they will continue as long as I am pleased with them. In short, I will build me a nest." Just as in building time you see the birds laying a tax upon the oxen for hair, upon the sheep for wool, upon other birds for down and feathers, and upon universal nature for just what she may have of suitable material—so men, in making their nests, tax all who will pay, gather together of all kinds and from all quarters, and build the whole into a treasure house, where their joys are kept, and where their portion is stored. In some cases the nest seems good and well built—the walls of it thick tenacious clay or of well-woven tissue, the lining of greenest moss or softest down, well canopied with leaves, well set in the safest cleft of the tree. Storms may blow, it will hardly rock. Evil beasts and envious creatures may pass below, it is out of sight or out of reach. Some men are not content indeed with less than a very eagle's nest, up among the rocks of the mountain, higher than any other nest, where they may survey the prospect and spread the wing, and be great and happy. And it is wonderful how happy men become sometimes in the worldly nest. A man gets the wife he wants. The children come, and prosperity, and kindliness, and health, and comfort, and reputation—and he says in his heart: " I shall die in my nest after living in it for long happy years." When lo! there comes somehow, and from some quarter, a "*stirring up*" *of the nest*—incitements, surprises, changes, losses, controversies, sorrows. The young birds are growing, and the nest is too small, and they crowd against each other, and *that* makes a stirring up. The eldest-born go out on the wing and do not fare very well, and come back again, and there is not room now, and the old child-welcome can never come back. Or there are storms that rock the tree and rend the nest; to drop the figure, there are griefs and losses that crush the unportioned heart and shake it all trembling out of its security. It were useless to attempt to describe all the ways by which God can shatter what man builds, drive away what man gathers, take what man in vain tries to hold.

The thing to be done is to persuade ourselves that all this is indeed sent for our good. The eagle does not stir up its nest with any ill design. God does not bring His forces of change and trouble upon men with a view to grieve and ruin them. He too has only good intent. His voices, His touches, His strokes, seem to say to men: "What mean ye, ye sleepers. Awake. Look around. Come away. You have enough of that. You have been long enough there. You have here no continuing city; seek one to come. You have in the creature no abiding portion; seek it, and you will find it in Me."

Divine Example.

"As an eagle stirreth up her nest, *fluttereth over her young;*" as showing them the way to fly; so God sets before us the examples of the good, the strivings of the great, the lives of the saints, and chiefly the perfect pattern—the perfect life of His incarnate Son. If the excitements and disturbances that come, the stirrings up of the nest, meant no more than "You must go out, you must go on," they would be of little or no value. But with the disturbances and dislodgements of life will be found very often (they will be seen and found if they are sought) invitations, and possibilities, and enlargements. When there are stirrings up in the nest, there will be flutterings over it— inducements, drawings, holy temptations of blessed example. The well-known lines of the poet express the thought exactly for us, if we apply them to the Divine incitements:

> "And, as a bird each fond endearment tries
> To tempt its new-fledged offspring to the skies;
> He tried each art, reproved each dull delay,
> Allured to brighter worlds, and led the way."

The allurements of God are wonderful, if we could but see them and believe in them.

"Let no man say, when he is tempted of evil, I am tempted of God, for God is not tempted with evil, neither tempteth He any man." The Devil, we are told, tempts men, draws them away, drowns them in destruction and perdition. And is God then practically out of the moral universe? Has He retired from the strife, and lapsed into a sublime and passionless inaction? Is there a tempting Devil, and is there no alluring God? Alas for man if it were so! No; God is always overcoming enticements to evil by His Divine allurements. He is always hovering over the world, as a bird over her young. He is Father and Mother of us all. He is always showing us the way; always rising into the purer air, that we may follow; always opening gates, and showing new paths, and pointing to high places: and never yet have the poor passing pleasures of earth been made to look so fair, as God makes goodness seem, shining in the lives of His holy ones and perfectly in Himself.

Divine Protection.

"The eagle spreadeth abroad her wings." This indeed may be no more than the full expansion of the meaning of the former phrase, the spreading abroad of the wings being the complete example of the method of flying. But the probability rather seems to be that the spreading of the wings is the promise of protection to the young birds, both while in the nest and while attempting to fly. This certainly is the usual sense of spreading the wing in Scripture. We are told how safe we are under "the shadow of the Almighty" and under "the covert of His wings." "He shall cover thee with His feathers, and under His wings shalt thou trust." So that whatever may be the true interpretation here, we have the divine protection amply promised and assured to us in the Word of God—promised, and yet under certain conditions.

This one great condition always holds—that we must be engaged in doing, or endeavouring after something worthy of divine protection, if we are to expect it to be extended to us. God protects—Whom? Not lazy selfish creatures whose chief aim is to make the world a nest and to find out the softest place in it for themselves, in which they may abide and rest, while food is provided and shelter found. God protects—What? Not indolence, cowardice, selfishness, fear, indifference. He protects those who stir themselves when the nest is stirred; those who spread the wing in answer to the outspread wings above them; those who try to fly; those who work; those who stay by the task; those who refuse to leave the field of duty; those who hunger and thirst after righteousness, and seek what they hunger for; those who follow on to know the Lord, and who serve Him as they can, although often in weariness; those, in a word, who try at least to mount up on wings as eagles, to run without being weary, to walk without fainting.

Ah, yes! if we would but try! But we are such bantlings in goodness! If we would but believe in the air as we do in the earth, or even in the high places of the earth as we do in the lower! What then must be done if we do not? Just what is done by the mother-eagle with the strong young birds when they are winged and feathered and fed, and yet keep the nest, they must *be* "*taken.*"

Divine Compulsion.

"As an eagle . . . taketh them," if they will, in helpfulness; if they will not, in compulsion; in one way or another, they must be got out of the nest. I have seen, not an eagle indeed, but a bird of some size, give a motherly or fatherly push to a strong young creature sitting on the edge of the nest engaged in a general survey of the world below. "It is time," said the mother, "that you should go down and see life more closely for yourself, and wing your way through the air, and try what you can find in the fields—be *a bird*, like your ancestors!"

"*Taketh* them!" These "takings" of God at certain periods and epochs of the individual life are very instructive, if you will observe them. I mean His takings of the stronger kind. His graspings. His expulsions. His banishments. Human history began with an expulsion. "He drove out the man" from a scene in which he would only too gladly have stayed. "Eden," God said to him, "is no more for you. It is a withered possession, a weedy garden now, a riven nest—you must away." He "took" Abraham from his native home and from his kindred, and sent him to wander as a stranger up and down in a strange land. He took Joseph from his aged father and sent him a lonely captive into Egypt; and He took Daniel into

Babylon; and the Pilgrim Fathers to the New England shores. So He "takes" oftentimes, blessed be His name, one and another in quiet common life, and by a kind of sacred violence forces them into new scenes, and almost into better states.

Then He is always ready with suitable and sufficient helps to those who are thus completely launched and started upon the new life. "As an Eagle . . . *beareth them on her wings.*" The mother-eagle comes beneath her young one in the air when it is about to sink, through fear or weakness, bears it up on her own outspread wings and carries it back to the nest or along through the air, until weakness is recruited and fear is overcome. God says: "Ye have seen what I did unto the Egyptians, and how I *bare you on eagles' wings*, and brought you unto myself." He had carried them safely out of Egypt, a poor defenceless people; Pharaoh's chariots, and horsemen, and armies were of no more account to Him than so many grasshoppers. He had brought them through the sea and through the wilderness, and here they were so far on their way, at Sinai, which God had chosen for the time as His throne. And from the past He means them to look with courage to the future, and believe that what He had done He would do still. Let us follow out the argument of faith. He helps yet with His almighty strength all His children, those who yield to His discipline, those who receive His nurture, and He helps them as He did Israel of old, at every stage of the process, from the first step to the last.

By the mighty help of God, we are carried out of the dark Egypt of our bondage and sin, through the wilderness of trial and temptation, into the Canaan of liberty and joy. And nothing but the almighty helps of God could carry men so high, so far, so well. But for His grace, men would never think of leaving Egypt at all. Their low thought would be: "We cannot leave the flesh-pots. We cannot go out on an unknown journey. We cannot cross the sea. We cannot fight against unmeasured odds. We must live and die where and as we are." But when the call comes from the voice of God, and when He pledges all His strength to meet whatever needs may come, those who hear the call have but to arise and begin. And many a time during the journey, exhaustion would come and utter failure but for the same eternal strength. All through the world and every day, such words of God as these, or the thoughts they contain, are whispered and breathed into weary sinking hearts. *"In the Lord Jehovah is everlasting strength." "Fear not, for I am with thee. I will strengthen thee. I will uphold thee with the right hand of my righteousness." My grace is sufficient for thee."*

True, this almighty help comes very quietly. It drops into the soul that is in need as the rain and distils as the dew. God's strongest forces in Nature are silent. So in the kingdom of grace. A thought! A memory! One gleam of light, one thrill of love, and the help is given. Nothing is more tender, nothing more gentle than the strength of God. Lean upon

Divine Expulsions. 229

it; breathe it; drink it in. It will bear you through the brunt of duty; unscathed through the fires of temptation; through the dark days of sorrow; and at last through the valley of the shadow of death.

Surely then, we may say, in conclusion, since thus the Lord alone does or can lead you, it ought to be your lifelong care that He alone *shall* lead you, and that there shall be no strange god admitted to the rule and conduct of your life.

XVIII.

On the Mountain.

"Then the eleven disciples went away into Galilee, into a mountain where Jesus had appointed them. And when they saw Him, they worshipped Him: but some doubted. And Jesus came and spake unto them, saying, All power is given unto me in heaven and in earth. Go ye therefore, and teach all nations, baptising them in the name of the Father, and of the Son, and of the Holy Ghost: Teaching them to observe all things whatsoever I have commanded you: and, lo, I am with you alway, even unto the end of the world. Amen."—MATT. xxviii. 16-20.

"After that, he was seen of above five hundred brethren at once; of whom the greater part remain unto this present, but some are fallen asleep."—1 COR. xv. 6.

BOTH these passages, I believe, refer to and narrate in a different manner one and the same event. Some think that the appearance of our Lord, mentioned by the Apostle Paul in writing to the Corinthians, when "He was seen of above five hundred brethren at once," could not have been in Galilee, because Galilee was, they think, too far from Jerusalem, where the multitude of believers were gathered.

This, however, is an objection of no great strength, and becomes, in our view, untenable when we consider more fully the facts and circumstances of the case. For one thing, remember how expressly Christ had told

His disciples before His death, that when He was risen He would go before them into Galilee. Remember also, that on the very morning of the resurrection, when He met the women who had been at the tomb, He said to them : " Go tell my brethren that they go before me into Galilee, *there* shall they see me." And accordingly they went away, expecting to meet Him on the day appointed, or that would soon be appointed, and on the mountain where He had fixed that the meeting should be.

It is very clear that the meeting on this mountain was a formally appointed one, that it was meant to be a meeting of the greatest importance, and that the impression of its importance was carefully and repeatedly made on the minds of the disciples. Could the intention to hold such a meeting be kept a secret? Was there not every reason for telling it, at least to the believers? Would not such news spread far and wide and fast among them? And would they not be drawn by a resistless attraction to the place where they might hope to see again the face and hear the voice of One who had been crucified, dead, and buried, but who was now risen from the dead to die no more? Who of them would willingly be absent on such an occasion?

Why then, if the case be so, does the Evangelist Matthew make no direct mention of it? Is it likely that he would speak only of eleven, if he knew (as he must have known if it were a fact) that there were five hundred persons present? Is it likely that he would have omitted so material a circumstance, a numeration so impressive as this? We answer that it is quite possible, it is even probable, that he did intentionally make such omission, as we are pleased to call it—he himself, however, never looking on his silence in that light. There are many such omissions in Matthew's Gospel. Here, and in other cases, he brings out the point of chief importance to his great object, which is to show how Jesus, although rejected of His own countrymen, was yet manifested and proved to be the true king of the great spiritual kingdom. The kingship of Jesus Christ and His kingdom, these are the subjects of Matthew's thought and of his pen. Anything that does not bear on these he leaves unchronicled. He does not mention either of the appearances in Jerusalem to the eleven, although he must have been present, simply because they did not directly bear on his object; and here he speaks of the eleven, making no mention of the far larger number, because the eleven were concerned as no others were in the founding of the Gospel kingdom, and in the planting and training of the Christian Church. But there are some indications in Matthew of the presence of others besides the eleven. The phrase "some doubted" (whether the doubt regarded the fact of the resurrection, or the identity of the person who appeared, with the risen Christ) is easily explained if it refers to some of the five hundred, many of whom may have had but slight opportunity of familiarly knowing the Lord. It is hardly conceivable that it applies to any of the eleven, after all that had happened in Jerusalem, where He had breathed on them, spoken to them, eaten in their presence, and where the unbelieving one of their number had been convinced by word and touch.

The appointment at first must have been only of a general kind. "At some time, soon after my resurrection, somewhere in Galilee, you shall see me." But the place, the day, the hour, must have been named at length. It could only be by a definite arrangement that more than five hundred brethren were brought together in a place by no means populous. It is very likely that Jesus made the appointment with the eleven on the shore of the lake, after the morning meal of bread and fish, before He left them. If it be so, they would be able on that occasion to let Him pass away from them with comparative content, hoping to see Him again so soon.

Of course, the news would be sent far and nigh to those concerned. No true disciple would be able to make his bosom the sepulchre of such tidings. Untold, they would be like a sword in his bones, like a burning fire in his heart; told out, they would taste like honey, and shine like light. Cannot we easily imagine many a runner bearing the announcement over the hills of Galilee, many a hamlet and many a house surprised and lighted up with the message, many a worker called from field and vineyard to hear it? Do we not see the net-mender dropping his work to listen, and the fisher drawing up his boat on the shore and getting ready for a little inland journey, and Martha stilled amid her bustling cares at the sound of the blessed name? Five hundred brethren were not in that early time found all in one place. From Nazareth, from Cana, from Bethsaida, from Capernaum, from both banks of the Jordan, from the other side of the sea, from the vineyards, from the sheepfolds, from the busy streets, and from the quiet hills, they come on the appointed day to the appointed place. The day is not known to us; it was one of the forty days after our Lord's passion—it matters not which. The place of meeting is a mountain; that is all we are told—a mountain in Galilee. It seems all but certain that it was Mount Tabor, the mountain which tradition has always favoured as the scene of the transfiguration, although there is really no evidence pointing specifically to it as the one on which our Lord then stood. It is, however, highly probable that it was on Mount Tabor that Jesus made this memorable appearance to His disciples, and where He laid on them the great commission to go into all the world and preach the Gospel to every creature.

Mount Tabor stands about six miles from Nazareth, to the south-east, rising up abruptly from the great plain of Esdraelon. It is defined, solitary, altar-like, grand to the sight, seen from the plain below. The sides of the mountain are covered with woods, beautiful in appearance and affording an excellent shade. The oak-tree, the walnut, the pistachio, rose-bushes, vines, abundant flowers, clothe it almost to the top. The crest of the mountain is table-land, although it looks at a distance like a cone. There is a small plain on the very top, and the view from thence is one of the most splendid to be found in the whole world. To the eye of the sacred poet, ages before the time of Christ, it had stood out in sublimity, and had drawn from him words which are to-day to have a wonderful fulfilment—"Tabor and Hermon shall rejoice in Thy name."

Imagine the expectant company toiling up the sides of the mountain by the several paths. It will take some hours for most of them to ascend, for it is nearly two thousand feet above the sea, although not so much above the plain. Imagine them resting under the shade of the trees, drinking from the tanks which catch and keep cool and pure the water that is filtered through the limestone rock, pulling the flowers that grow in the glades, listening to the birds among the branches; some of them, perhaps, remembering the Master's words, "Consider the lilies," or those other words, "They sow not, neither do they reap, nor gather into barns, yet your heavenly Father feedeth them." They talk together as they ascend, some of them no doubt thinking a good deal more than they speak. At length they are gathered on the summit; how many it is not easy to say. Five hundred *brethren* would almost seem to imply an outer circle of some hundreds more of those who were well-disposed and likely to become disciples.

And now He appears as quietly as when He entered the room in Jerusalem while all the doors remained shut; or shining out in transfiguration glory, which is also the glory of His risen life, and probably standing on some elevation so as to be seen of all. In whatever way the manifestation began, it seems soon to have glowed into celestial brightness. For "when they saw

Him, *they worshipped Him*," falling prostrate, many of them, at least, in the attitude of adoration. And He receives the worship as His due; and by no hint or whisper indicates that they have overestimated His dignity, or that to offer religious homage to Him is impiety or mistake. But there were some who "doubted" —doubted whether Christ had really risen from the dead; or doubted whether, if risen, this is He; or whether, if risen and if present, they ought to render Him divine honours. Whatever be the nature of the doubting, it is not without significance that it exists. The manifestation of His glory, therefore, although very bright and beautiful, and very helpful to weak faith or to faith just beginning, is not such as to overpower the rational faculties and compel the assent of the will and the conviction of the understanding without due perception of evidence. Men must think, reason, consider, weigh evidence, and come to conclusions by means of the faculties God has given them, even when materially they are in the presence of all that is most illustrious and divine. The outer senses cannot always rule the inner faculties of the spirit. Here is Christ in His glory! And here are poor doubting souls who cannot receive Him! so little does mere sense help the work of faith. "All power is given" to Him. What will He do with these men? Will He smite them down in some swift judgment? Or shut them out from the believing company? Or retire with some of His chosen ones, leaving them in the darkness of their doubting? Unbelief had companied with Him, in the persons of His dearest followers, all through His earthly life. He meets it now with the old patience. "*Jesus came and spake to them.*" It is very beautiful. The words are so few, and the narrative so simple and so much condensed, that we are apt enough to miss the gracious tender significance of this action of the Lord. He had been standing probably on an elevation and at some little distance. He came down into the company, went among the groups of the doubting, spoke to them in nearness, so that they could see His features, and hear the softness of His voice. I know not why we should not suppose that He came so near to them that they might, if they would, touch Him. And then He spake in the hearing of all these words, "All power is given unto me in heaven and in earth." Daniel "saw in the night visions, and, behold, one like the Son of Man came with the clouds of heaven, and came to the Ancient of days. . . . And there was given Him dominion and glory and a kingdom, that all people, nations, and languages should serve Him; His dominion is an everlasting dominion which shall not pass away, and His kingdom that which shall not be destroyed." Our Lord seems here to make reference to that passage in Daniel, and claims its begun fulfilment in Himself. Now and here He may be said, in some true measure, to "come in the clouds of heaven" with great majesty. He may be said to come to the "Ancient of days," to the eternal and unchangeable God, returning from the great enterprise of redemption on earth into the heavenly places a conqueror, having won supreme victory in the act of dying, and at the very central point of the battle of the ages. And here, according to His own express assurance, He receives "dominion and glory," "a dominion everlasting and a kingdom that shall not be destroyed." As much as this, assuredly, is implied in our Lord's words. If it be said that after all this mediatorial power of the risen Christ must be limited, since it is said to be "given," it is sufficient to reply, without entering further on the argument, that the Being who can take and keep and use all power in heaven and on earth must be as truly divine as He who gives it. This power, the chief purpose and use of which is to redeem and save, is "given" in fulfilment of the eternal covenant or purpose of redemption. That covenant is now fully and openly ratified. The resurrection is its final seal. The ascension, of which this scene on the mountain-top may be said to be almost a part (He is now so far on the upward way), will be the taking possession of the inheritance and the assumption of its royalties. And the first royal word is this—"Go ye therefore." "Because all power is mine, you who love and serve me, go, attended and defended by that power,"—to do what? To conquer? To enslave? No; to teach, to make disciples, "baptising them in the name of the Father, and of the Son, and of the Holy Ghost. Teaching them to observe all things whatsoever I have commanded you. And, lo, I am with you alway, or every day, or all the days, even unto the end of the world." Having spoken these ever-memorable words, He seems to have vanished from their sight, melting into the air or gliding swiftly away, by most of them probably never seen again on earth— by most of them, we may hope, joyfully recognised and worshipped, without any doubtings, on Mount Zion above.

The question meets us to-day, as we think of the whole narrative, How do *we* stand related to that assembly on the Galilean mountain and to that last command of our adored Lord? The answer which I trust we shall all feel disposed to give is this, that we are related to that assembly just as though we had formed part of it, to that last command as though we had heard it in audible words from the lips of our Lord. That we may be confirmed in this conviction, let us ask and answer some further questions.

First. Is the world's need any less now than it was then? Substantially, it is the same. It was great and urgent then, it is great and urgent now. The world, indeed, is in many ways a different world from that into which the first disciples were sent forth, and it concerns us, as Christian believers and honest men, frankly to admit and sincerely to rejoice in any steps of real progress which this world may have made. If there be such a thing as the education of the race, as such, with a view to its coming perfection, we ought surely, within the compass of eighteen centuries, to be able to see that some lessons have been learned not to be unlearned, some points of progress gained not to be lost.

Slavery has been all but extinguished. It lingers still only on the outskirts of civilisation, and is happily being pursued beyond these into its last retreats.

The condition of woman has been immensely improved, is still rising, and must rise in some grave respects yet more, if we are to have the best relief from some of our most appalling social difficulties. This is true; although it is also true that there are extreme and unnatural claims made on woman's behalf, which will cease just in proportion as the real and reasonable claims are seen and admitted.

I hardly know whether we may venture to specify as another point of advancement this (which is undoubtedly a fact), that the world to-day is immensely richer than that which was known to the first Christians. It is richer in stored-up wealth, in the accumulated fruits of human labour. That would be a benefit, as lessening the necessity for exhausting toil, if men were true and just to each other. All our wealth will be a benefit when it is held and used on Christian principles.

The world, on the whole, is more highly informed than it was then—not in everything: there are some spheres of knowledge in which we have never exceeded the ancients; but knowledge, in general, is far more widely spread among the peoples than heretofore, while within the realm of physical science great discoveries have been made, and great benefits of a material kind are accruing to man. But are we so simple, so shallow, so untrue to our better selves, as to put such things as these—good as they are in themselves, and as far as they go—as capable of meeting the deeper needs of the human soul? These needs are still unsupplied by any material satisfactions. Sin is yet sin, and cannot change its nature, and cannot be reasoned out of human hearts by any arguments, nor vanquished by the strength of human wills, nor washed away by human tears. The conscience of the world at this hour, in so far as it is an active and honest conscience, has cast upon it the old problem "How shall man deliver himself from the evil of his own nature? How shall man be just with God?" And if Christian people are silent, and if the Gospel of atonement and free forgiveness be withheld from the knowledge of mankind, the problem remains insoluble, however men may advance in general culture, and live amid the abundance of outward prosperity. "Go ye therefore;" go into all the world, preach the Gospel to every creature. He who died on the cross, rose from the grave, shone out on that mountain-top, and who lives now in heaven, King and Priest upon His throne, ever living to make intercession for us—" He is the propitiation for our sins, and not for ours only, but also for the sins of the whole world." Tell the world the news.

Whatever be the causes of it, is not the misery of man great upon him still? How sorrowful is life to many a one! How heavy the burden of personal existence! How dark are the shadows of affliction when they fall! What a fathomless pit is the grave! What realms of dread uncertainty lie beyond it! The world calls itself wise; but is not the world finding, as it has never yet found, the truth of the old saying, "in much wisdom is much grief," and that "he that increaseth knowledge increaseth sorrow?" You see it in the eagerness of human faces; you hear it in the tread of human feet along the busy streets; it throbs through all industry; it is proclaimed in the strain of new enterprises; it is painfully present in some of the deeper scepticisms; it goes like a sigh through a part of our best literature. If man will continue estranged from God and keep his soul unportioned, he must live in perpetual restlessness, and be the victim of a cureless sorrow. "His flesh upon him shall have pain, and his soul within him shall mourn."

"Go ye therefore" into the busy world immediately around you, and into the wider world beyond, with the good news of God. Tell men that God loves them; that all power is given to the Son of God to make love prevail; that all things are now ready; that each returning penitent is welcome when he comes; that whosoever cometh will be in no wise cast out; that "He is able to save to the uttermost all who come unto God by Him." Such is the great commission—the most important ever entrusted to men.

Look at *its universality.* "Its line goeth out into all the earth, and its word unto the end of the world." "Go ye unto all nations. Preach to every creature."

Look at *its intellectual character.* "Go *teach* all nations." The Gospel is, in the first instance, an appeal to the human intelligence. It is a message to the reason of man. It is not a mystery enacted, an imposing ritual with hidden meanings. It is, no doubt, divinely high and deep and far-reaching—in length and height and depth beyond human measurement—yet in its point of contact with man it is a clear and simple message. Its plainness is beautiful. Who dares to say that he cannot understand the Gospel of Christ?

Consider *its gentleness*. This will grow upon you as you look. The terms of this commission show us the divine condescension in act of bending down to reach men, stooping to the lowly, waiting for the slow, helping the weak. Go teach men; disciple them; bring them to His feet who alone can call up the dawning of the morning upon the tossings to and fro of troubled men; who can walk upon the wildest waves, and say "Peace be still" to the rudest winds that blow. Bring them to the place where the heavy-laden lay down their burdens, and the weary enter into rest. Disciple men, then put the sign upon the disciples, "baptising" them; give them the badge that men may know them; and that they may know themselves. Then teach again more fully and exhaustively; lead on into a further deeper peace; teaching them to observe all things commanded, until not faith only, but love and obedience possess the life, and "the peace of God which passeth all understanding shall *keep* the heart and mind." Peace shall mount guard (that is the meaning of the phrase; it is one of Paul's beautiful paradoxes), shall do the soldier's duty, shall keep the soul as a garrison keeps the fortress, beating off doubts, fears, distractions, cares, miseries, "shall keep the heart and mind through Christ Jesus."

Secondly. I ask: Are the encouragements given to those who put themselves instantly in a way of obedience to this last command, in any manner or degree less than they were at first or through the primitive ages? The followers of Christ had heavenly power on their side then, and felt that they had it. Have we any less? Has the power waned? Has it been withdrawn? Is it like any of the forces of material nature, capable of transmutation into another form, so that now it may have found some more congenial work than the salvation of men? Or is the promised presence withheld? Is Christ not with His people still "alway," "every day," and with especial nearness and fulness when they are faithfully and zealously engaged in His service? We should not dare to answer any of these questions in the affirmative. But let us make the test still more practical by applying it to the region of phenomena. Christ's assertions regarding His power and presence were immediately put to the proof by His followers, and in no long time they were able to point rejoicingly to certain definite results, not only in the inward experiences, but in the lives and characters of men. The most marvellous changes took place, such as had never been obtained under any other teaching or influence whatever. The apostle Paul, in writing to the Corinthians, enumerates some nine or ten of the worst vices and crimes which have ever disfigured human nature, and then he says, "Such were some of you, but ye are washed, ye are sanctified."[1]

[1] 1 Cor. vi. 9-11.

On the Mountain.

Every one of these men was a living witness for Christ, a living proof of the power of Christianity. In a state of society like ours, which has long been under more or less of the general Christian culture, we cannot expect to see many changes so visibly striking as those of the early times. But those who will look below the surface of things will see that changes the same in essence are being produced, that the same sanctifying grace is still at work. Take any of the foreign mission fields of any of the Christian Churches, and is it not true that, in the places where you have the most consecrated men—men of devout energy, of faith and prayer, other things being equal—there you have the surest and the richest harvest? Where Paul plants and Apollos waters, God gives the increase.

Or take the heathenism which, alas! exists at home. Would it be possible for any Christian society to take one of these dark, wretched neighbourhoods which can easily be found in any English city, or found even among the villages of the country, under culture and sympathetic care, giving—not much pecuniary help but much wise thought, much solicitude, much prayer, much personal presence—living men and women meeting living men and women, and all for the love of Christ, and in order to bring them to Him—would it be possible that any Christian company should do this without fruit and in vain? Can we believe that they would stand up and say, "We have tried the experiment faithfully, we have waited and laboured and prayed, and we have failed—there is no result." No, no. It is as it was at first. When men go forth and teach the true Gospel in the spirit of love and loyalty, the Lord works with them and confirms the word with signs following. It is a great work, so great that no other can be likened to it; all other good works are only parts of it. It will be a long and hard work, but it will be done. As surely as God is the Father, and Jesus Christ the Son, there will be "glory to God in the highest, on earth peace and goodwill towards men."

Go, therefore! Go, even if you doubt. "Some doubted" then; some doubt now. In a time like this, when all things are more or less on trial, and when doubt is in the very air, it is impossible, especially for young thinkers in the season of growth and susceptibility, to escape altogether its darkening paralysing influence. The practical question is how to deal with doubt so that it shall soon give place to faith. There is no way, on the whole, so good as the way of instant practical obedience. "Some doubted," and Jesus came near to them that they might have the practical proof they needed as to His identity. But He entered into no argument, He did not open to them the region of speculation, said nothing about principles or abstract religious truth—simply revealed Himself and the great fact of His resurrection, and then, in effect, said: "As to what remains of uncertainty, go and solve it in action, put the message to the proof, and see if your mists and questionings will not vanish away." The principle is applicable now as then. Beyond a certain point logic fails. Even the great facts of redemption lose their power when they are held solely in the sphere of contemplation, when they are not carried into the sphere of duty as practical force. Go, therefore, with the Gospel which perhaps you do not believe so fully as you could wish—you know it contributes to the purity of society, to the safety of states, to the relief of human suffering. If you dare not, in your present mental state, go alone, go with those who believe in it to the uttermost for themselves and others, and see whether it be indeed the deep, far-reaching cure for the world's malady. You will not go far, you will not work long, before the haunting shadows of your doubts will begin to flit away, and calm certainty to take their place.

Once before our Lord had seen the world and its kingdoms "from a high mountain." At least a certain phantasm and show of them passed through the air in vision before Him, called up, as it were, by the wand of the great enchanter. And He was asked to enter there and then into possession *on certain conditions!* He saw through the thin disguise. It was a mocking vision in delirious air; it was a fool's paradise; it was a despot's dream. He was indeed going to universal empire, but by another road—through the nightshades of Gethsemane, through the anguish of Calvary.

The temptation failed with the Master. Is it now going to succeed with the servants? "All the kingdoms of the world and the glory of them" are again put before us in a fair picture and as a great inheritance, into which not any single individuals, but the *race* is invited to enter. Modern progress sounds her trumpet and calls us to the mountain. "See," saith she, "how the countries are chequered with railways, how every ocean is 'shadowing with wings,' how the cities grow, how the axe fells the forest, how the ploughshare tears open the prairie, how homes soon to be filled with plenty spring up in many a far wilderness! In a moment London speaks to Manchester, Manchester to New York, New York to San Francisco. Look how on the wings of every morning the literature of the day spreads itself thick as the leaves of Vallambrosa! Science is multiplying her discoveries and applying them to practical uses—to vanquish diseases, to increase comforts. The world, in fact, is all yours on this simple and easy condition—that you satisfy your immortal manhood with these things, that you take possession, enjoy the present, and let the future provide for itself."

Can any who have been with Jesus Christ—on the mount of beatitudes, to listen to His teaching; on the mount of transfiguration, to behold His glory; on Mount Calvary, to see Him die; on the mountain in Galilee, to meet Him in His risen life and hear His last command—be held for one moment in any anxious suspense by such a vain and visionary offer as that? 'What would it profit a man," what would it profit the race, "to gain the whole world"—*thus?* Can matter be a portion for spirit? Can comfort satisfy a creature made for duty and the love of God? Can a brief gleam of mortal life, however splendid while it lasts, yet always soon stilled in a coffin and quenched in a grave, fill the desire of an immortal creature? We who have been with Jesus do not need to reconsider the question. "We know whom we have believed." Our philosophy of life is settled. We live to Him who lived and died for us. Ourselves subjects of His kingdom, we look for its appearance more and more among men. Not by natural knowledge, not by force, not by self-will or self-confidence, do men enter it, but by self-sacrifice, by dying unto sin and living unto righteousness. This is the kingdom that shall grow until it shall fill all the earth. And when that day shall come, when all material advantages of modern progress shall be caught up into the service of Christ, and earthly science and achievement shall come bending to His feet, then shall the old song be sung with a new name written on it.

"Thou hast made Him a little lower than the angels, and hast crowned Him with glory and honour. Thou madest Him to have dominion over the works of Thy hands ; Thou hast put all things under His feet . . . O Lord our Lord, how excellent is Thy name in all the earth!"

XIX.

The First Disciples.

"Again the next day after John stood, and two of his disciples; and looking upon Jesus as he walked, he saith, Behold the Lamb of God! And the two disciples heard him speak, and they followed Jesus. . . . One of the two which heard John speak, and followed him, was Andrew, Simon Peter's brother. He first findeth his own brother Simon, and saith unto him, We have found the Messias, which is, being interpreted, the Christ. And he brought him to Jesus."—JOHN i. 35-42.

DURING the time of our Lord's temptation, John the Baptist remained by the Jordan and continued his work, sometimes on this side the river, sometimes on that. After the baptism of Christ, although he still preached repentance, there was a change in the tone of his ministry. The coming One was now come, was baptized, inaugurated, and about to begin His work. John, therefore, probably felt that his own mission was drawing to a close, and was looking daily for the open manifestation of the Messiah.

Meantime, society was profoundly agitated. All kinds of rumours had been in circulation, and among them that which pointed to John himself as the Christ. Priests and Levites, sent expressly from Jerusalem,

The First Disciples. 251

arrive at the Jordan with the question, "Who art thou?" And "the next day," we are told (verse 29), after John's answer to these messengers, he pointed Jesus out in that memorable language which was at once a designation of the Saviour personally and a description for all time of His work—" Behold the Lamb of God, which taketh away the sins of the world." Our Saviour's long preparation is now fully over ; His days of seclusion are ended ; He must now appear publicly ; He must teach ; He must open His kingdom ; He must draw men to Himself : and He comes to the most likely place in all the world to find disciples. Among those who have accepted the teaching of John the Baptist will be found, in all probability, not the most learned men of the nation, not the most wealthy, but the most honest, the most susceptible religiously ; men with hearts best prepared to receive the seed-truth He will cast into them for their own salvation, and, by their instrumentality, for the salvation of the world.

Accordingly, He has but to appear, and the thing is done. A connection, vital and lasting, is formed between Him and those susceptive souls. He does not even speak. He says nothing, gives nothing, offers nothing. "Looking upon Jesus . . . John said to the two disciples who stood by his side, Behold the Lamb of God ! And they followed Jesus." The two disciples, undoubtedly, were John the Evangelist, and Andrew, the brother of Peter. Which of the two took the first step in following we are not told. One almost thinks it must have been John, with his swift and clear spiritual instinct; and if so, if John was the very first of all the human race who followed Him as the Messiah, that circumstance might be among the things which account for the Saviour's peculiarity of attachment to the beloved disciple. And yet we do not know; this world has held thousands of unknown heroes, and heaven has received tens of thousands of unknown saints; those names among the Apostles, which are only names to us, or little more, may, when we know everything, shine with unexpected lustre.

John and Andrew following, Jesus turns and speaks to them. The words are brief and simple—"What seek ye?" Very much would depend on the tone in which the words were uttered, and on the Saviour's aspect as He spoke. The question might easily have a forbidding sound—"What seek ye?" Why do ye trouble me? Why do ye presume to come into my presence? But it was certainly uttered in tones of kindness, and with looks of openness and love; for, in their reply, they venture to ask the place of His present abode, indicating a desire on their part to be taught, and especially, to find satisfaction on the great question of the Messiahship. His answer, prompt and kind, and with the winning "Come" in it, encouraged them to go with Him. It was about four o'clock in the afternoon, and they spent the remaining part of that day with Jesus. Ah, how honoured and how happy were those two first guests of the Redeemer of mankind! On that night there was many a scene of

The First Disciples. 253

festivity in royal court or stately hall; many a banquet prepared for favoured guests; many happy social gatherings in cities, and in hamlets, and homesteads, and tents; but not in the wide world was there a company so much to be envied as those two simple men, regarding whom it is written: "They came and saw where He dwelt, and abode with Him that day, for it was about the tenth hour." What passed in the interview will never be known here, although we may be sure it was never forgotten by the men themselves. And yet there is a sense in which we do know what transpired in that brief visit. We do not know the substance of the conversation, but we know the power that was in it; we do not know what words were uttered, but we know what a gift of life was given. Those men were confirmed in their hopes, and so far settled in their faith that they felt bound to go immediately and tell those nearest to them that they had made a great discovery—the great discovery for which the ages and economies had been waiting. Andrew was the first to tell, and his brother Peter the first to hear, the glad news that "the Christ" was found; and Andrew "brought him to Jesus." He too was received, was named "Cephas" in omniscient anticipation of the firm and stable character he was afterwards to attain; and so the first day of the ministry of Christ closes; John, Andrew, and Simon are disciples. The next day Jesus is ready to depart into Galilee. We cannot tell all the reasons which may have induced Him to leave Judæa so soon; probably He wished to avoid conflict with the ruling powers or parties among the Jews; besides, the Galilean, although comparatively rude and unlearned, was also less prejudiced and more open to His teaching than the Jew of Jerusalem. He is going to Galilee and He takes Galilee with Him. These men who are now gathered around Him are all Galileans. Philip was found by Jesus Himself, in what way we do not know; then, imitating the good example of Andrew, he found Nathanael and brought him to Jesus. He was received as an Israelite indeed, and was soon convinced that he stood in the presence of none other than the Son of God.

The simple narrative needs no further exposition, but some thoughts are suggested by it which may be of practical value.

We see here the very first beginnings of the Christian Church. It has been made a question indeed whether Jesus Christ had a conscious plan, whether He knew that this was the beginning visibly and before men of His own Church in the world. There can be but one answer to such a supposition from those who accept Him as a divine Saviour, in whom are hid all the treasures of wisdom and knowledge. And it is of deep interest to us to observe here, amongst things so quiet and natural, the beginnings of that Institution which is the greatest of all the institutions that have ever been or will ever be on earth. The beginning of anything that has grown into largeness and value always wins from us a special regard. If we sat under the shadow

The First Disciples. 255

of a great tree, which has fed on the soil and waved its branches in the air for centuries, it would interest us to have an authentic account of the planting of the acorn or of the little sapling from which the great monarch sprang. If we were sailing across the mighty mouth of the Amazon, one hundred and fifty miles in breadth, we would listen eagerly to any one who could tell us that he had seen the ripple of the mountain stream on the Andes' heights in which the great ocean-river began its course. An interest still deeper gathers round the beginnings of the great moral movements of the world. That little vessel, the Mayflower, speeding her lonely way westward, through wintry weather and stormy seas, to the bleak New England coast; bearing these brave warriors of the Cross, weak women as well as strong men, what a ship of glory she is to us now! For now we know that she carried the seeds of liberty and religion which have blossomed on that western continent. Or that lonely monk in his cell, thinking, praying, poring over an open Bible, is he a mere enthusiast or a reckless destroyer of old time-hallowed faiths? We know him now to be the prophet of light and freedom, the instrument used by God to bring in the blessed Reformation.

Ah! but with reverent interest how much deeper may we meetly regard this simple record of the beginning of that great Kingdom which has made every other feel its sway. It has affected the stability of empires, overthrown old idolatries, exploded philosophies, and, in spite of opposition, has outspread itself already into almost world-wide breadth. And its future will be yet greater than its past. It is a tree, and its branches shall stretch from sea to sea; a river, and the streams thereof shall make glad all the deserts of the earth; a heavenly leaven, it shall yet leaven the whole lump; a handful of corn, it shall wave on all mountain-tops, and its fruit shall shake like Lebanon! And it begins *here*—with the divine quietness which is characteristic of God's mightiest works. We have here no visible king, no wrapt prophet, no scribe even to make record at the time of the event. The only scroll is the heart of the simple, the only writer the unseen Spirit of God.

We see not only the beginning of the Church, but *also the beginning and first movements of personal religion.* How does spiritual life begin in the individual heart? It begins when the person comes to Christ. He saith to them "Come and see," "and *they came.*" Andrew finds Simon, and "*brought him to Jesus.*" "Jesus saw Nathanael *coming to Him.*" They all came; they were all received, and in that personal reception their higher life began. In saying this, we do not imply that everything is valueless which precedes this coming. In the case of these men, no doubt, the ministry of the Baptist had done much. They were penitent, they were prepared, they were expectant; in a sense, they were already accepted of God in that Saviour whom they as yet knew not. But as soon as opportunity was given they came, and so showed the but once, often looked upon them; the words of love seemed spoken again; and in a little while, when these memories and thoughts had had time to ripen in their hearts, the visible presence of the Master was given once more, and the *life*-call came, "Follow me." "And they arose, left all, and followed Him." Even so, there may be a true coming to the Saviour, and yet some pause between that and the full surrender. There is sometimes a great deal of work, as it were, with boats and fishing-nets, before a man can see clearly how he is to *follow* Him in whom he truly believes. Affairs of the family, affairs of business, personal friendships— all these require re-adjustment before religion takes the supreme place, and becomes the thing for every day and for all day long. We must not misjudge men, nor indeed judge at all, because we cannot. We ought only to judge ourselves, although that is the judicial work we are the least disposed to do; this, however, must be remembered, because this is clear and very important—that a true coming to Christ is always *with a view* to following Him; and that every one who has truly come ought to be seeing his way and working on through all difficulties, to a declared and full discipleship. A faith in Jesus Christ, held long in secrecy, is a very perilous thing. It is a thing "hard to be understood," and the danger is in such a case that it may prove to be not faith at all. We *come to Jesus*— that is the beginning and the spirit of religion for a sinner. We *follow Jesus*—that is the form and body which the spirit must take if it is real and true. The sincerity of their repentance, and their desire to be led by God. So it will be with us. All true repentance leads to Christ, all religion that is sincere finds its fulness only in Him. Early instruction, early impressions, longings of the heart, struggles of the will, breathings and soul-cries after a better life—all these are most valuable as preparations for an actual coming to Him who is the Truth and the Life ; but if they are rested in, and made the sum of religion, while He who is the fulness of the Godhead stands waiting still—then they are only miserable counterfeits of that life which is to be found only in Him.

It may be well to notice also that the first coming may be quite real and true, and yet not at once entire and decisive. It may be succeeded by apparent leavings and forsakings of Christ, and by returnings again, more or less, to old experiences and old ways. Coming to Christ truly is not of necessity coming all at once to clear views, to pure sanctity, to noble purposes, and to an all-consecrated life. There is often some wavering even after the first decisive act. These men came to Jesus Christ, but not *then* to stay ; the bond was real, but as yet it was not strong enough to hold them altogether and absolutely. And our Lord, who has long patience, and who makes no haste, does not interfere by any authoritative word. They went back to Bethsaida. They had houses there, and boats, and fishing-nets, and dear friends, and they went back to these for a while. But a strange invisible Presence went back with them. A face, such as they had never seen

The First Disciples. 259

"following" is in some respects (not in all) easier to us than it was to them. They were required literally to "leave all;" we are literally required to leave very little. Whatever is sinful, excessive, or dangerous—whatever is purely of the world—in habit, aim, or spirit, that must be left, and that will involve a very real and decisive renunciation. But as to external things, in many cases there is not much to give up. What is required is that most things shall be kept, but with other views and to other uses, kept in stewardship, with the seal of consecration on them for the Master's service.

We have here the *divine method of extending religion and of multiplying the number of disciples*. We have seen the beginning of the great kingdom, now let us see how the kingdom grows, and how the spiritual life passes from one to another. There is a beautiful exemplification here of the law of personal influence. The whole passage is full of "*findings*" by Christ and by the disciples. Simon is found, Philip is found, Nathanael is found, and they are brought to Him who came to seek that which was lost. It seems to be with a direct purpose that we have this minute mention of the finding of one disciple by another, of him who has not yet been with Jesus, by him who has. It is as if the Holy Spirit would set before us conspicuously, at the very opening of the Christian dispensation, one of the great laws by which the whole economy is to be replenished with new life and extended to still wider bounds. True, this is not the only law of growth;

the kingdom is to be extended in many ways—by writing, by preaching, by quiet living, by suffering—but through all these it will be found, if we examine closely, that the personal element of influence permeates and lives. The great Preacher of the desert points to Jesus and cries, "Behold the Lamb of God," and the preaching takes effect. But how small would that effect be if it reached no farther than the first hearers of it! It led to Christ these first disciples themselves, and then the power of personal influence and persuasion makes itself felt. One strong spirit, and another, and another still, is caught and held with these cords of love, these bands of a man. In this way, in little more than one day, Jesus has five disciples. Surely this has some instruction for us. It shows us what a sphere opens at once to every believing man. He has discovered the great secret; he has found the pearl of great price, and has sold all that he has to buy it; and yet without losing it himself (rather making it so more fully his own), he can offer it to his friend; he can enrich his house; he can find, at least he can try to find, a brother, a sister, a neighbour, a fellow-workmen, a fellow-man, to be a sharer with him in this great joy. It is too true that this blessed privilege is neglected, or timorously used, and with but little or slow results. There is reason to fear that the direct sense of this obligation in the minds of Christian people is not so strong as once it was. There never was so much evangelical preaching, never so much public teaching and work for Christ, as there is in our day, and perhaps

The First Disciples.

for this very reason we abate and slacken the quieter and more personal efforts.

We desire to discriminate here, and to consider the great difference in the circumstances in which we stand compared with those of the first disciples. Their example cannot be proposed, formally and literally, for our imitation. In Christian families, at least, we are born almost in the kingdom of Christ; we are, many of us, nursed amid divine things; we know from childhood the Holy Scriptures; and of course there is no need for one to speak personally to another in order to convey the literal information of Gospel truth. But after making all such allowance, the principle remains that whatever one possesses or attains in spiritual things he is bound, by the very law of the life he has received, to try to communicate to others who do not feel and possess as he does. Nor is it much to the point for any one to say that we ought not to be intrusive or rude in our spiritual zeal; that we ought not to take familiar liberties with human spirits even for Christ's sake. No, each man's personality is a thing so sacred and awful that we ought to approach it with reverence, and stay our foot as on the threshold of a holy place. Nor is it to the point to say that injury has been done in certain cases by a forward and officious manner of speaking on sacred subjects. I have seen some ingenuous and susceptible young people wince and tremble as if an iron hand had been laid on them, and then kindle into irrepressible resentment under such rough spiritual treatment. But are we to evade a duty by such excuses as these? Because unwise speaking is worse than silence sometimes, are we to keep silence always? We are to endeavour to use not the wrong speech but the right; not the rough self-righteous tone and the sound of theological phraseology, but the calm, earnest, wise, and winning voice; and on us, as Christians, rests the responsibility of finding out what is the best way to draw those around us to the Saviour.

It may be, after all we have said, the way of simple directness. There are some whom plain dealing suits, and who do not resent it: some persons who have not much delicacy either of nature or of culture, and who would not understand those cautious and considerate approaches to the subject of personal religion, which would be appropriate in other cases. And if this be so, you must take the direct way, if you are to be faithful. You must say: "I have found the Saviour, have you found Him? Let me bring you to Him. He is the Lamb of God. He takes away the sin of the world, mine and yours, if you will come." You must say this to husband or wife, to brother or sister, to son or daughter, if you see that only so can you fulfil the duty taught by inference in this passage. Or it may be by quite another way—the way of seeming circuitousness —of daily watchfulness, of quiet gentle suggestion, of earnest love, and of much self-denial. You may be required to discharge this duty, by inserting only as much as you can of your influence into the little openings of life as they occur, contenting yourself with a ministration as unobtrusive and invisible as that of the angels; only you must be sure that you stand firm at heart yourself for the Master, and that you render *this* as the best service you can offer. And He will bless you *so:* He will make your silence vocal, your love penetrative, your influence strong to win. There can be no doubt that in most families this kind of service will be the best and most appropriate, for it is a fact not easily explained, yet unquestionable, that the law of spiritual reserve holds nowhere so strongly as within the circle of the family, and in relation to those who are nearest and most loved. To them, last of all, can words be spoken on personal religion, and the things of God. Sometimes a member of a family may be a Christian for months, or even years, unknown to those in his own home. Perhaps the revelation comes at a parting, or a marriage, or beside a deathbed. Each, in choosing how to act in this matter, must be fully persuaded in his own mind, seeking wisdom from above, and it shall be given him.

One closing suggestion may be offered. When the organs of the body get into a chronic state of disorder, physicians tell us of the power of an alterative, something that changes for the time the habit or constitution, and so restores health. In this spiritual endeavour, if what you have done has not been successful, try an alterative—do the opposite, and see what will be the result. For years you have been speaking to sons and daughters, to others, with not much effect. They are accustomed to the earnest voice; they know all you have to say. *Cease to speak.* "Be dumb with silence. Hold your peace even from good." Think, watch, pray, cover them with kindness, and while they hear less of Christ's name, let them feel more of His power and presence in the quietness and constancy of your unselfish love.

On the other hand, you have been long silent; you have been afraid of wounding sensibilities, of exciting prejudices, of making religion repellant instead of attractive; and so you have said little or nothing perhaps for years. But you have been waiting all that time—perhaps more than they that watch for the morning—and longing, almost to heart-breaking sometimes, for the salvation of some who are very dear to you. You have been trying to reach that end in many quiet ways, putting books on the table, bringing friends to the house, trying to turn the conversation into a spiritual channel, praying that some particular providence might be blessed; but all things continue as they were. *Now, break the silence for once!* Speak tenderly and plainly; speak of Him of whom you are so often thinking—say, if it should be with some tremblings, or even with tears, "I have found Christ. Come and see." And thus the barrier may be broken down, and this Scripture may sound in your house like the voice of an angel. "And he brought him to Jesus."

XX.

The Gospel brought into Europe.

"And when they had seen the brethren, they comforted them and departed."—ACTS xvi. 40.

(*An Exposition*).

IT was to the Philippian Church that the Apostle Paul, who founded it, wrote the most tender and beautiful of all his epistles. And here is the nucleus and germ of that church: *Brethren in the house of Lydia.* How came they to be there? How were they in sorrow? How came the Apostle himself to be there to comfort them? We must go back somewhat in the history to answer these questions.

Paul is on his second great missionary journey. He has gone, with Silas for companion, "through Syria and Cilicia, confirming the churches." He has come again to Derbe and Lystra, has enlisted young Timothy in the service, has delivered the Jerusalem decrees to the churches in the several cities, and is bent on pursuing a certain line of travel with design to accomplish the greatest amount of usefulness, when he begins to be mysteriously hindered. He is hindered, not by earthly difficulties, of which, if they were in any manner superable, he was not apt to make much account; but hindered from the other world, by express withholdings and restraints of the Holy Ghost. They are "forbidden of the Holy Ghost" to go here, to go there in Asia. He would break into Bithynia, but "the Spirit suffers him not." Thus beat back from all his intended ways, he is brought at length down to Troas, a seaport near the ancient city of Troy, looking over to Europe, where as yet messenger of the Gospel has never been; and here he must wait. What can it mean? In no long time direction comes in this wise. In a vision of the night, not a dream, which—as the lowest form of divine communication, seems never to have been used with the Apostles—Paul saw, with the clear certainty of spiritual sight, a man of Macedonia standing and beseeching, and heard the words of his prayer, "Come over into Macedonia and help us." He probably knew the man to be a Macedonian from his dress. In Paul's native city, Cilicia, he had often seen Macedonian sailors and citizens. Perhaps in the vision he saw the man standing on the Macedonian shore beckoning to the Apostle and his company, as a shipwrecked creature on a desolate island would to a passing ship; or, more likely, standing by him he pointed to the Macedonian shore and cried, "Come over and help us." *Now* light begins to lie along the path of duty; now there is a way over the sea. This is the meaning of all these providential difficulties, and of these turnings back by the Spirit of God. These nearer doors are all shut just now; these cities must all do with what they have of divine truth at present. But see, here is the gate of a continent

The Gospel brought into Europe.

opening; here the way lies that leads to Rome, the mistress of the world! They assuredly gather that the Lord called them to preach the Gospel there; they loose from Troas, very likely with the first ship that sails, and make safe and swift passage to the other side.

Being landed on the European shore, they hasten on, according to Paul's invariable method, to some place that may be a radiating centre of Christian influence. The nearest important city is Philippi, and to that without delay they come. Philippi, as the name imports, was founded by the Macedonian king, the father of Alexander the Great. There were famous wells in the neighbourhood, and gold and silver mines at no great distance. A fertile plain lay around the city; and more than all, the high road from Europe to Asia went through it and could not be diverted. There is a continuous mountain range across the country between east and west, which at this single point is depressed into a plain, and, as has been said, forms a gateway in the great thoroughfare between the two continents. Forty-two years before the birth of Christ, a battle was fought here which settled the fate of the Roman Republic for the time. Brutus and Cassius were defeated by Octavius and Anthony. Brutus fell upon his sword, and Cassius, at his own request, was put to death by his freedman. The conqueror Augustus, in commemoration of his great victory, established here "a colony," *i.e.* a miniature Rome. Everything in it was organised after the pattern of the great metropolis—laws, government, language, and military defence. It was at first, and when Paul arrived, a civil-military settlement. Hither, then, he has come with his companions—Silas, Timothy, and Luke. He is on the great highway of nations; at one of the points of confluence between European and Asiatic life, where persons of many cities and many languages come and go. Some days elapse before anything is done; and when the Apostle begins to act it is in the quietest and simplest way. When the Sabbath comes round, he and his company go out of the city a little way to a river-side—not the river Strymon, but the small stream that flows into it. Upon the side of that stream there is—not a building, but a quiet favourable place for worship—where the Jews, or, at any rate, the Jewish women, come for prayer. We need not stay in the narrative to deal with curious questions, which can never be definitely settled. Was this a regular place of Jewish worship, fixed here by the side of the stream, because the laws of the colony did not permit a synagogue in the city? Or were the Jews so few in number that they could not afford a synagogue, and had the next best thing, a prayer-place? Were men present—although not named—separated, as is the custom in Jewish worship still, from the women? or were they late in arriving? or were they careless and neglectful, leaving divine service, as some Englishmen do, to their wives and daughters? or was this a voluntary gathering of the women—a simple woman's meeting? or did the Apostle and his fellow-missionaries, seeing the company of women by the river-side, think they were assembled for prayer, although that was not expressly or really the

The Gospel brought into Europe. 269

case? Some contend that the language will bear this interpretation. All these are matters of secondary moment. The certain thing is this, that the Apostolic missionaries and the thoughtful women met and talked, and that out of that meeting, blessed as it was of God, there sprang great results. It was the occasion of what has been called the conversion of Lydia, although the term is incorrectly applied in her case; for apparently she was a devout woman before she heard Paul, and simply embraced the Gospel as soon as it was made known to her. It is said "The Lord opened her heart," but that was the repetition of a process to which she was no stranger. She was residing here for purposes of trade, being either a seller of the purple Tyrian colour so much valued by the ancients, or more probably a dealer in the cloth or garments that were dyed by it. That Sabbath in Philippi would be eternally memorable to her. Immediately after Lydia's acceptance of the Gospel there followed her baptism and that of her household; and at once she persuaded Paul and his company to make her house their home during their stay in Philippi.

Here then, in the house of Lydia, the first Church in Europe is found. The brethren assemble here, and either go still to the river-side for prayer or transfer the place of prayer to the house. It is more likely that the little assembly went still to the old place on the stream, where, as Jews and Jewish proselytes, they had been used to worship. It was not the method of our Lord, and it was not Paul's method, to make sudden disruptive changes. "Not to destroy but to fulfil" was the rule. One thing was to glide into another: parts of the old forms were to enshrine the new ideas. The little company is Christian now, but that is no reason why they should not still resort to the old hallowed ground where they had so often sought and met with God.

On the way to it one day they are met by a damsel possessed by a spirit of divination—literally a spirit of Python, which was the name of a serpent said to guard a certain oracle on Mount Parnassus. It would seem from the narrative that this damsel was really possessed by an evil spirit, that she was not a lunatic or an impostor, but a demoniac in the sense used in the Gospels. She was a female slave probably, who had a plurality of masters, it being customary in ancient times to hold valuable slaves in joint ownership. The value in this case consisted in the soothsaying or fortune-telling power of this poor girl—a power which, whether real or not, was believed in by those who came to consult her. Here she is to-day, following close upon the footsteps of the Apostle and his company, and crying again and again, till the street rings with the sound of her well-known voice; "These men are the servants of the most high God, which show unto us the way of salvation." This cry may have been a repetition of Paul's own words, used now in irony or in scorn, or unwillingly, under that eternal necessity which makes even devils speak the truth. At first Paul took no notice of her words, but after this scene had been

The Gospel brought into Europe. 271

repeated day after day he—grieved not for himself and his friends, but for the poor possessed girl—commanded in the name of Christ the devil to come out of her, restored her to herself, and ultimately, as may be hoped, to her Saviour and her God.

In one hour all hope of further gain by her means is gone. Her masters are furious. They are slave-holders, who have vested interests—property, daily bread it may be, in the devilish business. Others sympathise with them. "Perhaps some other kinds of property may share a like fate." Paul and Silas, therefore, are seized and brought to the market-place or forum—the place where both commerce and justice have their seat—and are set there before the magistrates. When there they are charged, not with the actual thing they had done, but with the undefined crime of being disturbers of the peace, and of interfering by their teachings with the laws of the State. The charge is enforced by the phrase: "They, *being Jews*, have done this: they have come to force their poor religion upon us who are Romans." The pride of race is touched, and helps not a little to swell the excitement. The multitude or mob, crowding into the forum, are clamorous against the prisoners; and the magistrates, either not willing or not able to resist their importunity, anxious probably to take the easiest means of quelling the tumult, and, it may be also, with a view to the ultimate safety of the men thus charged, without process of trial, "rent off their clothes," not merely the outer garments, but all the upper garments, that, thus exposed, the strangers might receive the strokes of the Roman rods. The Apostle elsewhere writes: "Thrice was I beaten with rods;" this is one of the three times; the other two are not named. There he stood with his companion in the forum of Philippi with bared back, and, as the strokes fell from strong arms, bleeding and in pain. The shadow of Calvary stretches far! the servant drinks of the Master's cup. It is the gate of suffering that leads to the fairest parts of the realms of glory. After they had received many stripes, more than the forty save one of the Jews, they are hurried away to prison. It would almost seem that the magistrates went with them and headed the multitude; seeming for the time to be the leaders of the tumult, although really wishing to restrain and control it; and possibly they are thankful to lodge the prisoners in the gaol, although under a special charge that may lead to some severity of treatment.

They are soon in the inner prison, the central place, or the place farthest from the door, and from possibility of rescue or escape. And their feet are thrust into the great log or block of wood, which was used by the Romans sometimes for torture as well as for safe keeping. And there they lie or sit, while the multitude, appeased, disperse to their homes; and night comes down on the streets of the city, and silence and sleep; yes, even to the prisoners in the prison, some of whom may have been there before, and have learned to sleep anywhere. To-night they wondered perhaps, when they heard the roar of the people at the gates,

The Gospel brought into Europe. 273

what new crime had been committed, and who the malefactors might be who were led past their wards to the inmost and darkest place. But Sleep has mastered them, and they are sinking one by one into his drowsy balm; when at midnight they are roused and arrested, and held listening by sounds of singing which come from that inner prison, and from the men who a few hours before were cast in there. Strange sounds for such a place! Such sounds had never been heard there before. Blood had dript there from the limbs and backs of wounded men. Sighs and groans had crept round the unresponsive walls. Maddened curses, shrieks of pain, shouts of defiance, wild, half-maniac laughter may have come from that inner prison, but never till now a midnight psalm of praise to God.

While they listen, lo! the earth shakes: the doors fly open: the chains drop off. The keeper of the prison awakes, sees that the doors are open, and thinking that the prisoners have escaped, and that he is by Roman law a doomed man, prefers, being a soldier, the nobler issue as it was then deemed, and is about to fall upon his sword—like Cato, like Brutus and Cassius, and many of their followers, who had in that very city of Philippi consecrated suicide by their example—when he is arrested by a loud voice from the inner prison, enjoined to do himself no harm by such a vile and cowardly crime, and assured that his prisoners are all safe. Few scenes are better known than this of the jailor and his prisoner. We see the flash of the light. We see the man trembling and

T

falling at the Apostle's feet. We hear from his lips the everlasting question of conviction and anguish, "What must I do to be saved?" And we hear the answer that never grows old, that is repeated the world over and the ages through : " Believe on the Lord Jesus Christ and thou shalt be saved and thy house." Then came the fuller preaching of the Gospel, then the believing, then the baptism, and the midnight or early morning hospitality, and the wonderful joy of that jailor's home.

At early morning a serjeant comes from the magistrates to tell the jailor to let the men go : for they are by no means comfortable in their minds in the review of what has taken place. "Nay, nay," says the Apostle, "go back and tell them that we were shamefully entreated yesterday ; that we had no trial; that we were beaten openly as the vilest criminals are ; and say this, that *we are Romans*, and that as Roman magistrates they must, as far as may be, undo the wrong that has been done, and themselves bring us out of the prison as openly as we were put into it." And the magistrates had to do it. That one word "we are Romans" brought them as effectually as a message from a General would have done ; and they came and brought them out publicly; which was tantamount to an acknowledgment that they ought never to have been put in prison at all, and besought them, for the public peace, and for their own safety, to depart out of the city, which accordingly they did. After a brief visit to Lydia, and some words of consolation to the

The Gospel brought into Europe. 275

brethren there assembled, they said farewell and went away. Probably Luke was left to complete the work, so sadly yet so well begun, and to minister to the infant Church, while Paul, Timothy, and Silas went on.

Such is the narrative of the first, or if not the very first, the first open and full introduction of the Gospel into Europe. In view of its various incidents some reflections occur to us.

We have the old lesson of the power of small things, or rather the power of the earnest heart and steady purpose working by means of common things. Although the Apostle has come by divine sanction to far-famed Philippi, he comes like an ordinary traveller, goes out quietly to the bank of the little stream where he has heard that there is prayer, and even then he does not preach, but sits down and talks to the listening women. How many Christian people still have no other opportunity than just such as this, and could not use a greater if it were given! All they can do is to talk to a few simple folk, women or men, or young people. But how great the results may be! How one becomes many, and simplicity becomes grandeur! Call nothing little; call nothing common; if you can speak to fellow-mortals of Christ's grace and the Father's love know that you are standing at the source of rivers of immortal life. How close is the resemblance between the first Christian missions and the very latest; and how unlike these simple ways are the movements of the great powers and kingdoms of this world! Not by marching of armies or sailing of fleets, not by blare of trumpet or thunder of cannon, are triumphs won in the great kingdom. It "cometh not with observation." It lives and moves forward in single men, and they sometimes not distinguished by visible signs of power or dignity. A ship leaves some English port with passengers on board. By and by it is whispered that there is a missionary among them, going to a heathen country. He assumes no kind of prominence, perhaps speaks but little during the voyage, is somewhat given to gazing onwards in the direction in which the vessel sails, or at night, when no one can see him, *upwards* towards the stars. But the voyage is soon over, and the man is landed on an island among savage people, or on the shore of a continent, which he and others mean to occupy and take possession of for Christ. He seems a very picture and personification of helplessness. He is one among millions; a stranger in a strange land; not able at first to speak to the people in their own tongue; often weary; sometimes sick; misunderstood; suspected; in some instances still cast into prison. And yet by such men and by such means, just as at first—when Paul and Silas and Timothy sailed the Grecian seas and travelled the Roman roads, and talked with little groups of people as they met with them—by such men and by such means is the seed of eternal truth sown among the nations, and the kingdom of God brought down out of heaven to be among men.

If there be such a thing as apostolical succession in

The Gospel brought into Europe. 277

the world now, surely it is here! Those who with their own feet prolong apostolic travel, who continue apostolic suffering in their own persons, who sail the seas and traverse the countries, not knowing what is to befall them in any place, but simply and sublimely resolved to spend the whole of life in making known, as far as they can, the unsearchable riches of Christ, surely they among men have possession and charge of the grand inheritance and transmit the sacred entail. And they can tell us what comes of patience and prayer and good hard work. They can show in many places the reversal of the prophetic picture, for *before* them "is the desolate wilderness," and *behind* them "is the garden of Eden." True, they are only beginners, but God's beginnings even are beautiful and grand. More significant words are not heard in the world now than Tahiti, Madagascar, Kuruman, and others like them. These are names to charm with. They answer whole books of Philosophy. They keep alive the ancient hope. They rebuke the faithlessness of a worldly Church, and they bring to us all anew the assurance that Christ still fulfils the promise to be with His people alway—most nearly and most fully with those of them who come the nearest to Himself in work and suffering—" even unto the end of the world."

It is a notable thing that *the first European convert is a woman.* Lydia is a kind of personal Jerusalem—she is the "mother of us all!" She stands here at the gate of the western continent, is the first to receive the blessing, and to send it on. You may say that women and men being numerically equal, the chance that either of them should be the first believer of the Gospel is about equal. Not so—and for many reasons. At all events here is the fact that in this great Europe a woman's heart is first opened to receive God's message. In that fact we have the pledge and actual beginning of her elevation. She is no longer to be drudge, slave, plaything to man. She is to enter the kingdom by his side. Many questions concerning woman, her power, and place, and function in society, and in the Church as well as in the family, are stirring in our day. I take leave to think that some of these questions cannot have direct solution either by intellectual argument or by parliamentary legislation. But questions which can never be authoritatively settled may sometimes be indirectly disposed of in a most satisfactory manner. Half the women in the world are unblessed with the elevation that Christianity brings. They are yet in prison. Open the door and let them out into so much of social freedom and purity and happiness as Christian women enjoy. Teach them the music contained in that one word "home," and tell them of Him who will be a divine visitant there. "You without them cannot be made perfect." It is not given to any one part of the world to advance and continue very far in advance of any other part. We must give what we have, or we lose it. Hold out the hand of help to the vast sisterhood yet toiling and sorrowing in the darkness. Spread the Gospel over the sin-bound, caste-bound countries of

The Gospel brought into Europe. 279

the East; and when heathen women in great numbers have become Christian, the women of Christian states will have less difficulty in settling the questions which affect the details of their own liberties. Christ's kingdom is a kingdom of souls, of sacrifice, of virtues; and they stand highest in it who have the simplest faith, the largest charities, the tenderest hearts.

We have in *the deliverance of the slave-girl* another typical and prophetic circumstance. It would be almost universally allowed that the two most important social revolutions produced by Christianity are the amelioration of the condition of woman, and the abolition of slavery. And here in Philippi we have the second as well as the first. The poor slave-girl was delivered, we may hope, from a double bondage; and the same power that brought freedom to her on the street of Philippi has smitten slavery down, has banished it practically from the European and from the American Continents, and will yet banish it from the other two. Let all the nations know that the religion of Christ comes with justice and liberty in her hand, to break *every* yoke, and to let all the oppressed go free.

The conversion of the jailor, who was probably a Roman soldier, points to *the influence that the Christian religion was destined to exert over law, and political institutions, and prevailing idolatries, and civil governments.* This conquest over a soldier and servant of Rome is indicative of the subjection of the great empire herself to the sway of the Cross. That came in due time, and in due time "the kings of the earth shall set themselves, and the rulers take counsel together," not against but *for* the Lord and His anointed.

The order of the conversions is worthy of a moment's notice. The Proselyte, the Greek, the Roman—that has been the order of the diffusion of Christianity through the world; and it is so in principle at this day. We expect our first successes among those who have had some religious advantages, our next among the susceptible around, and our last among the men of the world. The varieties, too, are beautiful. These converts have nothing in common; probably not one of them before this time knew the other, nor would they have had the least interest in each other—the first an Asiatic, the second a Greek, the third a Roman. A merchant, a chattel, a soldier. And yet they are brought easily into the kingdom of harmony, into the brotherhood of the Gospel. So they come from the east and from the west, from the north and from the south, and sit down with Abraham and Isaac and Jacob in the kingdom of Heaven.

Observe also the recognised importance *of the family* in this wonderful narrative. There are three converts, and two of them bring in their households with them. The third had no household, or probably it also would have been brought. Lydia and "her house," the jailor and "his house," are baptized. The *house* goes with

The Gospel brought into Europe. 281

the father, goes with the mother; it goes with the master, with the mistress. The family is to be one—a field all under tillage, a garden with walks through and through. It is to be, in God's plan, one organic whole, not a number of separate and jarring individualities: and it can only have such harmonious wholeness by Christian baptism—not the baptism with water, but the baptism of the Spirit, which gives new life, and consecration of that life to Christ.

Finally, Jesus Christ stands out, here as everywhere, to be worshipped, trusted, loved, and followed. Believe on Him and thou shalt be saved. Honour Him and He will give thee honour. Open to Him thy house and He will fill it with the fragrance of His presence. Follow and serve Him truly, not only by the banks of quiet streams, and amid willing and sympathetic hearts, but in the noisy mart before a threatening world, while suffering injustice and wrong, when deep in darkness and night. Serve Him still, and serve Him truly, and He will hear your night song or your night sigh. He will shake the walls of the prison that holds you, and break your fetters with the strokes of His will. He will change your midnight into morning, and your shame into glory, for His own name's sake. Amen.

XXI.

The Humiliation and Glory of Christ.

"Let this mind be in you, which was also in Christ Jesus: who, being in the form of God, thought it not robbery to be equal with God: but made himself of no reputation, and took on him the form of a servant."—PHILIPPIANS ii. 5-7.

(An Exposition.)

IT will be well to keep in mind that the main object of the Apostle in this whole passage is the inculcation of Humility; or perhaps rather of the little group of virtues which are closely allied to it—unity, generosity, unselfishness: and this magnificent illustration, as we may well call it, is brought in simply with a view of commending and enforcing, in the highest degree, and in the most sacred manner, these divine qualities.

Let us briefly trace this humiliation of the Lord Jesus from the highest, the point of departure, whatever that may be, to the lowest—the act and moment of death: and thence His exaltation to the highest again.

The point of departure, where is it? On earth or in heaven? In humanity or in deity? The question has been much debated. Those who contend from the

The Humiliation and Glory of Christ. 283

simply human view of the character and nature of Jesus Christ, say that He began to condescend or come down somewhere in His earthly lifetime. The point chosen may be the beginning of His ministry, or soon after that—when, becoming conscious of His great power over the people, He did not use it for purposes of ambition or for selfish advancement. Bishop Burnet well observes that this interpretation is extremely cold and insipid, as if *that*, or anything like that, could be such a mighty argument for humility. No. We must begin where we believe the Apostle begins—in a preexistent state—in heaven—in God. "Being in the form of God" can only mean if we are to leave in it any real significance, possessing the attributes of God; being, as the Apostle says in his second epistle to the Corinthians (iv. 4), "the image of God:" or as in Hebrews i. 3, "the brightness of His glory, the express image of His person." Or as the Evangelist John says in the prologue to his gospel, "the Word of God—who was God." He being thus divine, did not deem His equality with God a thing to grasp at and eagerly retain. This is the proper rendering. As one puts it— "Though existing before the worlds in the eternal Godhead, yet He did not cling with avidity to the prerogatives of divine majesty—did not ambitiously display His equality with God." He emptied Himself of His heavenly glory, and took upon Him the nature of a servant, assuming the likeness of men. Nor was this all. Having appeared among men as a common man, He humbled Himself yet more; and became obedient unto death: and that the death which only the lowest malefactors die—the death of the Cross.

The Humiliation, according to this interpretation, began in heaven, and consisted in that change, to us almost inconceivable, which took place in the condition of the Son of God, when He left the bosom of the Father to begin the enterprise of human redemption. Of course any expression in human language descriptive of this change must be a simple figure, or a shadow of the thing itself, which, belonging to the sphere of the divine experience, must be always, in the nature of the case, beyond human cognisance. When the Scriptures say that He "came forth from God," that He left "the bosom of the Father," we feel at once that the *full* meaning is infinitely beyond our thought. We feel at the same time, however, that the outline of the idea is very intelligible to us—the idea of a voluntary condescension from all that is highest and best in divine life in heaven, to all that is dark, and poor, and mean, and shameful, in the life of man on earth.

Of course there could be no *essential* change in the whole course of this great humiliation. If Jesus Christ was originally divine He could never be less than divine. Birth in the flesh could make no difference; nor hunger, nor thirst, nor pain, nor death. The divine glory dwelt within the human nature, as within a veil; it shone out at times for a moment, and then was dark again. The glory of His boyhood was seen in the temple: the glory of His manhood on the mount of transfiguration. He gave but a look in the garden out of His divinity, and the soldiers fell back appalled. With a look he melted Peter's heart. These occasional acts were but escaping beams of that awful and unsullied brightness, which lay always within the veil of His earthly life.

Any human analogy must be very imperfect. But we have no difficulty in conceiving how a man of highest virtue, and noblest birth, and clearest intelligence, could assume an outward garb which would completely belie or hide his real character. A king need not always wear the royal robes and sit on a throne. He may become a shepherd on the hill, a sailor before the mast, a servant of his own servants. Missionaries—and in this case the moral analogy is more perfect—after learning the language of a barbarous people, have gone among them, conforming to all their habits as far as they could, living a dark rude life, submitting to every kind of trial and privation, in order to a great and beneficent end. Is it then to be said, in the ignorance of our pride, in the supercilious presumption of our poor narrow thought, that the Infinite One must always be in divine state and glory, in one manifestation, in one form of His infinite life, that whatever transpires in the history of the world or the universe, He can do *nothing* except what He has been for ever doing—speak no new word—make no new revelation of Himself. The assertion that God cannot lay aside some of what we may call the *accidents* of His being, and invest Himself in another way, is almost to assert that He is not God at all.

The conception is less difficult if we see the moral glory of it; if we see how worthy of God it is: how it adorns His name, reveals His nature; proves to us that "God is love." At the lowest point of the humiliation, the Cross, the ascent begins. "*Wherefore* God also hath highly exalted Him." The exaltation springs out of the humiliation. The ascent began even at the death-hour. New hopes for humanity were born at the very Cross, and new lights of love began to flicker even amid its darkness. We see this in the love and worship of the man dying at His side—in the ministry to His thirst, in the words of the Roman soldier, "Truly this man was the son of God." We see it in the reverence shown to His body; in His honourable grave and costly burial; in His resurrection, which rolled reproach away; in His entrance into heaven as a conqueror with spoils. "God highly exalted Him." In the abstract form it would be " God resumed His glory, put on His heavenly brightness—gave to the universe a new revelation of Himself in the Gospel; and made all this permanent and effective by enthroning the God-man Christ Jesus in the highest heavens."

"He gave Him a name that is above every name." There is no reference here to the actual name "Jesus." Many others bore that name as well as He. Nor is literal bowing at the name of Jesus, as though performing some heaven-required homage, at all enjoined. The meaning of the passage is large and wide. The "name" is the character, the influence; and to that name, that living "word" of God, all creation shall do homage.

Human history, nature, providence, this world and all worlds, bow at that name. Sun and moon and shining stars, all the beauty of the earth, and all the bounty of the seasons, are dim and dark compared with a crucified Saviour. This is the glory that excelleth. Here all divine attributes meet in surprising harmony; here righteousness stands untarnished; here love fights and wins; here is a new centre of power, from which flow forth energies which are seen and felt, not only by sinners redeemed on earth, nor only by saved men in heaven, but in some way and measure by all creatures, and through all worlds.

"Things in heaven and things on earth, and things under the earth :" that is, all things whatsoever and wheresoever they be, in extent unqualified and unlimited, are affected by what was done on the Cross, and by what is done by the Saviour now in heaven. Of course, the intelligent and the lower creation are affected in different manner and degree—unfallen heaven and fallen earth differently, and dark hell differently from either—but all in some way, all in a manner to call forth the praise and homage of the universe. May not angels be established in virtue by the Cross? Are not men recovered by it from their fall? And who will dare to say that in the case of spirits fallen and lost, some possible mitigation of their ruin may not come to them, or some possible escape may not be opened to them, through the sufferings and death of Jesus Christ? All we can say is, that we have no revelation on the subject, no certain teaching of Scripture either way; or rather we have Scripture teaching *both* ways. We shall be as near the truth as we can come at present if we frankly allow that we do not know the full truth on the subject; and we may take comfort in the reflection that God certainly designs us to be in comparative ignorance regarding it, and to *wait*, in humble faith, for light that may come hereafter.

In this passage we are on the large, hopeful side of the question; and we are to believe that the whole universe is, or is to be, subject to Christ—every knee bent, every tongue confessing that He is Lord. These celestial and infernal relations of redemption, these universal œcumenical applications of it, take away some force from the objection that has been urged against Christianity, founded on the littleness of man and of this world compared with the vastness of the universe, and the unlikelihood, therefore, that the Deity should make an interposition on man's behalf so stupendous as that which is involved in the incarnation. What abstract force there may be in that objection we shall not inquire; but at any rate, the argument fails. True, the incarnation takes place here in this world; but it has relations and transmits influences to other worlds. It begins on earth, but it is transferred into higher realms. The incarnation is God descending that He may ascend with His new creation, coming forth from eternal mystery and silence into manifestation, seeking that He may find, suffering that He may save. He thus educates the universe in the knowledge of Himself; He leads it along the "path that shineth more and more," and gives

The Humiliation and Glory of Christ. 289

to it the assurance that nothing can possibly happen in the evolution of the ages, or by any multiplication of celestial or terrestrial populations, for which His own nature will not make provision. For all creatures, for all worlds, and for all the ages, the God and Father of our Lord Jesus Christ will be sufficient.

Let us look now at the practical purposes of the Apostle in bringing all this before us. Among the chief of these is the inculcation of humility. This whole marvellous passage is brought before us, not for dogmatic teaching, but for moral example. The main intention is not to reveal Jesus Christ as the foundation of a sinner's hope (although that is implied), but it is to point out the wonderful moral beauty of His condescension, and to enforce it upon the regards of His followers for their devout and diligent imitation. As if the Apostle said : " You see what Christ has done. Let the same mind be in you that was in Him. Do likewise ; be lowly ; condescend ; go down ; seek, and suffer, and give ; and be patient to the end. Lay by dignity, and forget pleasure and the finer delights of life, and go help the poor and lift up the fallen, and strengthen the struggling. Search out the cause you do not know. Make the widow's heart sing for joy." *Go down !* That is the secret of moral greatness as revealed here: down to shame, to suffering, to death itself—die rather than fail !—die rather than turn in your course !

Ah, the contrast in this, between Christ and many who bear His name ! He, in His greatness and glory, coming down so far! We, in our blindness, and narrowness, and littleness, all struggling to rise! "Let me get up!" is one of the very canons of our social strife. It is even proposed by social teachers as a worthy end of much exertion. Be industrious, honest, careful, persevering, and you will certainly rise; you will succeed; you will be rich; you will be a man of influence, wearing one knows not what badge or title or robes of office and dignity. This is the too-prevalent sentiment in the whole community; and it affects Christian people as well as others. There are only some elect souls, as it were, who see this thing as it is—and they only in select moments of their life see it clearly—that the way to the higher duty and to the nobler dignity is to *put off* and not to put on, to go down and not to climb. As long as one is poor, I am to relieve or help him in some way to the extent of my ability; I am to go down, miser that I am, from this mountain or it may be from only this little hillock of my gettings, with a portion of it in my hand, that it may not be quite so high when I come up to it again. As long as one is ignorant I am not to lap me in soft airs of culture and refinement, and draw off from rude contact with darker minds, seeking what is called "congenial society;" I am to go with what light and delicacy of feeling God has given me, and shine and breathe these out in the darkness, although for a while the darkness may not comprehend. As long as one is in the guilt and bitter misery of sin I am not to wrap myself in the clean mantle of my virtues, and go in a stately manner along the well-swept roads of respectability; but I am to go down and gauge the guilt, which I can do very well by estimating my own; I am to go and speak to the misery, and draw it away from those who suffer it, even by the channel of my own tears. And unless I am ready to *make an effort* to do this, let me never say "*Master*" to Him who came from afar; from the highest, from the fairest—glory trailing with Him down the sky—and who went past us down to the lowest, to the foulest, to darkness and shame and horror, on our behoof.

But if I am breathing His spirit: if His life is the model of my own: if His Cross repeats itself in the cross I bear for Him: then there comes to me a truer elevation. *Now* I can look up; now it will be safe to rise. "*Wherefore?*"—because He humbled Himself; because He pleased God, expressed the very mind of God—"God also hath highly exalted Him;" and we are allowed to reason that with and in Him, we too shall rise. The Master and the disciple, treading the valley of humiliation "*together*," shall together sit on the throne. To be partaker of the sufferings is the sure pledge of participation in the glory. What that glory is we know not now, but we shall know hereafter. We must look through all earthly images, and put aside the dreams of sense, if we would think of it truly; and, perhaps, we can come no nearer to it than *this*: "We shall be like Him." We shall be perfectly conformed to His will. "For he that doeth the will of God abideth for ever."

"*Wherefore*" (12) (the practical weight of this

sentiment is carried on into the next verses) : "*Work out your own salvation with fear and trembling, for it is God that worketh in you, to will and to do of His good pleasure.*" Paraphrased, the words might be rendered : " Seeing that these things are so, as you have been obedient hitherto, so continue. Labour earnestly, not only when I am with you, but now when I am far away. With a nervous trembling anxiety, work out salvation for yourselves : for *yourselves*, did I say? Nay, ye are not alone. God works in you from first to last : God inspires the earliest impulse : God secures the final achievment : for such is His good pleasure." This seems to be the course of thought in the passage.

"*Work out your salvation*"—this moral conformity to God—by following Christ; by cross-bearing; by self-denial; by descents into darkness with your lights, into misery with your joys; by holding yourself at the service of others; by making life a sacrifice, and yourself a living victim; by filling your soul with the tenderness, and Divine passion, and unutterable love of the Cross.

"*With fear and trembling.*"—Yes, literally so; for, indeed, it is the one thing to fear about. There is nothing else that need give us much anxiety. We are not told to be afraid of sickness, or to tremble at death, or at any mortal calamity. All these are shadowy and unimportant, if only immortal life be growing in us; and this immortal life is likeness to Christ—is denial of the lower self and service of our fellows. Ah! to

The Humiliation and Glory of Christ. 293

lose *this*, or to put this in peril, is to risk all! The face of the helmsman in coming down the rapids of the St. Lawrence in the great vessel is a sight to see. He takes in, as it were, all the conditions of the case, in one inevitable glance — the bank ; the bend ; the shallowing or deepening bed ; the amount of way on the vessel ; the hurry of the waters ; the calm spread of the deep river lying like a peaceful haven yonder in the distance! There he stands—fearful, yet firm—distrustful, yet confident—until the danger is past. With a similar feeling—not slavishly afraid—but intent, earnest, bending all the powers in concentrated effort towards the ultimate object—*so* "work out your salvation."

"*Work it out for yourselves.*"—That is the meaning, rather than as it is put in our translation, "your own salvation." There is no appeal here to the principle of personality — the idea is, *Do it for yourselves.* Do not depend on me, or on Timothy. He may never come. I may never see you more. Do not let the chief motive force in this great life process be lodged in circumstances, or in human persons. Keep that force alive in your own hearts ; work it out into success, in and of yourselves. And that this may not tend to self-righteousness, and self-trust, we read in the next verse (13), "*For it is God that worketh in you.*" If only your working be such as I am now describing, it is the working of God. Every Christlike thing in you is from Him. A Christian thought kindles within you—it is God. A Christian feeling glows—it is God. A conflict springs up in your heart—there is wrestling among the motives, old and new—it is God who animates the right, and shames and wounds and weakens the wrong. What a beautiful stimulus have we here! It is not necessary, if it even were possible, for you to labour at the intellectual construction and conception of this thing, settling to your own satisfaction *how* it may be; you have only to follow Christ, and lo! God is within you—His Spirit the light of every holy thought, the breath of every pure desire, the throb of every generous emotion. The phrase "*to will and to do*" seems to cover the whole ground. Here we have what theologians call the "prevenient" and the "co-operating" grace of God; grace at the first act of will, grace all through, and to the end. The first good is the germ and pledge of all that follows. When the little leaven of better thought and purpose begins to work, it is that it may leaven the whole lump; that it may fill all thought, and feeling, and action with the sacred power.

"*His good pleasure.*"—And *what is* that good pleasure of God manifested to the world in the coming of Christ? It is this: "That God so loved the world, that He gave His only begotten Son, that whosoever believeth on Him might have eternal life." It is this: "The grace of God which bringeth salvation." It is this: that "He will have all men to be saved." All this is in the full sense "The good pleasure of God.

When we get an assured knowledge of what is God's will in a large world-embracing question like this, we get the key of the whole position. Until I know God's good will and good pleasure—not to this or that individual, but to the whole great family of men—I know nothing on which to rest my spirit. I look with my natural vision, and I see all the world solemn and dark with mystery which I cannot solve. Joy and grief, hope and fear, success and failure, life and death, are strangely mingled. I hear sounds of effort, aspiration, passion, despair! And men pass silently but swiftly on—thousands of them every day—like an army in march, out of life; all bone of my bone, and flesh of my flesh. What does it all mean? What is *God* thinking all the while? What is His purpose in it all?

Behold the disclosure of the secret! We have it in the Gospel. We have it in God *coming down;* in the suffering, dying, rising Saviour; in His people who breath His Spirit, and follow in His steps. And—consider it well—what He is to any one of these: the most gracious, the most heavenly soul that lives, He will be to any other who takes Him at His word. There is no difference, His "good will" is to save you, and it is only by putting your own evil will against His that you can miss salvation. All things are now ready; you have nothing to do *in preparation* for beginning; you have only *to begin;* to begin with what you already have. You have a conscience—let it speak, and lo! God works in you, and your salvation is begun! You have a heart—listen to its lonely cry! You have some honour left, you have some nobleness, you have some sense of truth; bring them all, such as they are, to the

Cross, to be purified and filled with a higher spirit. Begin *anywhere* in your nature, and in things however faint and small—so be you begin truly—with your good will to meet the good will of God, and all will be well. The Author will be the Finisher of your faith. "To will and to do," will be married in your life for ever more.

XXII.

Receiving the Grace of God in Vain.

"We then, as workers together with him, beseech you also that ye receive not the grace of God in vain."—2 COR. vi. 1.

THIS world, or one of its continents, is discovered by its inhabitants very slowly. Long ages elapse before even a general map of the country can be drawn up with anything like correctness. One traveller discovers a mountain-chain, and is immortalised. Another pursues a great river a few hundreds of miles towards its source, and its waters ever afterwards murmur his name. A third casts himself into the untrodden wilderness, and, after years of wandering, returns as from fairyland to tell the wonders he has seen. Along these first tracks other feet soon follow. The geologist comes to seek worlds long since dead, that he may know how they bloomed and faded, and laid themselves in long death-sleep, one upon another; the last dead always drawing the living down into its arms. The mineralogist forces his way into many a long-closed laboratory. The botanist is hungry for the flowers that bloom only there, and will so far trench on the domain of another as to snatch with eagerness even the stony image and corpse of flowers that bloom no more. Then more practical men come—the scientific money-maker, to sink for coal and iron; and the agriculturist, to see what crops can be raised; and the contractor, who, alas! is a contractor in another sense; for he chases away the poetical illusions, laughs at imaginary heights, and so-called impassable barriers, and in the face of nature's ramparts and bastions, and underneath frowning clouds he takes his gradients and lays down the way by inches, along which he will bring his victorious snorting engine. Yet, after all this, the country is not conquered, is not even discovered. Let any one travel through it for himself, awake and impressionable, and he will find not only, if at all, the country he has read of in books, but a new country, as though it came fresh from creating hands; blooming in its first spring beauty, or yellow in the ripeness of an autumn that has had no predecessor. He will find that the half had not been told him, that there are surprises and discoveries at every step. This house which God has built for the human race has rooms so many, and so variously furnished, that no man can go through them all, or even observe all that is in any one of them. No age can inhabit the whole house; children and children's children come, and pass by degrees into the empty rooms and find in them all abundant proofs of the great Father's forecasting love; and when the last fires are kindled, more unknown

Receiving the Grace of God in Vain. 299

wealth will sink in the burning house, and more unseen beauty be consumed, than all the ages have ever found.

So it is with this great, this unmeasurable, this exhaustless thing called here the "*Grace of God.*" Since it was first made known men have been searching it out, and it is yet unexplored; they have been defining it, and it is yet unknown. It is greater than all descriptions of it, and better far than all conceptions of it. Its first developments are here on earth—in Time; but for its completer manifestations, for the opening out of all its wealth and glory, a vaster theatre is needed, "new heavens and a new earth, wherein dwelleth righteousness."

"*The Grace of God.*" We know it means the Gospel, its provisions, its promises, and its very present helps. It means Christ and the Cross, and the Holy Ghost, and the new life, and heaven, and all that is contained in that great remedial dispensation under which we live. But there is a sense in which the grace of God is more than the Gospel. In this world we have "the Gospel of the grace of God." In the next world there will be another Gospel of that grace: and then another and another still, by which will come to us the revelation of God's deeper thoughts, and the accomplishment of His greater purposes. So that we come to this, as perhaps the best definition we can reach of what is really undefinable, that "the grace of God" means His gracious disposition. It means, no doubt, what He has done in the great transactions of redemption, but it means far more, *i.e. what He is in Himself*, and must be eternally. Historical Christianity is only the scaffolding by means of which true Christianity is built up. It is not, so to speak, the Christ who died on Calvary, who saved the world by that act, and then left it. It is the living Christ in heaven, who carried up with Him thither the whole passion of earth and the whole virtue of Calvary enshrined in His own being, who saves the world every day. What concerns us most nearly is not what God was on the day of the crucifixion, but what God is to us to-day, and what He will be to-morrow, and through all the never-ending days of our need. God *gave* His Son—that is true ; God *gives* His Son—that is truer still. God poured out His Spirit once in rushing wind and tongues of flame. But ah, how little were that to me if there were no celestial breathings and burnings left, to cleanse and fire my soul to-day ! This is not, we believe, a mere refinement on the text, rather it is the essential heart-meaning of it : "See that ye receive not the grace of God in vain." It is something you *are* receiving every day ; it hangs around you, it is within your reach, it waits your appropriation. It is being given perpetually. It is a daily donation. It is a vast possibility. It may be everything to you, or it may be nothing, as you will. See that you receive it not in vain.

What is it then to receive the grace of God in vain? To this question a threefold answer may be given. A thing of value is received in vain if it is not used at all. It is received in vain if it is perverted and turned to some alien use. It is received *almost* in vain if it is used very little and very imperfectly.

There is the non-use of grace—the neglect of a "great salvation."

In vain is it here, within the sphere of our knowledge, and within the possible grasp of our faith; ready for immediate application to all the uses of life, and to all its heart-needs, if it be simply ignored. Here is gold, in a casket or bag, put in free gift within my reach, and I am poor, and I am hungry, yet I will not unloose the strings or open the casket. Of what avail to me is that locked-up wealth? Here is seed-corn, and I have fields about my house where it might be sown, and where it would grow to a rich harvest. But I will not sow it, I will not plough the land even, but leave all to chance, and drift on towards the cold dark winter of want. Of what avail to me is the seed, or the soil, the sun, or the shower? I am going on a journey long and difficult, through an unknown country, and here is a guide-book, written with great plainness, and describing the very road I am to take. But I never open it, never ask what it contains, but go wandering on by day, and stumbling on dark mountains by night. That guide-book is as utterly "in vain" to me as if it were in the depths of the ocean. "Ah yes," you say, "but the grace of God is not so definite, so tangible, so near, or so available, as the money, as the seed-corn, as the written book." Yes, it is. It is as definite as any message of God to man can be. It is as tangible as anything can be to the mind and heart. It is as near as omnipotence, working by wisdom and love, can bring it. It hangs in the very air. It speaks in a thousand books, and overflows in fountain-fulness from the one Book. It has made laws, institutions,—all that is most Christian and most humane in social life. It shines out in the light of every Sabbath day—it is the keynote of every true sermon—it is in every providence, whether dark or bright—it is everywhere, and always, abundant, sufficient, and free. It is sad that many will not be persuaded of this, and still think of the Gospel, and of God's grace in it (if indeed they think of it at all), as a vague uncertain thing, not given to all nor to each in free overture, but held mysteriously off in distant heights; in the grasp of divine sovereignty which will not easily let it go! O! it were everything if we could but carry home to a man's heart the practical, inevitable assurance that the love of God is *for him;* and that he "receives" it with all the wealth it contains, potentially, and as far as it can be given to free, responsible creatures, when it is thus brought down to his level, laid within his reach, and pressed on his acceptance. Nothing more can even God accomplish than this, until the individual will moves and bends to His. When the sleeping mind begins to awake; when the dull heart begins to feel, and the glad discovery breaks on the soul that all this is a present and sure gift of eternal love—then begins, in the nature of the case, the practical and actual reception of the manifold blessings of the Gospel; but *until then* " the grace of

Receiving the Grace of God in Vain.

God," with all its riches which we proclaim and set forth as common property, and free alike to all, is "in vain." Receive it we certainly do—one and all—as a dispensation, an offer, a free gift from God, of possible redemption and eternal life ; and it is sad now, and will be sorrowful for ever, if in the case of any it has been so received " in vain."

A thing is received in vain *if it is perverted and turned to some alien use.* Such perversion of the Gospel is, alas! too easy and too common. It may be made *a cloak for sin*—a mere covering for that from which it is express and peremptory deliverance. It is easy practically to give another reading of that remarkable Scripture, and think of Jesus as of one who " saves His people," not from, but *in* their sins. This may be done in degrees far short of antinomianism; but in whatever degree it is done it makes the grace of God in vain, The very richest and most precious expressions of Holy Scripture have this peril lurking in them to those who bring certain predispositions to the interpretation of them. " There is no condemnation to them that are in Christ Jesus." I rest in that: my moral condition is a secondary matter. "Thou hast clothed me with the garments of salvation ; " the garments are seen, not the man beneath them. "Ye are complete in Him." Then *in Him* I am safe ; my personal character is lost in His. The danger is that we magnify God's grace and slur over, or pass lightly by, the evils of our own hearts. The grace of God is in vain to us if we make it support any moral dishonesty in ourselves or if by its means we impute any moral dishonesty to God. He sees things as they are. He calls everything by its right name, and treats it according to its nature. He performs no judicial fiction; puts us under no cover or shield that will enable Him to call us what we are not. However we may read the blessed doctrine of Christ's atonement, at least there is no false pretence in it. God brings us *as we are*, sinners and unworthy, into the great sphere of His mercy, and for Christ's sake, in whom that mercy is expressed, and by whom it is brought near to us all—" He pardoneth and absolveth all who sincerely repent, and unfeignedly believe His holy Gospel." But those who are thus pardoned, are in that very act, the most godlike of all divine acts, declared to be sinful and guilty, and are bound over to watch and war against sin in themselves, whilst still repenting of it, until by the Almighty aids of grace it is vanquished and surmounted, and left for ever behind.

Or, the Gospel may be made *a tent for indolence*, and so its grace may be received in vain. In this perversion we do not tamper with moral distinctions; we do not disguise our real condition; we acknowledge these things as they are—the sin, the grace, the moral obligation, but we fail in those practical applications and activities which alone can bring out from the whole a vital result. We see how much must be done in us, and by us; but somehow we get the comfortable conviction, and rest in it, that it *will* be done soon or late; by greater or lesser acts of God's mercy; by gentler or mightier forth-puttings of divine power : we shall rise into settled safety, and have full entrance at length into perfect purity and eternal life. The tabernacle of God is with men; and we come into it, and compose ourselves there to rest, as travellers who have come to an inn. We say, "When the tabernacle is lifted up from earth to Heaven, we shall go in it." No, not necessarily. You will be dropped out and left behind, if you are not careful. Some day, perhaps when you are sleeping, the great tabernacle will be lifted and borne away; and the awaking will be in the wilderness—in the winter— in the darkness! Take heed that ye receive not the grace of God in vain.

What is that grace? It is living will of God to strengthen and guide the faltering will of man. It is Spirit to rule flesh. It is life to quicken death. It is power to animate weakness. It is law to inform conscience. It is love to breathe perpetual summer through the heart. It is cross-bearing up a Calvary as high as all the days of life. It is fire to burn on the inward altar until all evil lies in ashes there. It is a race which no one has run until he has died. It is a still growing knowledge; a still enlarging love; a putting on of the image of God, until in every secret principle and through every thrilling sense, there is participation of the divine holiness. Let none of us receive this grace in vain.

Again. The Gospel may be made *the signal for perpetual controversy*, and *so* be turned from its highest use. This is more likely to be, in a controversial age like the present, when things are moving on and changing in their aspects with great rapidity. Truth is always in danger in this world, but the danger seems more real and close at hand when there is a great variety of human opinion, and great freedom in the expression of it. All kinds of witnessing is going on for and against particular points. All kinds of assertions and denials are made : old beliefs are being modified, new faiths are springing up : and *no*-faith demands tolerance and attempts its own justification as boldly as if it were the oldest creed. All this, of course, is discomposing to those who are resting their own hearts in the things which have for so long been "most surely believed," and which they still see to be most sure, and feel to be most precious. And it is not unnatural that some impatience should be felt with such a state of things, and a kind of sacred intolerance indulged in, which will find expression now and again in strong words. We need not wonder at this. We dare not utter blame. We may even be very thankful that courage on behalf of the old faith is not dying out, and is not likely to die. The sceptics are not the only heroes of the time. The faith of our fathers has yet defence in the hearts and by the hands of many of their sons ; and we may depend upon it, that when the smoke of this great nineteenth century battle somewhat clears away, the old towers will reappear, and the old palaces of Zion will shine in the light once more. So we are glad of controversy, in proper spirit and measure ;—it braces the soul ; it clears the air ; it defends and instrumentally perpetuates the truth among men. But there is hardly anything which runs more easily to excess, and becomes a perversion, and no longer a defence of the grace of God. When a man is preternaturally sure of his own infallibility; when he will not re-examine any of the points of his faith, either for the satisfaction of others or for his own; when he is ready with suggestions and imputations of heresy in others, and *not* ready to give a reason for his own hope; when he is on the watch for the emergence of error in opinion, as if he had received some special divine appointment to that kind of police service; when he is keen on the scent of the evil, and almost blind to the sight of the good; when he lives in perpetual consciousness of the secondary differences of good men, and is nearly insensible to their far larger central agreements; and when all this finds expression in the language and the acts of bigotry,—there is, of course, to that whole extent, a receiving of grace in vain. The grace of God *is gracious;* and in its prevailing influence ought to lead us into gracious ways, and words, and dispositions. It ought to fill our breasts with kindness, and cheerfulness, and charity.

There is yet another way of perverting the grace of God, and one which comes closely home to ourselves. *The very little and imperfect use we make of it as Christians.*

A thing of value may be applied to its right purpose, but used very seldom and very feebly, and in so far it comes to be partly "in vain." This supposition meets the case, more or less, of all Christian people, although it is true of some much more than of others. The plough is taken to the field, but does not plough the whole day; or it ploughs *one* little field, and leaves all the rest fallow. The seed-corn is cast in only in patches, and some of these but thinly sown. The well-built ship is launched, and chart and compass are on board; and the sails catch the wind, and the helm obeys the hand, but she is kept shifting and tacking, and even lying-to, when she might sail swiftly and straight to her haven. Here is a great world of grace brought down to us, brooding about us, touching us, waiting for us, and we may have as much or as little as we will. It is impossible to exaggerate here, for it is literally true that no man as yet has even seen from afar the loftiest summits of the mountains of the grace of God. No man has drunk of the uppermost springs, or found the deepest treasures, or tasted the ripest fruit. When a company of travellers go up a mountain-side, a few will outstrip the rest, and you see them far above, diminished by distance, standing on or near what seems to be the summit. But when you come up with them they are found to be only on a lower height, and the true mountain-top yet shines high and far away among the dazzling snows. So it is with the spiritual elevations of grace. A few athletic climbers have gone before and beyond the great company of the faithful. We see Abraham, as from afar, looking for the God-built city. We see Moses on the Pisgah-mount of vision and of death. We see Elijah wrapt in burning splendours, and we think "who can reach or follow that chariot of fire?" We see Daniel—the faithful and fearless—turning monarchs by his word, ruling the world by his very dreams; and then dismissed, without one visible spot or taint of earth, to his eternal rest. We see Mary at the Master's feet, and John on His bosom, and Paul in the field of service, and we sink down discouraged at the sight of the giants.

Yet what is the truth? It is this, that compared with attainments that are possible, these saints are only a little way above us. The last heights (but indeed in this world of grace there are *no* last heights) are far above both us and them; and if we would but press on earnestly we should soon be nearer them than we dream of now. Indeed it may well be, that some whose names are unknown, may have reached *their* stand-point, and even gone beyond it. But however this may be, it cannot for a moment be allowed that even the saintliest of these historic men have risen in this great world of divine grace, as high as any man can live and breathe. They saw nothing that we may not see, and still more clearly. They had nothing for personal life and progress that we may not have, and in still greater fulness. Do we forget the words, or do we disbelieve them—in which our Lord describes the new over-brimming cup of redemptive grace, "I am come that they might have life, and that they might have it *more abundantly?*" or the words which fit closely to the text, "He giveth *more* grace?"

In saying this, I do not forget what Christian men

really are, nor what are the limitations of their life and endowments. Not every man can be an intellectual giant. Every one is not fitted even to be a moral hero. Some have more mind to begin with than others. Some have more conscience, and some more power of will than their fellows; and those who have five talents can do what he of the single talent cannot—they can trade them, they can grow them into ten. But in the world of grace, methinks *this* judgment will be given, that to change one into two is as noble as to change five into ten; and to be faithful in little is to secure the Master's "well done" as surely as to be faithful in much. Here is the point: that each has a world of grace unlimited, to draw from, to live in; and there is the corresponding point, that each has a growing, ever expanding nature by which to receive the grace, and grow by it to gigantic stature. As a matter of fact, the expansion may be much or little, the growth may be that of the hyssop on the wall or that of the cedar on Lebanon. But the root-life is there in each case, and the normal capacity, to be drawn up if we will, into actual attainment. By the grace we receive we may grow ourselves up into heaven, or, not using it, we may dwarf ourselves down to the very brink of hell. We may use the one talent (and no man is without the one), so that it shall, by the law of moral increase and progression, which is as sure as any mathematical law, become two, five, ten, a hundred in the end. Let each be true to himself, and to his own circumstances, and to the tasks and claims they bring; not coveting the circumstances of another. Let each bear his own cross, more and yet more patiently, never forgetting to take the strength in which alone it can be borne. Let each fill his own heart day by day anew with those divine truths and consolations which are born each day anew for him, and which will come to him fresh as morning sunlight, and free as the running brook, from the very heart of God; and so he will for himself most happily fulfil this injunction—solemnly given to us now in these sacred words—that we "receive not the grace of God in vain."

XXIII.

The Creed of Christendom.

"I believe in Jesus Christ, His only Son, our Lord."

THE Apostle's Creed, as it is undoubtedly the most ancient, so it is the grandest and the simplest of all the creeds. The simplicity in form and purpose is in part the grandeur of it. Yet in beginning to think of a single clause, one soon becomes sensible of the great difficulty, indeed the impossibility, of keeping within that alone. This difficulty is, of course, not peculiar to religious or theological writing. Truth is manifold and all-related. At whatever point of its great realm we are for the moment placed, we are, of necessity, in intellectual contact, consciously or unconsciously, with the truth that is nearest, and by means of that, with all that is beyond. But there is in this creed an organic completeness which is almost unique. As, in the body, one member cannot say to another "I have no need of thee," so each clause here is related to all, and all to each. We will try, as far as possible, for our present purpose to keep within this first clause.

"I believe in Jesus Christ" plants us at once,

The Creed of Christendom.

surely, on the plain historic ground. There can be no doubt that He "appeared"—that he was born, lived, died, as a man. That the life of Jesus Christ was a semblance and not a reality, was an early heresy, naturally enough bred of the philosophies and religions of the time, and held in considerable variety of form. It were a waste of words to attempt now any formal refutation of a long-extinct heresy. Some of the difficulties which aided in the production of Docetism are perpetual, arising out of the limitations of human knowledge. It is impossible to have a perfect *intellectual* comprehension of the mysteries of divine existence, or of the modes of divine manifestation among men. But the Church has long ago recognised this impossibility, and has found in such recognition an aid rather than a hindrance to her faith. "Great is the mystery of Godliness,—God was manifest in the flesh."

The mythical theory of the life of Christ lies much nearer to us, and is only now dying. But the process of dissolution is going on rapidly; and soon that whole theory—pretentious, shadowy, changeful—whose bold aim was to leave the world without a personal Saviour, will have followed the trooping shadows of the past, and gone to the oblivion it deserves. Not learned men only, but the simplest adherents of the Christian faith, can see how Jesus Christ—the Christ of the Gospels—survives, as a historical character, all these successive attacks, and shines out again, in the view of the world, in undiminished majesty, in unruffled serenity and sweetness, in glory that has not lost a ray. The Christian history is like some grand mountain, "whose pinnacles pierce the clouds, whose foundations are beneath the waves," which sits silently for a while amid the gloom of passing shadows, or is lost to sight in the rack of hurrying storms, but soon shines out again from the same place, and with the same lights on its brow, upon the plains below. There are many unsolved difficulties. There are discrepancies and apparent contradictions in the accounts we have of the person and life of Christ; and these may well exercise the ingenuity of the learned—may even in a small measure try the faith of the devout;—but the preponderance of evidence in favour of the historic verity of the life of Christ, according to the Gospel records, is meanwhile rather increasing than diminishing. The trust of the multitudes is not impaired. No day dawns and sets on Christendom, without hearing audibly or silently from millions of trustful hearts the one confession, "I believe in Jesus Christ."

Every reader of the Gospels knows how often the phrase "Son of Man" occurs in them. But it is likely enough that many have not observed how almost exclusively the phrase is used *by the Lord Himself.* His disciples never call Him "the Son of Man." It is His own favourite description of Himself; and, no doubt, one of the principal reasons for such frequent use of the phrase is His desire to be known among men, *as truly one of them.* Is it too much to say that He loves the title because He loves the thing—because it pleases Him well to be a man ? It is not that He casts humanity around Him like a mantle, in a little while to be put off. He could have done that, as the angels do when they come on brief messages to earth. They can come without being born. They can go without dying; and yet look like men when they show themselves here. But "forasmuch as the children are partakers of flesh and blood, He also Himself likewise took part of the same," and in this phrase "Son of Man," so often on His lips, gladly owns the "part" He has taken, says in effect that He is thankful to have been born, that it rejoices Him to live, that He is willing to die.

But now it would be a complete perversion of this phrase to make it mean, according to the misapprehensions of some, that He was *only* human, and not also divine. Rather, it means that He is not only divine, but *also* human. For the phrase is, not "Son of Man," "a Son of Man," or "the Son of a Man," but, in the way of excellence and sole peculiarity, "THE Son of Man." "Son of Man," said the angel to Ezekiel, indicating nothing more than his participation of human nature. "The Son of Man," says Christ, pointing to His divinity while asserting His humanity. Peter's Confession, in and for the making of which he was pronounced blessed by our Lord Himself, puts the matter above question :—" Thou art the Christ, *the Son of the living God.*" Of course the disciples never had any doubt concerning the proper humanity of their Master; but His divinity seems to have dawned upon them by degrees. It came in gleams, and in softer shinings. It filled the air about them; it troubled them; it cheered them; it cast them down, and lifted them up, and at length stood out—although perhaps not perfectly until after the Resurrection—with unwavering clearness to their faith for ever. I have spoken of the inductive gropings of the disciples from the human, which was visible, up to the divine, which, although generally invisible, shone through and down upon them "as they were able to bear it." But when Jesus was glorified they not only had full revelation of the great fact and mystery of our redemption, God manifest in the flesh, but they then remembered how he had told them of all this before, in words which they had allowed to drop out of mind, or to lie there unrecognised and unknown—how plainly He had spoken of His divine Sonship to men, how He had put it into actions, how He had expressed it in prayer to His Father—and then they wrote all this down, that we "also might believe."

There is another, a more abstract way of approaching the divine meaning of the phrase, "His only Son." It may be deduced as a necessary inference from the Fatherhood of God. If there be an eternal "Father Almighty" there must be an eternal Son, or Sons. The terms are strictly correlative. As there can be no husband without a wife, no king without a subject, so there cannot be a father without a son, an eternal father without an eternal son. No creature is eternal. There must therefore be a sonship far above ours, a Son quite other than we. And, as in the nature of the case we need not look anywhere in the created universe for

The Creed of Christendom. 317

such a being, we can look nowhere else but into "the bosom of the Father, to find His only Son."

I am aware that this kind of reasoning, like some philosophical arguments for the doctrine of the Trinity, takes us along a dim pathway towards heights too giddy for us. "Who can by searching find out God?" For nothing can we be more incompetent than for any sufficient discovery of the divine nature by means of abstract speculation. But, surely, all that we have ventured to say is in accordance with the inspired declaration—"The only begotten Son which is in the bosom of the Father He hath declared Him;" and with our blessed Lord's own declaration—"He that hath seen me hath seen the Father."

This revelation of the fatherhood of God through the sonship of Christ is for nothing less than the world's redemption. It is that "knowing the only true God and Jesus Christ whom he hath sent," we might have eternal life in this knowledge. This great manifestation of God in Christ is not intended for our instruction simply, for the communication of religious knowledge to men by means of their natural faculties,— as knowledge of other kinds is conveyed among men themselves, by the teacher to the taught, by the man of experience to the novice. If this were all, as far as we are able to judge, the means are too great for the end. This stupendous interposition of the Deity, if indeed it be what all Christendom has ever believed it to be— very God coming down to man through bending heavens to a wondering earth: infinite wealth and glory exchanged for the meanest, and darkest, and bitterest things that earth could give—does it all issue in only this, that Jesus Christ becomes the world's chief schoolmaster?

"The Father of lights" is, of course, always shedding them forth in this as in other worlds. But He is, so to speak, in no haste to do this. He has time enough, and He takes time. The general progress of the world—may we not say of the universe?—is slow. And if nothing more than education and development were needed, is it likely that He would interrupt, or at any rate, immeasurably elevate the process by a miraculous and strictly personal advent upon the scene? If nothing were going wrong in this world, if men were taking no harm except of temporary kinds, it seems every way likely, judging from the analogies, that whatever other manifestations might have been made, *this* manifestation in the flesh—in order to humiliation and death—would have been withheld. His very coming, therefore, is a proclamation that danger is abroad, and of the most serious kind. His very appearance, in such guise, is a revelation of our sins. His name Jesus— "the Saviour," shows our name to be "the lost." We cannot have the full meaning of the name Jesus which the angel, at His birth, declared it to contain. "Thou shalt call His name JESUS; for He shall save His people from their sins," without assuming the dark corresponding truth, that in this sin, the world, without Him, is utterly "lost."

"Our lost state by nature" has always, as might be expected, held a chief place in the writings of divines; and it has always been a favourite theme, as it is a very necessary one, with practical preachers of the Gospel. Yet, perhaps there is no religious subject on which it is more difficult to write or speak with wisdom, and to any gracious and wholesome issues. It is so easy to exaggerate, although when the truth is rightly conceived, exaggeration is hardly possible. It is so easy to misstate the case and press the charges in a form to which the conscience makes little or no response. There is a way of vilifying human nature, and depreciating all its qualities down to so low a level, that the greatness of the loss vanishes from the mind, for there remains practically *very little* to be saved. Not only has the gold become dim and tarnished, but, according to the representation, it has ceased *to be* gold. The ring of the noble metal can be heard no more; nor its yellow lustre seen. It is not merely lost, it is destroyed. The corrosion has gone through and through and eaten it up. Jesus, the Saviour, never puts the case so. The woman has "lost" her silver piece, and knows not in what mire, or dust, or dark corner it may be found; but she never doubts that when it is found it will be silver still. The shepherd has "lost a sheep in the wilderness, and goes seeking it by height, and hollow, and thorny thicket, but "when he hath found it," bruised, it may be, and exhausted, "he carries it home rejoicing." For the time, at least, it is nearer to his heart "than the ninety and nine that went not astray."

God forbid that we should be understood as seeking in any way to lessen the guilt of human sin. That guilt, rightly conceived, is more intense and profound than our most serious thought can make it. Apart from Him who seeks and saves, the case is one of irretrievable calamity. It is not that there is a shadow falling here and there. It is that the night has come. It is not that some hindrances have happened to humanity in its progress onwards and upwards. It is that it has fallen utterly down to a quite lower level. It is not that man is troubled, tried, unfortunate, baffled, and mistaken for a little. It is that he is "*lost.*" Ah, that word "lost," coming from *His* lips, tells all. It is as when a man, tossing in sickness, but hoping to be well again in a few days, sees suddenly at his bedside the face of a physician who is called only in cases of emergency and danger, and knows then in a moment that he is very ill. When "the only Son" of the Father comes into the world as "Jesus Christ," the Saviour, and says, looking us in the face, "I am come to seek and save that which is lost," can we be less than deeply troubled and utterly serious? Dare we try then to mitigate the case, or gild over the misery, or deny the guilt?

Lost! What a word is this even in those applications and uses of it which, alas, are not uncommon among us! It is often brimful of sorrow and anguish. It is perhaps the saddest word we ever speak. It expresses privation, desolateness, misery. It is like a wail from the wilderness in which some helpless pilgrim-company are wandering, or lying down to perish. It is like the dirge of a stormy midnight over sinking ships and drowning men; like the sighs which come from the windows of a prison where lie captives doomed to death.

Take it even in the lighter cases and it is sad. Property is in danger; the case fluctuates from day to day, and the man whose property it is, says often to his friends, "I am very anxious." Then some day the thing is settled, and one word expresses all, "Lost!" A young man shows signs of giddiness and instability, yet for a while is held back, or drawn back, from the brink of folly and destruction; but at last makes the fatal plunge, and heart-broken friends say with a more bitter grief than they would feel at a Christian's grave, "Lost." Tennyson makes a very touching use of this word in the case of Enoch Arden, when he brings him home after long absence, only to hear tidings and see sights that will sink him into his grave. The widow tells him, not knowing—Enoch was so brown, so bowed, so broken—all the story of his house.

> "And o'er his countenance
> No shadow past, nor motion: any one,
> Regarding, well had deem'd he felt the tale
> Less than the teller: only when she closed
> 'Enoch, poor man, was cast away and lost'
> He, shaking his gray head pathetically,
> Repeated muttering 'cast away and—lost;'
> Again in deeper inward whispers 'lost!'"

I cannot help feeling that these nearer senses of the word catch some of the pathos that is in them, from the farther and wider sense of it which underlies all others —that signification which our Lord expresses when, looking on humanity, and speaking to men, he says, "I am come to seek and save that which is lost"—that sense which we also express when, in grateful response we say, each for himself, "I believe in Jesus Christ." Too gratefully has no man ever yet made that confession. Nor has any man ever thought of himself and his sinful state with too much shame and grief. As a matter of fact, and apart from all theory on the subject, it is now as it has ever been,—he who has the profoundest sense of unworthiness and impotence comes most naturally and easily to the realisation of the highest ideas and the best attainments of the Christian life. "He that humbleth himself is exalted." That purified moral sense which enables us to see sin with a sorrowing heart, also gives us the vision of purity and the thirst for God. Those who "cry from the depths" soon follow their cries and looks, they come to sit on thrones, they are men after God's own heart. Those who, sinking in the waves, cry "Lord, save," become rocks on which, historically, churches are built; pillars in the house of God; men whose shadows will be wholesome as they pass along city streets.

We shall not now attempt to put into definite form any *plan* of salvation. In our inner thought we must all have something that may be called a plan, some systematic arrangement of our beliefs and opinions, some logical concatenation of our thoughts. We must, too, with the nature God has given us, see some reasons for His declarations and procedure in regard to the forgiveness and restoration of humanity. He clearly recognises and honours this moral quality of our nature by giving so many explanations, by telling us so much. He puts us by His revelations amid the great facts, relations, powers of the universe—law, sin, grace, flesh, spirit, angels, devils, God incarnate, heaven, hell. We have our part to play, and our destiny to work out amid all these, and it is indolence or pusillanimity to shrink from knowing and verifying as far as we can. But on the other hand, it is a profitless presumption to attempt to pursue our knowledge within the lines and beyond the lights of revelation. We are soon " at our wits'," and our reason's "end." We soon touch infinity. We soon gaze on mystery. Our measuring lines are too short; our penetrative faculty too forceless. Baffled and blinded we turn again to Him who is the light of the world, and the life of men. We watch His coming and His going, and in the facts of His wondrous life, holding, as they do, in solution or in dependence all the doctrines of our faith, we accept the free, full, salvation of God; we say with Christendom that we "believe in Jesus Christ."

The proof and fruit of this acknowledgment and experience of His redemptive power will be seen in practical and hearty submission to His sovereignty as "OUR LORD." In homelier phrase, He is still "The Master,"—laying law and rule upon the daily life of each one of His followers. We may look at this truth for a moment in the larger, and then in the limited individual aspect. In the largest sense, "He is Lord of all,"—"set at the right hand of God,"—"In the heavenlies"—supreme in heavenly places and in heavenly things. "Above all principality and power, and might, and dominion,"—"Having all things under His feet,"—"Head over all to the Church,"—Gatherer together of all things in Himself, as the centre and power of universal conciliation and harmony. All this is substantially acknowledged by all Christendom. On the part of some Churches there are what others regard, viewed controversially, as perilous qualifications of this supremacy, in the setting up of rivalries to his sole authority. It admits, however, of little practical doubt that the almost unanimous assent of Christendom is given to the proposition that "*He is Lord of all.*" Even weak and dark souls see HIS glory shining high over all, and, in proportion as they are earnest, find a way to *Him.*

It is encouraging also to observe how increasingly Christendom *is* ruled by her Lord. We are far from wishing to deny that heathendom yet lingers, even entrenches itself, in dark places and things, and offers stout resistance to the law and the spirit of Christianity.

There remains yet much to be done in all departments of our complex life; there is before us yet a long and arduous struggle before there can be any final proclamation of victory for the truth, and for the Lord.

The Creed of Christendom.

But on the other hand it concerns us to mark all real progress, and to lose no encouragement that legitimately comes to us from the achievements already won, or from the probable successes of the future. HIS words, who once spake on earth, who now reigns in heaven, are found embodied in the jurisprudence of nations, inscribed on the pages of the historian, enshrined by the moralist among his first principles, set by the poet in his pictures of choicest beauty, recognised and exhibited continually in even the most ephemeral productions. He reigns; He rules—not only by divine overmastering power—but by the ideas, the principles, the sentiments of the Christian faith. By the truth and gentleness of His kingdom He restrains and rules the spirits of men, and the councils of nations. He assuages even the fierce spirit of war, tempers the passions of multitudes, and, slowly it may be, yet surely, is moulding the forms of society and directing its hidden processes, with a view to the civic and social perfection of the future.

The same blessed rule of law and grace is over each individual life. The Saviour becomes the Lord. The love that saves has in it the law that rules; and the law that rules still breathes the love that saves. When a man "comes to himself,"—be it suddenly, like the prodigal, in some far country of sin, or, what is still better and more to be desired, insensibly, in the growing and under the nurture of grace,—he feels instinctively that he is called to obedience in active and passive conformity to the perfect will. He is "found" for this.

He lives for this. This is salvation. By how much there is of conformity to the will and the rule of "the Lord," by so much and no more is salvation attained. Escape is of value to us only if we advance into freedom. Safety is a blessing, indeed we may say is *a fact*, only as we translate and expand it into progress. We are not to stay in our very service—until we climb to its highest places, where the servant becomes the son, with conscious part in the great inheritance; and we stand forth at length—awful elevation!—"heirs of God, and joint-heirs with Christ."

XXIV.

Quenching the Spirit.

" Quench not the Spirit."—1 THESS. v. 19.

AWFUL, and yet when fully realised, most blessed is the thought of the indwelling of God in the spirit of man. It is more than "Emmanuel, God with us." It is God *in* us; it is more than divine manifestation in the flesh; it is God dwelling in the human spirit. Until He so comes, we are ruined, we are lost! When He comes the ruin becomes a living temple, and holy fires burn on the altar of the heart.

No man can explain this as a psychological fact. The natural mind and the natural philosophy do not at all receive it. It cannot be proved by logical demonstration. The Infinite in the finite must always seem a contradiction in terms : nor does it seem less a *moral* contradiction, that the Holy One should dwell in the unholy heart. And yet every Christian believes it— every striving expanding soul exults in the sacred belief that God dwells in him, and he in God. This fact lifts our mean nature higher than ever Paul ascended ; it throws a light of hopefulness and even glory on the future, which never could shine were human nature left to its own resources.

If the fact of the divine indwelling be awful and sublime—still more awful is the power given to a man to "resist," to "grieve," or to "quench" the Spirit of God. If we may well rejoice with a sacred reverential joy at the thought of God's indwelling, we may well tremble at the possession of that dread freedom, whereby we can oppose divine agencies, and even "quench the Spirit" in our hearts.

How can any one quench the Spirit? To answer this question we must try to understand, in our limited measure, what His work is, and how it is carried on. There is no direct consciousness in any human spirit of the contactual presence of God with and in it. A man is conscious of himself, but not internally of any other creature, nor of the Creator. Even a Christian man in serene devoutness, in burning earnestness or heavenly rapture—is still only conscious *of himself.* He believes that God is within him; by faith he knows it, by sure spiritual instincts, and by quick reasonings from gracious effects to their cause—but he is not *conscious* of God in the same way as he is of himself. It follows, that if the Spirit of God be really in us, He must act by means of the laws of our own nature; giving thoughts to the intellect, affections to the heart, and holy purposes by the tension and nerve of our own will. Suppose a city to have a perfect machinery of conduits for the supply of water; but the actual supply is—none at all, or very bad. There is abundant water at a distance, in some mountain lake, fed by clouds and snows, and that, let us suppose, is brought to be distributed in the city. There may be much labour and expense before the water can be brought, but once there, the pipes and conduits are ready to receive it. These could never make the pure water; they could not purify it, but they are capable of transmitting it. So—(forgive the humble figure, I think it is true and fair)—the natural faculties and feelings constitute a perfect instrumentality for the reception and distribution of the divine gift. They cannot generate the living water. They never can purify thought and feeling so that these shall become divine. But when, by the coming of the blessed Spirit, the well of living water is opened deep within, and begins to "spring up into everlasting life," then these faculties and feelings are the channels along which the heaven-fed streams will flow.

Thus we conclude that any unfair dealing with our own nature, with its laws or principles, is really quenching the Spirit of God. He acts through our nature. He uses memory for our conviction, conscience for our condemnation or justification, the understanding for our enlightenment, the will for our invigoration, the affections for our happiness; and if we refuse to allow these faculties to be so used, we are quenching the Spirit of God.

To illustrate this—we are told by our Lord Himself that the Spirit *convinces men of sin*. He takes a sinner at some solemn time, brings his whole life to remembrance, and makes memory a scourge to him. He touches his conscience, and it flames like Mount Sinai! He shows him the holiness of God and the sinfulness of sin. It is a most gracious opportunity—a very door of life to the man. But alas! he closes the door with his own hand. He misses the opportunity. He stifles memory and silences conscience. He quenches the Spirit of God. But such an one may ask—"Then is it God who is making me miserable?" Yes, as a surgeon probes the wound he wishes to heal; as God has dealt with some of His noblest servants—casting them down into the depths — almost overwhelming them with a sense of sin. Then they cried unto the Lord, and He heard them, and delivered them from all their fears. To you, if you obey the Spirit's leadings, there will come a like deliverance, and as much elevation as your nature will permit. Weeping may endure for a night, but the joy that is already travelling on will be here in the morning.

Christian people too are convinced of sin, and they too may quench the Spirit of God if they do not take heed. Sin is sin, in whomsoever it is found; and however painful the process, it must be searched out and abandoned. We are going on a long and hard journey, in weakness and disease; and we are apt to murmur when God makes us *feel* weak, that He may help us. We are going out into the night, and the oil in our vessels is low,—shall we be angry when a dear heavenly Friend lifts them up, and shows us how empty they are? Precious to a true saint are the convicting visitations of God, even at latest life? Strength and joy come with them, or after them. Angel-like in purity is the strength that springs out of humiliation! Sweet the joy of God which godly sorrow brings! Welcome be that viewless agent, who comes to make a holy trouble in the soul, that there may be afterwards a holy triumph.

Again, the Spirit's work is eminently *a revealing work*, or, to use a Scriptural phrase, a work of *shewing*. "He will receive of mine, and shew it unto you." "He will shew you things to come." In conducting this great work, He uses every kind of suitable instrumentality—the written and inspired word; the spoken word of the ministry; the thoughtful books of men; conversation with Christian people or even with those who are not so; quiet reflection. These are some of the media through which He sheds His heavenly lights. It follows that if we do not search the Scriptures,—if we do not take kindly the ministries of divine truth that come to us in providence, if we never read books with good thoughts in them, if we do not try to get some added wisdom from our intercourse with friends, if we never "meditate at eventide" or at dawn,—we are shutting out of our hearts the waiting Spirit of God.

These are His revealing instruments, but He is not confined to these. He can give revealing grace without them. Who has told any body of divines that the Spirit of God is limited to a book—although the book be of His own inspiration? Who has told philosophers that the Spirit of God cannot enter into the spirit of a man, and show there the highest truth, without previous processes of reasoning, and a great noise of intellectual machinery? Let us be careful not to trench on the royalty of the Spirit. Let us not put human bars and limits to His viewless, windlike course. Let Him blow as He listeth—in rushing, mighty wind; or let Him brood and rest in the still, moveless air. Let us rejoice to think that God can speak without Bible, without logic, without spoken word, *if He will:* to the little child—filling the infant soul with wonder and prayer; to the savage—solemnized amid the forest glooms; to the sailor—out on the sunny or stormy sea; to the slave—fainting in the hot plantation; to the traveller—amid the mountain-snows; to any man of the ten thousands who throng the streets every day; to *any* man, *anywhere*, as He will, God can speak.

Have you never felt a revealing time come to you suddenly, you knew not how? The common busy world about you seemed to grow still, almost to sink out of sight; while the other world, and the everlasting kingdom, rose gently, sublimely into view? Have you not had flashes of the better light thrown in upon you sometimes, through dark clouds of trouble? Or in moods of meditation, or even of vacancy, has there not arisen to your perception some great truth, glorious and distinct as you never saw it before—in self-evidencing light? All this is the "shewing" of the Spirit.

Life is a school, in which the lessons are always going on. But now and again the Master speaks expressly to *one* of the scholars; teaches him some new thing, or confirms him in some old lesson. The world is a many-stringed instrument, and the divine hand sometimes lingers on a special chord, and a man does not know it till the music thrills out on his ear. Providence in personal history is like the unrolling of a map or a picture, of many scenes and colours. For days and days there is little or nothing that has not been there before,—all things continue as they were. Then suddenly comes a new scene rolling out on the view like daybreak, or like the falling of unexpected night. In short, not only when God uses His greatest and most honoured instruments of illumination—Bible, books, living ministry, fellowship of saints, charities of home—but also in regard to every other way by which He reveals truth to the soul, let us carry in our minds, and put in practice, this solemn exhortation, "*Quench not the Spirit.*"

One thought more. The Spirit's work is to "seal" or set apart. He is said to "*seal*" believers "unto the day of redemption." He is Himself the earnest of their immortal inheritance. When by His creative regenerating power they are born from above, they are immediately marked and sealed (by what mystic signs and impressions we cannot tell) for their celestial destination. They are set apart for God. "The Lord knoweth them that are His." More. He renews that sealing process again and again; retouching His work, bringing out the divine inscriptions, clothing His children with robes of purity, making them manifest as "children of the light and of the day." Any one who resists this process, who does not often think of the Father and the Father's house, who seldom looks within the veil, who "minds earthly things" too much, is opposing the gracious work of the Spirit of God.

Christ, our Redeemer, has ascended into heaven, that we may follow Him thither, in thought, in faith, in love and longing; and by these upward-drawn affections we are sealed for the heaven where He is. Our friends are taken from us, not only because they are ripe and ready for the better life, but also because by their departure hence, and entrance into the blessed company, God would make us susceptible of another sealing touch. By taking them home He takes us, morally and in affection, one stage nearer home also.

I believe—although on such a subject, hanging almost over the verge of our dull mortal faculties, one would wish to speak with reverence—I believe that Christian people have thoughts given them sometimes, purely as *sealing thoughts*: they are not needed for their daily duty, nor for this life, so far as we can see: they are anticipative: they are needed for the higher service, and for the life to come. Spaces are made for these, unaccountably, in the present life—moments of silence, when this mysterious preparation is carried on. One is earlier down some morning than usual,—sees the rosy flushing of the sky,—and in the short moment of quietness looks far away beyond the gates of the earthly morning into the land of sunless light. *It is the sealing of the Spirit.*

Or one is struck suddenly—at high noon of city-life —with the utter vanity of all the fever, toil, and strife; of all the activities and hopes seething around him. Then the conviction comes—more profound than can be put into words—that all this is in itself as hollow as the sounding tomb, and that it can have significance and value only by its relations to the "powers of the world to come." Again, *it is the touch of the sealing Spirit.*

Or at night, when the toils of the day are over, when the social communications of the evening are ended, when the friends have all left and gone home;— there falls upon the house or upon one room in it, a little visitation of silence—a wonderful silence with a sadness in it, and yet no fear;—almost as if the friends had all died;—as if the thinker were walking into the grave, or away beyond the grave;—as if the shadow of the end had come. This, too, is *the sealing of the Spirit*—another deeper impression—"unto the day of redemption."

"*Quench not the Spirit*" in any of these, or in any other of His gracious comings. He moves in us only for our good. He leads us ever onwards. The worst He ever does to us is to retire. The most awful thing we can do to ourselves is to grieve the Spirit and drive Him away. O the misery, solitude, and ultimate despair of a human spirit when forsaken of the Spirit of God! O the rush of a God-forsaken life over the black cataract of death, away to the unknown darkness! What a fall, what a ruin we have here! Lament over it, ye heavens, and weep, O earth, because your sons are thus destroyed! And you, O ye children of the Spirit—arise and do what in you lies to avert this doom from others, to keep about them the lights of hope!

"*Quench not the Spirit.*" Follow the gentle inward motion. Listen to the still small voice. Yield to the stronger drawings. Watch for each beam of light. Be thankful for each drop of softening dew. Keep burning the holy fires, until they consume the last relics of corruption in their searching flames, until they have refined the soul to a celestial temper, and made it meet for heaven.

XXV.

Strength as the Days.

"Thy shoes shall be iron and brass; and as thy days, so shall thy strength be."—DEUT. xxxiii. 25.

(*For the New Year.*)

THE whole prophecy concerning Asher is a happy commentary on the name "Asher"—*Prosperity*. It is not always that the omen or suggestion contained in a name is fulfilled, but in this case the fulfilment is remarkable. Jacob's prophecy, long before, was this: "Out of Asher thy bread shall be fat, and he shall yield royal dainties." The words of Moses here are the confirmation and amplification of those of Jacob. The fulfilment came in due time in territorial advantages. "The fifth lot came out for the children of Asher . . . and reacheth to Carmel westward . . . and the outgoings thereof are at the sea." Carmel! "It shall blossom abundantly." "The excellency of Carmel and Sharon" was a type of the highest blessing. Asher not only possessed these places of fruitfulness, as well as harbours and outlets by sea, but his portion stretched away to Lebanon in the north, and held in its soil the "brass" and "iron" mentioned here. "Thy shoes"—some render it "*thy towers*"—iron-girt, brass-locked, *i.e.* strong, impregnable. Or, if we keep to the usual rendering, the idea is the familiar one of a journey, a pilgrimage; but not across the green sward and amid soft and flowery ways, but over rough roads, among rocks and stones, where the ordinary sandals will be an insufficient protection for the foot; where the shoes must be, as it were, keeled with iron, ribbed and nailed with brass. The thing of importance is—what is conveyed in either case—*i.e.* that sufficient help will be given for the journey of life or for its conflict, as we have it in the closing words of the text—"*As thy days, so shall thy strength be.*"

The instinctive sense of the Church has turned these words into a spiritual promise amid the changes and trials of this mortal life. As such we use it. We are now once again at the beginning of days. The year is new. The future spreads out before us in a long line of "*days,*" if we look on to the end of the year—365 of them—measured portions of time, cut off by the circling of the sun from eternal duration for human education and earthly use. That long line is the line of our march; we must leave footmarks on the surface of *every* day, *i.e.* moral impressions made in Time, which will be opened like a book, and read in Eternity. And here is a promise which comes every day and every hour to the last of the year—nay, to the last of life itself: "*As thy days, so shall thy strength be.*"

Of course in making a spiritual use of this promise

for ourselves a great deal is presupposed. The whole Gospel stands in presupposition; the whole Gospel possessed and obeyed, although not perfectly, yet with the will and the heart. It is to those and to those only who thus accept God's mercy and bow to His will that such a promise *can* be true. I see it, indeed, stretching over all alike, in general availableness. But the real helpfulness of it can come down only on a religious life. It is to those who say, at least in heart-intention, "As our days, so shall our service be," that God says, "As your days, so shall your strength be."

Let us see what this promise *is not*, and then what *it is*.

This promise has no direct relation to the past. It has in it no power of retrieval and recovery. These "days" along which we have come, where our footmarks may be seen, if they have been well spent, it is well; but if not, this promise will not alter that. Negligence *is* negligence, and no spiritual alchemy can change it into diligence. No promise or even power of God can alter the actuality of the moral character of the time that is past. *This* only may be done: precious lessons may be drawn out of that which has been; and thus the moral continuity of the results of what was evil may be in a measure interrupted, and good drawn out of the evil. But there can be no annihilation of what has actually happened; and the probability is that out of a careless, fruitless past there will come much disadvantage and much hindrance in the present and the future. Thanks be to God—those who truly repent can say, "He has forgiven it all," but not the less certainly will it live in some of its moral results. I mention this with a view to the future. We put a kind of fallacy upon ourselves sometimes, and go on in a mist in this matter. We believe that "the blood of Jesus Christ cleanseth us from all sin," but we do *not* always believe that "as a man soweth so shall he also reap." Both are true and equally full of import.

Some one looks on through this coming year, and says within himself, "If I get the fulfilment of this good promise it will be a happy year for me, but if not, the promise will be still waiting for me at the beginning of the year beyond, and I may have the full benefit of it then." No; you cannot have *so* full a benefit of it then, as you may have if you go on through this year in the full possession of it. The years grow on the same stem, are held in the same rind; grow into each other. They have a moral continuity running through them, and it is folly and presumption to go on in practical carelessness under the vain idea that some magical change will take place, by which danger and penalty and evil consequences will be warded off.

This promise does not bring us into any immediate connection with the future. Of course it has respect to the future; indeed, as has been said, it stretches all over the future; but it does not put into our own possession to-day the strength we shall need to use to-morrow. It reserves to-morrow's supply *until* to-morrow comes. It is, strictly rendered, a promise simply *for the day*. A great and daily unhappiness comes to some people by their failing to recognise this. They are not content with the *assurance* that the strength will be given. They want the strength itself. They want to feel brave in the face of the danger that will not be here for weeks. They want to feel resigned under the trouble, a mere thin, projected shadow of which only has fallen yet. They want to-morrow's grace before to-morrow comes. And if there be anything urgent coming on—duty, or temptation, or trial, or change—the desire to feel and be sure of possessing the needed strength grows urgent and importunate in like degree. Just as people gather and lay up material substance for years, for life if they can, until they are able to say, "*now we are provided for*," so these persons want to have grace in stock and capital, to hold it, as it were, under lock and key, and live on the interest of the same. It cannot be done.

No doubt there is what may be called grace in stock; in capital if you will, in the existence and operation of gracious principles and dispositions. You may reckon with certainty on getting large interest from these. But even that is on condition of continued faithfulness, and in order to secure that God gives *by the day*. It *is* only in the day itself—in the dispensation—in the duty—in the melting of the heart-grief; in the bitterness of the disappointment, or in the fierceness of the temptation, that you can fully know what strength you will require—and only *then*, in the nature of things, can you receive it.

At the beginning of a year, a man feels that he would like to know that there shall be no reverse in his circumstances—or if such a reverse shall come to him, that he will be brave to bear it, and be, at least in his own esteem, none the less a man. But God will not satisfy any such curiosity as that. The man must wait to see. He must depend on providence *every* day. He must accept what comes, yield what God wishes to take away, frame his mind to his circumstances, and whether paucity or plenty preside over his table and his stores, he must pray, if he is to be true and childlike, "Give me *this* day my daily bread," and day by day God will answer him.

Or one may much desire to know whether any personal or relative affliction is to come during the year. "Is there to be a weakening of strength in the way? Will there be pain, weariness, exhaustion in my life? Shall the moan of sickness be heard in my house? Shall I, or any dear to me, say through the night, 'would God it were morning?' or through the day, 'would God it were evening?'" Neither to this solicitude does God vouchsafe any answer; at least in the way of prophetic knowledge. He gives *this* answer—that nothing shall happen by chance—that nothing shall be sent in cruelty —that nothing shall come without grace in its company; and that if we thankfully receive the grace, it matters less than we are apt to suppose whether the things that convey it be health or sickness, natural joy or grief.

And so of all other things that lie in the unknown future of the coming year, or of the coming life, to its close. The most solemn anxiety of all is that which relates to the time and manner of departure from the world. When shall I die? And where? And how? In peace or trouble? In doubt or triumph? Clinging in fear to the life I am leaving, or soaring in the ardour of the triumphant hope, to be "with Christ, which is far better?" God has made no arrangement for answering such anxieties. He does not think them of sufficient importance to be answered. It does not matter where, or when, or how, as to feeling, death finds us. The *state* in which we die matters everything; the feeling matters very little. O what slaves we are to our feelings!

You are going some distance to a banquet. It will, of course, be pleasant if the sun shines by the way, and all the world looks fair. But if the clouds hang heavy, and the air is dark and cold, you will go to the banquet just the same. You are going across the sea to claim a property, and you are to sail in a ship that cannot sink. It will be pleasant if there is only the ripple of quiet waters from the prow of the ship, and the flashing of the sunlight from the scarcely-crested waves. But if even there should come the roar and hurly of the storm, and the dash of the angry waves against the sides of the vessel, until the very masts are white with spray, you will none the less, and probably even none the later, see and claim your good estate. If a man lives well *each day*—die well he must, whatever his feeling be. Death will be to him a very chariot of fire to take him to the banquet of heaven; or a ship that turns back for no weather, nor ever strikes sail till she enters the harbour.

The subject is all practical, and we might draw out of it many needful lessons, such as these :—

(a.) It says to us—*Do not be managing and masterful* over circumstances and providence; hammering and hewing at the "days" to compel them into a certain shape. Take them as they come; for they come as they are sent, arrayed darkly or brightly by the hand of God, and filled with such elements as His wisdom and goodness have put into them. Never did the most bountiful affection of a happy home fill with precious things the box that is to be sent in new year's gift, from under the old roof-tree, to son or daughter who cannot get home—than the hand of God fills our several days with the things that are needed, and the things that will work for the best. Take them as they come. When the door is low, bow the head; when the dust is blowing, shut your eyes; when the road is rough, look to your steps; when all is pleasant, give thanks and sing; when things are full of mystery, wait. Lift up this promise and fit it to each day as it comes, and you will find there is not one which it will not cover. "As thy days, so shall thy strength be."

(b.) Do not be timorous and fearful, and full of anxious care; you see how little need there is for it, how well you are provided for! "The young lions do lack and suffer hunger"—the greedy, the ravenous, the passionate, the self-willed—do suffer hunger; the more they have the hungrier they become. "But they that fear the Lord shall not lack any good thing." "*All things are yours*, and ye are Christ's, and Christ is God's."

(*c.*) Such a subject and such a promise is surely a call to diligence. For here you see is an unlimited promise of strength—strength to match the "days"— that is God's side of it. Our part is to try to raise the "days" to match the strengths. We have said, "take the days as they come," submissively; but it is equally necessary to say "*make the days*, as they come, full of energy that God will sustain; full of needs that He will supply; full of hungers that He will feed; of growths that He will beautify; of living channels along which He may pour the living streams of grace. This is the last text in the Bible under which a man or a Church may sit down in indolence. It invites to enterprise and activity. When a man has good backing in mercantile or political life—what does he? Why, he goes right up the ladder if he can; or right away on a career of progress until he touches the bound of his opportunity. When Christian men and Christian Churches begin to act fully on that principle in the Lord's business—when they act according to the backing they have in immovable promise; according to the strengths laid up for them, and almost pressing them on—then the world will begin to believe that they mean what they say, and that they are going to do and be, at length, what they have so long professed.

The past year has gone from us for ever. It is but a little way behind; but who can bring it back? Gone with all that it held—its dark days and its bright. The smiles are faded; the tears are shed; pain and struggle and joy are alike over; and surely we can say with some humble thankfulness, "As our days," three hundred and sixty-five of them, not omitting one, "so has our strength been." "O God of our Father Abraham, and God of our Father Isaac—the Lord which saidst unto each of us, 'Return to thy true country, and to thy heavenly kindred, and I will deal well with thee'—we are not worthy of the least of all the mercies, and of all the truth which Thou hast caused to pass before Thy servants." But we are thus far on the road by which we must go. We set up another stone to-day to Thy praise. "*Ebenezer!*" And we go on beneath the shadow of the good word Thou hast given us. "*As thy days, so shall thy strength be.*"

XXVI.

Paul, Timothy, and Epaphroditus.

"But I trust in the Lord Jesus to send Timotheus shortly unto you . . . For I have no man like minded who will naturally care for your state. For all seek their own, not the things which are Jesus Christ's . . . Him therefore I hope to send presently . . . Epaphroditus, my brother, and companion in labour, and fellow soldier."—PHILIPPIANS ii. 19 to end.

IN these verses we are brought into close contact with persons more than with principles, or rather we have the advantage of watching the working of the principles, good and evil, in the persons. This passage reads like a chapter in the autobiography of the apostle Paul, and at the same time it is a chapter in the biography of Timothy, of Epaphroditus, and of some persons unknown. We shall best reach its various teachings by taking these several personages as they stand in succession.

Paul himself is the chief figure in the group, and his condition, his desire and purpose, are here incidentally made known to us; but in fact the persons are so closely related that it is impossible to speak of one without having one or more of the others in view, and impossible to speak of any of them without recognising the chief around whom they cluster, and under whom they act or refuse to act.

Paul is still in Rome, and is still a prisoner; wishing to be free, hoping and even strongly expecting to be free, we might even say assured that he will be so in no long time; but *not* so sure, as we see in a previous verse, whether his liberty, when it comes, will lead him out again upon the earth, or usher him into heaven. Still his hope is that before long he will get away from Rome a free man, and that he will be with his friends in Philippi. Meantime, hither has come to him in his imprisonment a messenger from Philippi, bearing from the beloved church there material help, rich messages of affection, and abundant proofs of the continuance of the work of grace among them. He wants to send fitting answer back, and to send it *now*. He desires not simply to send an acknowledgment of their kindness,—any messenger could take that,—but apparently he wishes to send some person or persons who would be able to help them in the highest sense,—to give them divine instruction, to console, direct, and strengthen them in the work and way of the Lord.

Here in Rome there are a number of persons professing the Christian faith, who in general capability are quite equal to a service of this kind; many of them are in fact already engaged in preaching the gospel, although we learn that their motives in doing so are very various—some preaching Christ from "goodwill," some from "envy and strife;" and it would almost seem that the Apostle had made overtures more or less direct and personal to some of them. It is not indeed conceivable that he had made proposals of this kind to those who preached the Gospel from "contention:" they would be quite unfit for a high and delicate mission like this. But among those who preached from "good-will" there may well have been some quite capable of undertaking it, and to one and another, and another still, we can imagine the question put by Paul himself as they came to him in his lodging—"Will you go to Philippi? Will you render to me and to the Master this great service? A great service it will be, for the Church there must always be important. Philippi will always be a centre of influence, and it is of great consequence to the Christian cause that incipient evils there should be checked, rising differences composed, that their knowledge and spiritual strength should be increased, and that they should be made happy among themselves. Will you go?" "No," replies one, "it is a long journey by land, and perilous by sea; it would be all hardship and difficulty, and, after all, success would be uncertain." "No," again from another, "I do not so much dislike travel, I do not fear difficulty, perhaps I might succeed in the mission; but I prefer Rome. No place is so good to live in as this great city, with its hills, and arches, and busy streets; the seat of universal government, the meeting-place of all the nations, the mistress of the world; I can preach here, and be as useful as if I went to Philippi." "No," yet again from another, "I am not so much affected by these outward things, but I prefer *home*. If I were at home in Philippi, I should object to come to Rome; since I am at home here, I would rather not go to Philippi." And so one after another declines the mission, and the Apostle is sad, and the day is dark about him, and the chain on his wrist is heavier as he writes, "*All seek their own and not the things which are Jesus Christ's.*"

This then is the dark group we have to look at first. They are unnamed, happily, but they are the men whose conduct suggested the sorrowful complaint "*All seek their own.*" The term "all" is used here evidently in a limited sense. It refers only to some of those persons who were requested to undertake this special service, not of course to all the Christians in Rome. There may have been many among them wholly consecrated in spirit, but who were, from various causes, quite incapable of doing this particular work. This condemning sentence is written against only a few, comparatively. Again, even in this case the sentence must be limited to the thing on which the decisive words of condemnation were pronounced. It is not an absolute verdict on character; it is a verdict in relation to one point of duty, and *only* in relation to that. It declares these men in Rome to be lacking in the requisite measure of faith and self-sacrifice, for a service which the Master in His providence required of them; and that is all. It is quite enough; it is serious and very sad; but not so sad as in the wider view it would be. If it be insisted that the interpretation of this twenty-first verse must be in conformity with the verbal and mechanical theory of inspiration, then all the professing Christians in Rome were hypocrites; there were no faithful men there except Paul and Timothy, and two or three who were with them. "*All* seek their own!" No man who seeks his own supremely can be a Christian; his profession must be a mere pretence. That this was so, we cannot for a moment suppose. The whole estimate is a comparative one. The Apostle had a standard of action and service by which he ruled his own life. It was the true standard. He applied it here to some of the most privileged and capable of his fellow-servants, and they drew back; they would not accept the burden; they refused to wear the yoke.

Charity and a true interpretation require us to say so much as this: but faithfulness requires us to add that the failure is a very great one. It could not be a light thing for Christian men thus to shrink from duty; and it cannot be a light thing for any of us to fail in the same way—to fall, by our own choice, clearly below the highest and best service it is possible for us to render. Each of us has some Philippi to which we may go, God-sent: or from which we may hold back, self-hindered. The place, the service, may bear no great name; it may be some ordinary place, some plain service in common life; but whatever tests motives and principles, whatever tests especially the purity of the motives and the strength of the principles, is as great to us as if the service were an Apostolic mission, as if the place were historical Philippi or imperial Rome. The essence of all New Testament teaching, reduced to practical form, is this—*Life in Christ and for men*, an entire consecration to Him, and through Him to our fellows. This life is to be simple and whole-hearted—a life of complete abandonment. It is to have in it no checks or withholdings: it is to be without reserve. "To the uttermost" He saves, and to the uttermost we are to serve. Indeed there can be no saving to the uttermost unless there be a corresponding service: for this—and nothing less—*is salvation;* that we seek no more "our own things,"—as we are apt to deem them — some personal advantage, some mere worldly gain, some transient glory of this earthly life; but that we seek rather "the things which are Jesus Christ's." Thus we shall find, in fact, "our own things" in the true and deep sense. In Him and in His service, when we take it *all*, we find our true selves. This other self—that is so watchful, and so busy, and so greedy— is a mere usurper: the nobler self, the true ideal within us, answers to the appeal from Calvary; bows low in the presence of a crucified Saviour; bears itself a cross; serves, suffers, knows nor limit nor reserve; has for its motto "unto death," and "for evermore."

Happy are we if this higher law has full force in our life, or anything at all *like* full force! For it is too much to suppose that it is perfect yet in any of us. But it is a great matter, indeed it is everything, if we perceive its beauty, and if our desire and endeavour be to make it really the law of our own life. If this be so indeed, then the promises are ours, and we shall grow stronger and stronger, until one day (how far off sometimes it seems!) we shall be perfect in Christ Jesus.

It is a great point always, in moral education, to be brought into the presence of our superiors. In our life-progress nothing is more helpful than the sight of those who are more advanced than we. Let us therefore turn from these Christians in Rome, who cannot help us except as beacons and warnings, and look for a little at one of a very different spirit.

Here is Timothy: *he* will go to Philippi: he will go *anywhere* for Christ. He is with Paul in Rome now; no doubt in daily attendance; and the Apostle declares that among those who could by their abilities and gifts render great Christian service, he stands quite alone. There is "no man like-minded," no man minded like Timothy: he is, as it were, Paul's own only image, his other self: we see no shade upon him: we hear no whisper of any defect. He is fit for this service, or for any service. Let us look at him well—there are not many such men to look at even in the history of the true Church. You go into a gallery of pictures, and they are all good in some way,—a bad picture would not be admitted there,—but perhaps out of many hundreds on the walls there are not more than two or three that approach the highest mark. So every Christian has a light of God upon him, has some portion of the spirit of Christ in him. But ah! how few shine with unwavering lustre! How few are dressed in the beauty of the Lord their God! How few are ready for *every* call of duty! How few will go to Philippi when they are well settled in Rome! There are many who will serve the Lord and "seek their own," who "fear the Lord their God and serve idols." There are not a few John Marks in the Church, ready to take the homeward road if the journey is long and the fare but scant. Not a few also, thank God, of a better type than he. But of this *noblest*, most beautiful type there are not many! There is no attempt made here at anything like a full delineation of the character of Timothy, yet taking this outline as it is given us, and the few lines and features in other Scriptures which help to fill up the sketch, we have as the result one of the fairest, sweetest, and most perfect of human characters.

Some lines in the picture are worthy of note; this among others, that *he has grown into this perfectness from his youth*. He has not leaped into it suddenly. No moral excellence can be achieved in that way, but must be reached through growing. It cannot be the lot of every one to be born like Timothy, of a godly stock; to know from a child the holy Scriptures; to be tenderly reared under a pious mother's care, with a venerable grandmother's blessing: nor can every one have, as it were, a Grecian father to give inheritance of his own culture and manliness. Such pre-requisites as these would exclude many from the consecrated life. But this I say—that if you want to be a good soldier of Jesus Christ you must enter the service early and continue in it steadfastly. If you want to be fit for anything to which God may call you, begin at once and work your way up to that fitness. Probably when you are *ready* for it the call will come.

Another line in this fair character is the line of *obedience*. Timothy has "served" in the Gospel under another. A good many years have now gone by since Paul found him at Derbe and led him out, not much more than a lad, into the great field; and he has been "serving" all that time. No doubt he has been before now guide and master to many; but he has never ceased to be a servant himself, and in this way has his character grown to its high excellence. If you have a holy ambition to follow in his steps—and a nobler cannot warm your breast—leave it to others to command in the Gospel—to speculate, to dispute in the Gospel, even to rest in it and enjoy it. A nobler and more fruitful use to make of it than any of these is *to serve* in the Gospel. Out of service will come strength, beauty, manhood, higher service still, and so fitness for heaven when the time of entrance shall come.

Yet another line is added to the picture when we are told that Timothy had been with Paul as "a son with a father" in the gospel service. This spiritual relation between them is more than once referred to elsewhere. "Mine own son in the faith," Paul calls him in writing to himself, and there seems to be a delicate allusion here to the same thing when he says, "I have no man like-minded who will *naturally* care for your state," *i.e.* as a birthright, as inheriting the interests and labours of his spiritual father. This fatherhood does not necessarily imply an agency in conversion.

Timothy seems to have been a Christian before Paul knew him. It was a fascination, a leadership to which it was both a necessity and a pleasure to yield; and we know that such loyal allegiance and spirit-service given to one so worthy of it must have called into yet fuller life all that was good and true in him who gave it.

This is he whom the Apostle designs to send to Philippi: and Timothy stands ready for the service, quite in the spirit and mood of him, who on being chosen to command the Indian army in a time of extremity, and asked when he could leave England, answered with a soldier's promptitude, "*To-morrow!*" As we look at him—all his wealth of youth, and gifts of nature and of grace laid at the feet of Christ, we can imagine what a mitigation his very presence would be to the sufferings and troubles of Paul; we can imagine too, although not a word of this is said, how great was the sacrifice to the Apostle in the loneliness of his captivity, when he sent Timothy from his side, uncertain, as he must have been, whether the parting might not be final.

The other figure in the group, of whom we get but one glimpse, is Epaphroditus. He was pastor, or one of the pastors of the Philippian Church. He has come now to Rome, the willing bearer of a precious gift from the Church in Philippi to the Apostle—not the first they have sent him, nor the second, nor the third. For years there had been no opportunity to give him any fresh token of their affection; but now, again, having heard of his arrival in Rome a prisoner, the old affectionate care of him revives, and perhaps much to his surprise, one day Epaphras comes to his lodging and lays the gift in his hands. We are not told whether, having done so, he wandered out to look at the shows, the statues, the temples of Rome—to see Old Tiber and his bridges; but this we do know, that he gave himself to Christian labour under the Apostle's direction, without stint, in the spirit of a true devotion. Paul claims him as a "brother, a companion in labour, a fellow-soldier;" the words are arranged in an ascending scale, indicating a threefold spiritual sympathy, in faith, in work, and in suffering.

He gave himself with such eagerness to the work in Rome, that he seems to have undermined his health; indeed, he almost lost his life:—"For the work of Christ he was nigh unto death." And the Apostle could not cure him. He could smite a sorcerer with blindness; he could cure the father of Publius at Melita; he could cast out a demon from one possessed on the streets of Philippi; but he could not raise up a dear fellow-labourer from a dangerous sickness in Rome. The miracle-power is for public uses, and not for private satisfactions. Those who preach the Cross must bear the cross, and must themselves be crucified to all their dearest earthly desires, and hold themselves entirely obedient to the good Master's will.

At length, after many fears, and many a prayer, the danger passes away. God had mercy on Epaphroditus, and on Paul also, "lest he should have sorrow upon sorrow." With convalescence came home-sickness. He knew that the Church in Philippi had heard of his illness; he knew that they would be troubled by the tidings; and he is troubled in their trouble. He longs after them all, he is "full of heaviness," and earnestly desires to be at home. And Paul heartily approves his purpose, and makes him in fact the bearer of this epistle.

Now surely we have been in good company. Seldom, even in sacred history, do we find such a triad as we have here; and they come before us incidentally in the course of the writing of a letter, with no intention to depict them; and so we see them the more naturally. One could almost wish that some artist's faithful pencil had preserved for us the group—Paul, with his severe yet chastened countenance and silver hair, about to dictate his letter: Timothy, with fresh ingenuous face, and unwasted courage; Epaphroditus, thin and pale with sickness, but eager and tender with affection. But we have what is immeasurably more and better than any painter or artist could have given us—the *moral* portraiture of the group thus sweetly limned, drawn artlessly and unconsciously by one of their number. We ought to be purer and better for spending a little time in their company. The lessons we may learn in such society are very many and very good. Amongst others we find such as these :—

First. *The great importance of a sincere and thorough self-denial in the Christian character:* or in the words of the passage, the importance of subordinating " our own things" to "the things of Jesus Christ." Renunciation of the world, complete and full; crucifixion of self; subjugation of the personal will to the declared will of God; in each of these three men we see all this: it lies ever close to the heart of what we call the Christian goodness, and without it there cannot be a pure or strong development of the Christian character.

The second lesson is the positive form of the first: viz. *the exceeding beauty of a consecrated life*. A human life is in a sense beautiful when it is wholly consecrated to any great object, even if there be in it no declared regard to any single person—when it is given to patriotism, or to charity, or to duty. We can all admire the old words of resolve and courage: "It is necessary that I should go; it is not necessary that I should live." This great sentiment is translated and intensified in the Christian life, and exalted into the Christian courage: "To me to live is Christ,"—"I can live or die *for Him!*"

Lastly. *We have the use and value of suffering* here brought out in a striking way. Take away the suffering and you take away the beauty and the nobleness, or at any rate you can have small revelation of these. Strike the chain from the wrist of the captive Apostle. Let young Timothy be here only to see the sights of Rome. Let Epaphroditus have no sickness, and his Philippian friends no distress on his account, and how do you steal all the sweets of the story away! The delicate interplay of mutual affection is gone! The tender flittings of hope and fear! The life-grasp of the life-purpose by each one, come what may! Faithfulness to each other, sustained by a common fealty to the Master—these things are all gone. The sadness and the sacredness are closely allied: the glory comes out of the suffering, at least on the earthly side of things, and we are told that it is so on the heavenly side too. For those who come "out of great tribulation" shall stand in celestial eminence, "clothed in white robes, and with palms in their hands."

XXVII.

"*Jesus Christ the same yesterday, and to-day, and for ever.*"

HEB. xiii. 8.

SAMENESS is not a quality of things much loved for its own sake. In common things and in common life we soon grow wearied of sameness, and the whole earthly system of things is founded on the principle of variety and change.

In what department of this universe shall we find immobility? In the clouds of the sky, in the colours of the earth, in the successive periods of man's life, and in its inevitable close—we see the law of change. The objects in nature that we call fixed are all in motion. The fixed stars move; the mountains are moving, not only with the earth in its course, but they are in constant process of decay. Take your stand on the quietest day, in the stillest place you can find—change is going on around you with every moment of time, so movable and restless is nature down to its very heart.

The same law holds in providence. Indeed, there could be no providence without change; no providing and no rule would be possible if no new circumstances arose. A providence over an unchanging society! We might as well speak of a government over the still occupants of a graveyard.

The same constitution of things holds in the higher sphere of man's moral progress and religious life. True, a man may change for the worse as well as for the better, and that is one of the dread possibilities arising out of a state of freedom. But it would be far worse for us, on the whole, if no such change were possible. We make progress only in change—we put off the old and put on the new—we learn and unlearn—we fall and rise again—we leave the things behind and press on to those before; and as nature and providence are never the same on two successive days, so our souls are never in exactly the same moral state on one day as they were on the day before. The difference may be very little, and altogether inappreciable to our moral sense, but it *is* something, and it tells, to Him who knows all, of a living approach to Himself, or of departure from His fellowship.

Instead of giving pleasure, it would inflict a keen pang on the lover of nature to be told regarding any beautiful or grand prospect, "That is fixed for ever; no other light shall play on it, no other shade shall fall over it, no aspect shall it present to you but this aspect for evermore." And it would give no man pleasure to have his providential life stayed and circumstances congealed around him. The brightest day would darken soon, the happiest allotment would wither in his sight like an autumn leaf if the fiat went forth, "*that shall be, and none other for ever;*" for "the eye is not satisfied with seeing nor the ear with hearing." Least of all could any good man feel gratification in being told that his moral progress was finally stayed. The prayer of every Christian heart is: "Oh! unchanging One, let *me* change from day to day, until I gain Thine image and reach Thy presence!" And may we not believe this to be the prayer of angels too? Are they not thirsting for change "from glory to glory, as by the Spirit of the Lord?" The more deeply we think of heaven—of its amplitude, its inhabitants, its employments—the less shall we be disposed to lift it above the beneficent law of change.

And yet many hearts thrill with a sacred and awful joy on hearing the words, "Jesus Christ the same yesterday, and to-day, and for ever."

Why? How comes it that when we are pleased and profited by variety everywhere else, we are conscious of a sublime and awful satisfaction in finding fixedness here? Is it not because we are created to find rest and portion only in God? Behind all changes in nature we press to unchanging power and law, and feel that these can reside only in an unchanging God. Behind all the flux of providence there must be a hand which shapes and determines its events, and, beyond all human progress, there must be One who can make no progress Himself, because He is absolutely perfect. Take this thought from us, and the whole universe, and all our human life, is at once darkened and degraded.

Nature's beautiful changes become nothing better in purpose than the mazes and whirlings of a fantastic dance; providence becomes a system of falsehood and mockery; and human progress is impossible for ever, for there is no longer any standard by which to measure it, nor any effectual help whereby it can be promoted.

The text is a declaration of the immutability of *Jesus Christ*, and so takes for granted His divinity. It can be said of no creature that he is the same yesterday and to-day. Apart from changes that occur in every created being's history, it never can be said of any that they are the same yesterday and to-day, because "yesterday" they all began to be. The spirits which have existed longest had, each of them, a natal day. And to come out of nothing into being is the greatest possible change, and precludes for ever the application of the language of the text. That language can only have reference to a divine Being, and it can only be with regard to His divine qualities that Jesus Christ can be said to be immutable. In fact, He is *not* the same yesterday and to-day in the forms and aspects of His existence. In these there has been great change. He was "with God," then with man, now with God again. He was born. He grew up to manhood, went from place to place, suffered, died, was buried, rose again, ascended on high, and entered heaven—not as He left it, but in that human form which He still wears, and in which He pleads our cause, rules the nations, and will judge the world. In regard to these visible, sensible manifestations, Jesus Christ is different to-day was rich, and for our sakes He became poor." He was "the brightness of the Father's glory, and the express image of His person," and yet "His visage was so marred more than any man, and His form more than the sons of men." "He was in the form of God, and thought it not robbery to be equal with God, but made Himself of no reputation, and took on Him the form of a servant." These scriptures tell us of the most wonderful change as to outward state and condition that has ever been witnessed. This condescension is unparalleled. This love "passeth knowledge." We cannot on the one hand see the brightness of the glory from which He came down, nor, on the other, can we penetrate the depths of that humiliation which He found at our side. We can only wonder at the love which brought Him from the one to the other, and at the zeal and constancy which sustained Him through all His earthly work, until He ascended up where He was before.

There were heretics in primitive times who regarded the incarnation and the life of Christ as only a historical representation—a mode of expressing divine purposes and affections. Jesus Christ did not really (in their view) become a man, did not really suffer, did not really die because, as they presumed to imagine, He *could* not. He only *seemed* to do these things. His was but a shadowy life, but it expressed all that Christians believe, as to His love, and grace, and saving power. There is no need now to refute a heresy like that, for no one believes it now. There is danger, rather, of overlooking the truth which that heresy involves, or from what he was yesterday, and (we speak with reverence), for anything said in the Scriptures, He may be different to-morrow from what He is to-day. Some such change may be suggested in that passage in 1 Cor. where the Apostle says: "Then cometh the end, when He shall have delivered up the kingdom to God, even the Father, when He shall have put down all rule, and all authority, and power." "And when all things shall be subdued under Him, then *shall the Son also Himself* be subject unto Him that put all things under Him, that God may be all in all." But these mortal, formal changes, whatever they are, do not affect the substantial meaning of the text. Jesus Christ, in all that constitutes His personality and in all that pertains to His character, is the same, and cannot change. In His will, in His purposes, in His principles, in His affections, He is for ever the same. These things constitute being and character, and these in Him are without change. What, then, was Jesus Christ "yesterday?" what did He do "yesterday," expressive of His character, of His will, of His relation to us, of His feeling towards us? For that He is, and that He is doing, still, to-day.

Yesterday He became incarnate.—He left the bosom of the Father, and became a man with men. The glories and joys of heaven, all its vast honours and regalities, were left, nay, exchanged for their opposites—for royalty, subjection—for honour, shame—for praise, reviling—for joy, ever-darkening sorrow—for the highest heights of life, the valley of the shadow of death. "He at any rate, suggests, and which the text strongly expresses, that Jesus Christ is the same, that amid the varying modes of manifestation there are fixed principles and undecaying affections of the divine mind in which we may trust for ever.

The gospel history of Jesus Christ is a true history, confirmed as no other history has ever been. But is there not a constant tendency in our minds to make it history and nothing more? We reduce the wondrous story from its great dimensions in our too literal thought. We divest it of some of its living significance. We think "it is all over and gone; it happened long ago. The story is becoming venerable by its antiquity; eighteen hundred years is a vast intervening space between us and 'God manifest in the flesh.' The very Cross is dim, for the mists of centuries are around it. It is long since the song of the Ascension died away, and the ascended One has vanished from our sight, and is lost to us in a far-off heaven."

Not thus would the Saviour have us to conceive of His coming and incarnation. It was not on a transient visit He came. It was not to discharge some official formal business, which being done, might stand recorded in a book—while He, having done it, might pass away into distance and invisibility. *He came to stay.* He entered into relations with us of perpetual love and nearness, and when in bodily vision He was going away He assured His disciples again and again that spiritually He would never leave them; that in divine loving presence He would be with them in all their labours and journeyings for His sake—and that He would make His grace sufficient for them all, even to the end. Almost His latest word to them was, "Lo, I am with you alway, even to the end of the world." And so, if there is truth in His promise, He is with us as He was with them. He is Emmanuel still. In a spiritual sense, He is continually becoming incarnate; He is always condescending to our low estate; often is He looking into the places where we dwell; He still pities our miseries—still laments our degradation—still yearns and labours for our elevation to the joys and glories of the higher life.

Jesus Christ is not far away. There still "standeth One among us whom we know not." Mystically, yet really, He walks with the pilgrim, toils with the worker, looks down with pity on the sufferer's bed, stands beside the grave where mourners weep, touches tenderly all human interests, has this great world in constant care—as the mother has her children—as the shepherd has his sheep; and all who accept His care and tendance may live in His presence and rejoice in His smile.

The fisher on the sea may have Him in the ship with him; as He was with the sons of Zebedee on the lake of Galilee. The husbandman in his farm may have Him as near as He was to the disciples, when He went through the cornfields on the Sabbath day. The drawer of water will find Him still sitting by the well. The traveller may walk and talk with Him by the way, until his heart burn within him. The mistress may give Him, like Martha, evening welcome into the house.

Every learner may sit down at His feet like Mary; and the children in their helplessness may be put by their mothers into His arms. The humblest scene in all the round of this mortal life He will not disdain. The farthest spot on earth or sea He will not refuse to visit. The strangest experience of a human soul He will turn to the highest account—everywhere, between the cradle and the grave, we may find Him, for what He was, He is—" *the same.*"

Some of Christ's people are waiting for His coming visibly, and they expect but little improvement in the state of the world until He comes. All who love Him will rejoice when He appears. But what will He give us then that we may not have *now*, if we seek it? A brighter picture for the eye, but not a fuller portion for the heart—scenes of more dazzling splendour, but not a richer inheritance. He is present now with all who love Him—He cannot be more than present then. His perfection, like His work, is finished, and if we will but prove it, we shall find that we are complete in Him for all our need and for all our endless time; for our sinful and sorrowful yesterday, for our "to-day," be it dark or bright, hard or easy; and for our vast overmastering "for ever," for He will guide us through it all, and turn lower into higher and last into first, until sun has faded and moon no more endures.

Yesterday He received sinners.—We have been considering his earthly life as one of love and nearness to man. But there was one act and habit of that life, characteristic and distinctive. "This man receiveth sinners, and eateth with them." The usual actions of His life showed Him to be a true man—fellow-worker, fellow-sufferer—fellow-traveller with the race; but this peculiar and distinctive act revealed Him in a higher light and aspect, as the Redeemer and Saviour of men. There can be no doubt at all that this was the Saviour's habit. He was charged with it as a crime, and He accepted the charge and justified the habit, by explaining that He had come to call "not the righteous but sinners to repentance." It were easy to call up to view some of the individual sinners whom the Saviour received, but it is more encouraging to know that this was the habit of His life. He was known to his enemies by this, that he received sinners, without distinction and without exception. To some of the worst—broken, bleeding, lost—He spoke with peculiar tenderness, and accorded to them a most holy yet gracious welcome. The Pharisees and formalists of the day looked on them with disdain and aversion; Jesus Christ went into their houses, sat down with them at table in friendly repast, allowed them to offer, before all, the proofs of their penitence and love, assuaged the bitter agonies of remorse with assurances of mercy and donations of peace, and secured all the interests of morality and their own subsequent moral progress, by putting on them the claims of His high service, by attaching them to Himself, and by solemnly enjoining them "to go and sin no more."

They were received as sinners, but they did not

continue what they were at the moment of reception. They began immediately to grow into goodness; they followed Him, they were taught of Him, they served Him, suffered for Him, and some of them died for His name's sake. All were welcome who turned to Him, and implored either in language or only in look, His redeeming help. It mattered not from what depths, from what darkness they came, nor how, if only they did come. And it matters not now, for Jesus Christ is the same to-day as He was yesterday. There is no hindrance put by Him; there can be no disqualification in us. The doctrine or teaching of the Scriptures is that all sin is exceeding sinful, and the object of the Scriptures is to strike the awful sense of sin home upon every heart, that none may be soothed into a false peace, but that all may seek the sovereign healing which the physician of souls alone can bring. We talk of better and worse in sin, and there is no doubt a difference; there is a bad, a worse, and a worst; but probably the worst of all is this—that a sinner shall feel and act as if he had no sin, as if his nature were whole when it is broken, as if his heart were pure when it is polluted. The worst may be to be strong in impenitence—to feel no sorrow for the sin that we have done, and for the sin we carry within us —to be thinking of our virtues in the Saviour's very presence—to look into His face as though we could have fellowship or friendship with Him, without being received as "sinners"—*that* is the worst! May God save us from that? On the other hand, may He save us from sinking into despair, or even hopelessness, under the impression that our sin is too great to be pardoned, that we have sinned too much and too long to be forgiven. Think as much as you will of the dark peculiarity of your guilt, and of its aggravations, if these thoughts are made the food of repentance, if they hasten and compel you to the deliverer's feet. But if you keep these gloomy thoughts and perversely try to make a salvation *out of them*, you will never succeed, you will but make deeper ruin, and none can hinder you.

"*Look to Him* and be lightened." "*Come to Him* and be saved." He is "the same yesterday, to-day, and for ever." Ten thousand sinners are at this moment bending at His feet. Ten thousand pardons are flowing from His lips. All the instrumentalities of His grace are working for the recovery of the lost; and there are angels waiting to rejoice over one sinner more, repenting and turning home to God. Do not think in your heart that because He is high in glory now, and because only the sinless and the pure are around Him, that *you* must not come into His presence with your nature all stained and soiled, and your heart wounded and broken, through the sin you can neither bear nor cure. It is because you feel yourself in this evil case, in this dread extremity, that you are welcome. Nay, this very feeling of concern is from Him. This misery is His gift and it is the harbinger of joy. This may be the dawn of the brightest day of your history. One thing is sure, that if you follow on to know the Lord you *shall* know Him, and the sin which now stands like a mountain will melt away like a cloud, and the bitter sorrow of your heart will change into joy and praise.

Yesterday He died.—We are not using figurative language. There is *no Time* in His existence. It is but as yesterday to Him since He looked up through the olive-trees of Gethsemane, and saw the moon shining calmly on high, while His soul grew "exceeding sorrowful even unto death." It is but as "yesterday" that He saw Pilate's face in the judgment-hall—but as "yesterday" since the crowning and the scourging and the bitter reviling came in quick succession, and passed that the crucifixion might follow. And that darkest sublimest hour is yet clear in His sight. He sees Calvary again. He sees the Cross. Travellers cannot now tell where it stood, but He knows the very spot, and has the whole scene always in His view—the mocking, maddened priests, the watching soldiers, the trembling disciples, the weeping women; and what is still more to our purpose, He remembers the very feelings of His soul, and all that constituted that inscrutable experience of love and sorrow in which He accomplished the great work of man's redemption. Remembers! It is truer to say that He *has* those feelings still—the suffering is over, but the sentiments that led to the suffering, the purposes to be attained by it, the principles which it expressed—these all continue now as then. He feels towards all the persons concerned in His death exactly as He did when He died. Sin is as dark and bitter, law as bright and good, God as glorious, and human souls as precious, and their salvation as much to be desired, "to-day," as on that wonderful "yesterday."

Men sometimes rise to heroic actions under the impulsion of rare circumstances. They dare and do, while the excitement continues, while the purpose lasts, and then sink down again to commonness, and even feel regret that they were so much moved; on reflection, their enthusiasm seems to have been unwarranted, and their minds to have been unduly affected. But Jesus Christ is "the same." There is no refluence of feeling in His heart. He died—and He contemplates the act with undying complacency. He died—and would die again if it were needful. A finished work cannot be improved. A soul unaffected by one Cross would not yield to a thousand, and He is risen from the dead to die no more. But yonder, in far glory, while angels bow, and the ransomed arrive from every clime, He has the same heart from which the life-blood flowed—nay, as we have said, it is as if He had just died and His blood "cleanseth us from all sin."

It was a glorious discovery that came to the Church and to the world—after our Lord's ascension—the discovery of the adaptation and sufficiency of the death of Jesus Christ, for complete atonement and the reconciliation of man to God. That death, so strange and sad, so destructive of all the hopes of His disciples, soon became vast and luminous to them in its joyful significance. And they went out to tell the tidings—to preach to Jew and Gentile free forgiveness of sins through the Cross.

We say this was a great doctrine at first; the power

of it was immense. It drew the Jews away from sacrifice, altar, and priesthood. It drew the Gentiles from their distance, and, through all their disabilities, into the one family of God. Little churches sang for joy, as they thought of the perfect sacrifice, and whole cities were glad because of this word of the Lord. There is no reason why there should be less confidence in preaching Christ, or less joy in believing now. He died only "yesterday." The incense of His death is as fragrant as when it ascended at first, and the inherent power of it as great as when, on the day of Pentecost, repenting thousands hailed the Crucified as their Saviour. If amid all the changes of your lot you turn to the Cross, it will become to you the very centre of your dearest life; you will go to that place of seeming weakness to renew your strength, to that scene of darkest sorrow to assuage your own; and as the vision of the heavenly life breaks upon you out of the Cross and the earthly dying, all blessed hopes will awaken in your heart never to slumber again.

Yesterday He cared for His disciples.—Their needs were very various, and ever recurring. Sometimes that need came upon them with surprising suddenness and force, but He was always near, and ready with the appropriate help. Peter cannot be allowed to sink, although his own presumption has brought him into danger. The disciples must not be lost as they cross the lake. Mary and Martha may have four days of grief, but the fifth must set in joy. All men forsook Paul, and he stood alone at his first appearance. "Notwithstanding the

Lord stood with me and strengthened me." And so it was always and in everything, as between Him and them. He was always ready with new teachings for new circumstances, with a new leading for the new path, and in all the gospel history not one is left to faint and perish without the needed help.

Now this is the one thing which the Apostle has here especially in view, the Saviour's tender, faithful care over all who trust in Him. These Hebrew Christians were in extreme necessity—they were persecuted, tempted, tried—and some of them were on the very brink of ultimate and complete apostacy. A little more pressure of adverse circumstances, and their faith would loose its hold. A little more lingering, and the lights would burn dimly, and then all would be dark. "Hold on," says the apostle to them, "steadfast to the end." "Cast not away your confidence." "Be not of them who draw back unto perdition." "Behold the footsteps of those who taught you, and who have gone on before, marking the way *you* are going with their faithful feet. Follow then, consider the end of their conversation; that end they have reached at last, after many a struggle—in that end they are blessed for ever. No more watching, no more weeping, no more weary working, no cloudy mornings, no despairing nights, they are away now beyond the shadows into the eternal light. And if the very contrast between their state and yours be discouraging, then remember (so the text seems to come in) that Jesus Christ is 'the same yesterday, to-day, and for ever.' He helped them, He will help you ; He never forsook them, He will not forsake you; you have the same foundation to rest on, the same arguments to plead at the throne, the same promises to grasp, and the same tender open heart of love into which you may pour your sorrows and your fears."

We are warranted by the spirit of the text to recall and use for our help in the stress of life, the experiences of our fathers and friends who have gone to heaven—*all* their experiences, the best and the worst alike. Indeed their worst experiences will at some times be more helpful to us than their best, for they got safely out of them; out of the deep pit and the miry clay, to stable footing on the rock; out of the halting into the running; out of the night into the morning; out of cold, carnal, miserable days—the continuance of which would have been perdition itself—into newness of life, with earth and heaven combining to help them on to the sublime "end of their conversation." Ah! we remember that our sainted fathers did not lead always the glorious life they are living now, and many of the days and scenes of their history here gave to our view no indication or promise of the glory which has followed. What conclusion then do we draw from the fact, that after all, they have reached that end at last? *This*—that "Jesus Christ is the same." He was their Saviour, and He will be ours. Let this be our confidence. How far we are from the end we cannot tell, and we do not surely wish to know; but let us journey on to reach it in good heart, and as we go from place to place in the pilgrimage, pitching our tent now here, and then yonder; when we are strong, and when we are weak, in joy and sorrow, in pain, and in health; when we go down to the river with friends who are to be parted from us, and carried over to the "end of their conversation;" and when, with the whole of life behind us at last, all its bright scenes, and all its sinful and sorrowful days over and gone, we touch the chill waters with our own feet, be this the word on which we live, and in the faith of which we die, "*Jesus Christ the same yesterday, to-day, and for ever.*"

XXVIII.

Our Years.

"We spend our years as a tale that is told."—PSALM xc. 9.

(*Watchnight Address.*)

A GROUP gathers around the fire, or around the table, and the tale is begun. But stragglers drop into the room and slightly disturb the attention of the listeners; the children exchange quick secrets and take a little time to settle into their places, and still the tale runs on; a messenger enters with a letter, and perhaps by a sign is told to lay it on the table silently and retire; the attention becomes more earnest as the story runs on, and the company, forgetting that there is such a thing as time, has worked itself into a mood of unconscious expectation that the story will be as long as it is interesting, when lo!—the lips of the narrator cease to move—and "the tale is told."

Thus do we "spend our years as a tale that is told." "Our years." How silently they come! Approaching us as from a distance in shadowy noiseless procession, and then gliding away from us, as quietly but as swiftly as they came. We never have Time in secure present possession; it is always something to come, or it is something past and gone by. "I once was lord of yesterday, and if I live I shall be king of to-morrow, but there is no to-day. Every moment passed is really in the soul's yesterday : every moment to come is in the soul's to-morrow." So silent, so swift is time! So glides away from us the procession of our years!

Our years are "determined" as God says: give entertainment to this thought, close as we are upon the end of another year. Job, speaking of mortal sinful man, says, "His days are determined, the number of his months are with Thee; Thou hast appointed his bounds that he cannot pass." Do not think this truth a dismal thing to contemplate at the close of a year. Like many other things its character will depend on how we take it. We may make it like an iron band of fate around us; or we may regard it as a staff on which to stay our feebleness, or an arm on which we may lean through all our earthly time—through danger, darkness, and death. Put it the other way; will that mend the matter? Say that nothing has been determined, or foreseen, or provided for! We are not guided, we are not upheld, we are not corrected, we are not expected yonder at the end of the journey of the years—no one is waiting for us—no one knows when we are to arrive, ourselves least of all. We go groping through the mist, and stumbling over the stones, and chilled by this world's wintry weather; not without gleams of sunshine, not without what men call summer days, and gatherings of what men call autumn fruit. But alas, how little is it all! For still we spend our years. The tale is being told, day after day, and year after year; and it will, with some of us, in no long time, be told to the last syllable and the last sigh.

A gracious purpose of God about our life—about the length of it, and the close of it—if rightly regarded, so far from being a burden or a terror, will be comfort and stimulus and help; it will be especial help in an hour like this, when we feel the last shadows of another year gathering thick around us; and when the uncertainties and possibilities of the year that is coming are touched somewhat perhaps with the same shade. Out of that shade there comes a firm but sweet and tender voice. It is the voice of one who knows us altogether, and who loves us well. "Fear not, fret not, weary not, poor pilgrim of a day. The pilgrimage will soon be over. Thy days *are determined.* The number of thy months is with me. I have appointed thy bounds that thou canst not pass. Thou wilt soon accomplish as an hireling thy day. There is a time to be born, and a time to die."

Our years are connected the one with the other. These years of our earthly life are not really separated the one from the other. They are not like adjacent islands, deep water flowing around and between. There is no severance between the one and the other at all. We go right onwards, treading on the same kind of ground to the end. The next striking of the clock will be to our imagination the knell of the year, and we do wisely in entering into the human ideas of the thing and into the solemnities of the time. God himself, the changeless and eternal, speaks of "years," of our years and of His. But this is only in condescension to our infirmity and to our mortality: a thousand of our years to Him are but "as yesterday when it is past, and as a watch in the night:" and accordingly, when our year ends, there is no notice taken of the circumstance by the celestial worlds. There is no disturbance in nature, no tremor in the earth, no supernatural blackness or brightness in the sky; not any audible whisper from heaven or sigh from hell comes over the earth. The midnight to which we are now just coming, will be as ten thousand midnights before it. This world-ship will sail on quietly through the seas of time and space, among the many star-ships that sail through the grand heavens of God. And if we were not here with our faculties awake, and our hearts worshipping, we should not know the moment of transition.

Such too, usually, is the growth of character in the individual man. It flows on silently, giving to others, and even to the individual himself, but little note of its growing. Character in a man is not formed by conscious leaps and bounds, by single actions of splendour or meanness, by heroic words, or by agonies of pain. It is like the kingdom of heaven in this, that usually it "cometh not with observation." It goes on growing through the year, and it will not stop growing at the end of one year, and then begin again to-morrow morning when the year is new. The growing may be quickened or it may be confirmed a little, by the impressions and the sanctities of this last hour; quickened or confirmed in goodness; or else, alas, the heart, passing through these solemnities and agitations without a real religious faith, will be hardened in evil, and made more impervious to the impressions of any future season. We shall (to put it plainly and briefly) carry *ourselves* through this midnight hour, and be beyond it, probably, in the main what we are now.

And yet here let us be careful, else we shall come near to the acceptance of the very worst intellectual doctrine of this time—the doctrine of inevitable necessity, or, religiously viewed, the doctrine of a moral continuity in character and being, which nothing can break. "We are what we are, and that we must continue to be for ever!" A dismal message that would be for the midnight that comes between the years; a dismal message for any day in the year, even the brightest day in June. The whole Bible is a contradiction of such hopeless fatalism as this. If there be forgiveness of sin, that is one dark and perilous thing over and gone. If there be renewal of the heart, that is a good thing begun that will never have an end. He who says, "Ye must be born again," does not tantalise and mock us with the picture and shadow of a thing that never can be. He urges us to the realisation of the greatest possibility of our life; and all the "powers of the world to come" are brought to bear upon the accomplishment of this. We never lose our personal identity, character runs on, the same thinking substance, the same immortal soul continues; but grace, that renovating, cleansing, saving power, is introduced into the consciousness, transforms the character, lives in the experience, brings out the divine image, makes the "new creature in Christ Jesus." I cannot leave *myself* behind, to be floated down the stream of time with the year that is now almost gone. I must be myself—but blessed be God! I may be my true self and not my false one. I may be a child and not an alien. I may have the light of heaven on my face to-morrow morning, and the love of heaven beginning to stir in my heart. Turn back I cannot, to live the years over again. Stop the flow of time at this point I cannot, or myself upon its bosom; but through the infinite mercy and almighty power of Him who made me, and sent His Son to die for my redemption, from this hour I may begin to live anew. If I have spent all the months, and all the weeks, and all the days, and all the hours but the last, and more than half of that, of this year in unregeneracy and unbelief—I may yet complete the grandest transaction of my life, and have the seal of God set to it—and before the bells shall ring in another year, I may cause rejoicing in heaven and call forth the angels to chant afresh their never-ending song. I, a poor mortal creature sinking in the waves of change and trouble, I can cry, "Lord, save me, I perish!" and that Lord to whom I thus cry would leave heaven again and come to the earth, rather than allow me to perish looking to Him and naming His name. Lord Jesus, come to us, come to all of us gathered here,—in Thy saving power, and ere the bells shall sound midnight, claim us for Thine own, and be henceforth the

Lord of all our time! Creating Spirit, Thou Eternal Light and Life! from this time scatter our darkness, and pour the light of day about our steps! Slay all our enmity and deign to make us Thine own temples for evermore! Eternal God, Fountain of unwearying energies, Giver of all good, Thou that sittest upon the throne of eternity surrounded by all the glories of heaven, give us this much of heaven here, that every one of us shall hear Thy voice, and know it to be Thine, sounding through the darkness of our midnight hour, saying, "Behold, I make all things new!"

And thou O my heart, plead not, I entreat thee, for longer delay. Wilt thou lead me forth again through the dark of another year? Wilt thou wile me forth again over the wild moorland where nothing grows, and where there is no path? Wilt thou lure me into the thickets where stings follow fast on pleasures, and poison lurks in all sweetness? Wilt thou falsely persuade me that "there is time enough," while all the wise, and all the good, and all the angels, and even God Himself, is saying, "Behold, *now!*" O myself, have mercy on myself! Yield thee at last, my soul, to Him who made thee, who redeemed thee, who loves thee, who, father-like, keeps a place for thee at home, and would have thee home into thy place to bring in the new year with Him.

Need I say how prophetic our years become when we thus begin them in grace? Grace is the earthly name for glory. Glory is the heavenly name for grace.

The evil years also are prophetic of evil years to come after them in a sense and to a degree, and alas they do reproduce themselves in many and many a one on to the end. But here is the difference. There is always the gracious possibility that they may change at any time and become years of good. There is no such possibility when the years of goodness begin that they will change to evil. "We know whom we have believed, and that He is able to keep that we have committed unto Him."

Have we now the new heart?—that is the well of living water within us which will spring up into everlasting life. Do we really take unto us the whole armour of God? That is victory. Have we the true pilgrim-staff in our hands? Then into the kingdom we shall go in spite of all the storms of earth, and all the legions of hell. What is the best, or if not the best, the happiest promise of future life and heavenly blessedness? Surely it is the blessedness begun here in the breast. I am a prophet. There is something working in me, to more and more, and better and brighter. I know what is coming, for I have it in part, through God's mercy, already. These years of my pilgrimage here are born into each other, reproduce each other, and when I come into the year in which I shall die, that will give birth to endlessness and heaven.

Pass on then, O mysterious Time, with silent pinion, from year to year! Thou art our friend and not our enemy. Thou art taking us to our portion, our rest, and our home. Flow down, sands of life, until the glass that holds them is empty! we would neither retard nor quicken thy motion; thou wilt stop in the right time. Tale of our life, run on through what years, or days, are left for the telling of thee; and when thou art told again in the review of the judgment, and in the memories of eternity, may it be with joy and not with grief!

>Life is swift : the years go by :
>A story told and then we die.
>Life is glory—all things holy :
>Conflict done—victory won :
>Clad in white—crowned with light :
>Angel songs shall tell its story.

XXIX.

The General Assembly written in Heaven.

"But ye are come . . . to the general assembly and church of the first-born, which are written in heaven . . . and to the spirits of just men made perfect."—HEB. xii. 22, 23.

WE have in this whole passage a description of the Catholic Church as it is now revealed to us under the Gospel. And this is put in contrast with the state of the Church under the law. That state, with all its boasted advantages, was yet only a condition of terror and bondage. It brought no full freedom and no perfect peace. But now, says the Apostle to those whom he addresses, "ye are come" unto the state of freedom and spiritual perfection. The kingdom is now united, the Church is catholic; and those who come into it are not only joined in mutual earthly fellowship, but they come into union, as real, although not so conscious and apparent, with the Church invisible and glorified. They come to Mount Zion, to the city of the living God, the heavenly Jerusalem, and to an innumerable company of angels; "to the general assembly and church of the first-born, which are written in Heaven . . . and to the spirits of just men made perfect." In several of these expressions there is manifest allusion to the visible, or, as we say, the militant Church. The terms "Mount Zion," "The city of the living God," "The heavenly Jerusalem," have application and fulfilment here as well as hereafter. But even these expressions do carry the higher meaning as well as the lower; the celestial and eternal meaning; while some of the others—that one especially—" the spirits of just men made perfect," have reference solely and exclusively to the heavenly and unseen state. The assertion, therefore, is that we are come to that state— that in some true and important sense we are come to that which yet we see not—to the Church triumphant in heaven.

As we consider some aspects of this subject, let us try to think and feel ourselves into that higher fellowship.

We come to that unseen and glorious company *by our knowledge.*

Our knowledge of the invisible world, and of heaven, the happy part of it, may be considered little or much, according to the standard of judgment or comparison we adopt. It is little compared with what we might know, or with what we shall know hereafter: it is very little compared with the great reality. But it is much compared with absolute ignorance. It is much compared with the knowledge of the ancient Church. It is much when we consider how little worthy we are of the knowledge, and how little is our practical realisation of it. We have far more actual knowledge of the invisible world than we vivify and use. "Whither I go ye know, and the way ye know," Jesus says still to His Church on earth, and she dares not make answer with Thomas, "Lord we know not whither thou goest, and how can we know the way?" "for," answers one of the first-born in that Church, "*we know*, that if the earthly house of this tabernacle were dissolved, we have a building of God, an house not made with hands, eternal in the heavens." We know, that when flitting like shadows here, from place to place, and ever nearer to the grave, there is a city which hath foundations, in the records of which our names may be enrolled. We know that when struggling and crowding here—striving for space and room, and particular standing—there is a house of many mansions, and a place prepared for each, large enough for the developments of the immortal life. Our knowledge of heaven is in some respects limited enough. We cannot see it; we cannot come to it in the flesh; flesh and blood shall not inherit it; no mortal hand can draw aside the veil, nor pierce it, although it sometimes seems so thin. We must check our impatience and still our murmurs. We must wait. Yet perhaps we are apt to forget the extent to which the moral characteristics and spiritual aspects of the life to come are revealed to us in the Gospel. We know that it is purchased for us by the death of Christ. We know that it is pure and permanent; that it is vast to meet expanding capacities; that it is fair to feed the sense of beauty; that it is to be enjoyed by the saints in fellowship. We know that angels are there, or will be there, and that there will be an eternal mingling of the two races, the celestial and terrestrial, in worship and work and joy. We know that the Redeemer Himself will be visible, as the Lamb slain, yet as the King of kings; retaining the marks and mementoes of His earthly suffering, and wearing the symbols of royalty; all these things, and they are considerable, "we know in part." Perhaps if we were better, purer, more saintly, we could safely be trusted with more light on the future, and it is certain that if we ask and look and wait we shall attain to more. We are like men gazing towards the land from the deck of a ship. A dim outline appears, like a cloud, at which they strain their sight; until by the movement of the vessel and the custom of the eye, it becomes clearer and clearer still. The mountains gradually reveal their peaks; then the valleys show; then the corn; then the smoke of the cottage; the group by the cottage door; the apples on the tree; and then—the vessel is in port. So, by looking, heaven becomes clearer; *as* we look, it comes more near. This knowledge is a thing of degrees and measures. The veil hangs thick to the careless and the carnal, but to those who desire and wait, it grows ever thinner; this world, which is to most so solid and hard, seems to waver and fade, and that world which stands off so dim and far to the eye of sense, shines out to them in calm and sweet reality.

This our knowledge of the unseen state will never be lost. It is not much, and in individual cases it may practically almost disappear. A man may have faith in Christ, and yet be so unspiritual as to have very little commerce of thought and knowledge with the world in which Christ is. But the knowledge of the life to come, which is the inheritance of the Church, bequeathed to her by Jesus Christ, cannot be lost. To say nothing of the purpose of God to keep it alive in the world, or of the declaration that "life and immortality are brought to light," not for a time, but for ever, "by the Gospel,"— I think it may be affirmed that the Christian revelations of a future life, although dim and vague, are yet so vast, so full of interest and importance, that, not only the Church by her faith and love, but the world by its wisdom, its inevitable curiosity and speculative thought, will never allow them to drop out of sight. To us as individuals, this revelation will be much or little, according to our personal realisation of it. Our knowledge may be a lamp unlighted as well as burning. It may be a map of a country on which we seldom look, or on which we trace with careful finger every mountain ridge, and every river and plain. Central Africa is now opened, and to the world it can never be a blank any more. Some individuals may know very little of it, yet that knowledge is a possession to the race for ever. And so, to the world has been given the unalienable possession of the knowledge of the "better country, the heavenly," which is on the other side of death, in which the Saviour is, into which he has already gathered myriads of his friends, to which so many of our own friends have gone, and to which we ourselves are travelling.

We come to the invisible Church *by our faith.* We come to it more by our faith than by our knowledge. Faith is knowledge glorified, and vitalised; it is, as the former chapter tells us, the "substance of things hoped for." It makes the objects of our cognition so real and vivid that we possess in our thought the very substance of them. We have such assured confidence in their existence that the removal of them from the realm of faith would be something like taking away the solid world from our senses. "Faith is the evidence of things not seen." It proves them, and presents them so that the mind feels their presence; sees them; is solemnised by them; holds them fast! It redeems our humanity from its degradation to know that there are men, who, while living here, are also living yonder—who have a life hidden as well as visible "with Christ in God." Many a one in the full stress of toil is yet by faith somewhat within the eternal rest; many a weary pilgrim is already at home, many a mourner keeps company in his heart with those who have left him, and his thoughts sometimes pass the mortal boundary, and almost enter into the holy calm of the blessed.

Figures and symbols abound in the Scriptures, founded many of them on our earthly experiences, by which the unseen life is brought near. They are no doubt poor and faint pictures of that exceeding beauty, but we have nothing better; we cannot surmount the limitations of our mortal thought, nor speak the language of heaven while we are still on earth. These are to faith the ladders by which she climbs to the super-sensuous truth, to the place of holy vision. They are the alphabet by which she spells out something of the celestial meanings. In this passage we have "a mount," "a city," "companies of angels," a "general assembly" of the selected and noblest—while elsewhere we have "house," and "temple," and "throne," and "country,"—rivers and fruit-bearing trees, fountains of living water, the wiping away of tears, the fine linen clean and white—and palms for triumph, and harps for song, and setting sun and waning moon no longer, but the Lord the Everlasting light, and God the glory. Our faith uses all that wealth of metaphor, and yet surmounts it far. These are but figures, the reality is more and better than they. We feel that the facts of the future must be personal and moral, not scenic or physical; our faith travels forwards to find persons and states—not pictures or processions. We believe there will be a "spiritual body," and that there will be a suitable home for it; but the celestial things will be far better than the terrestrial, and our true heaven will ever be in and around our Lord. "I have a desire to depart," says the Apostle Paul, "and" see heaven? Prove the untried life? Realise the sinless consciousness? No. "To be *with Christ*, which is far better."

So "we are come," supremely, in our faith *to Jesus*, the Mediator of the new covenant, and also to all those who are being assembled in His presence. We believe that He is. We believe that our friends are with Him; and if we can come to Him, and to them, in our daily faith—in the seekings, strivings, and settlings of our souls, then we are believers indeed. We may form what views we will on the time and nature of the resurrection—on the intermediate state, or on the physical characteristics of the life to come. If only we come to Him—our High priest within the veil, and our forerunner there—we shall in due time stand rejoicing in His presence.

"We are come" to that invisible triumphant church, *in our love,* as truly as in our knowledge and our faith. All heaven-born souls love the place of their birth. Born again, or born from above, is to have enrolment and citizenship there—it is to have our treasure there and our heart there also. It is a common but an erroneous impression, that if any one thus desires, longs for, and makes way into another life, he must, as a consequence, have his attention and activities turned away from his earthly sphere of duty. In other words, that if a man becomes very spiritual and heavenly-minded, he will not be fit for much in this world; he will neglect his business, have no relish for social joys, no hand for daily work, no eye for the happenings and doings of this present world. There could hardly be a greater misconception. There may be some Christians of that stamp, some lives of that colour and complexion. But that is not the desire or plan of God. His plan is that we shall see the next world, not by turning away from the present one, but in it and through it, rising by a moral expansion from the lower to the higher. It would not be the most popular picture and type of Christian character, but it may be questioned whether there is any other much nobler than that of one who is weighted every day with tasks, and shadowed inevitably with cares; but who at the same time is regaled with many enjoyments, and thoroughly interested in all that happens around him; and yet who looks with a longing heart through the atmosphere of hurry and the spaces of calm, through pleasures and through cares, to the things which are unseen and eternal. All this may coexist with a very real and hearty interest in all that goes to make up the earthly life. The young should wish to live, and the strong should wish to labour, and without reason, none should wish to get away.

But reasons multiply naturally, as life goes on. Strength fails; some cross grows heavier by the failure of the strength; disappointment comes again and again in things temporal and spiritual; strange misunderstandings cloud the life; conflicts, explanations, mistakes, weary the spirit. Then there is the loss of friends by death; one and another goes away, and a little and still a little more of the heart goes with them; until the home is half in heaven by the going thither of those who made home on earth. Then personal sickness comes; pain, inability to labour, which is worse to some natures than the sharpest pain; and then the death-summons, sometimes received before the death itself, and the dying learn to love that world out of which they cannot die, and in which they hope to find all that has been dearest and best to them in this. And so it is, that by one means and another, Christ prepares His true followers for going to Himself, for lifting the anchor gladly, and letting the vessel slip away to the land of life. Perhaps it would be some surprise to us if we knew how common this experience is among men. Probably there are always more than we are apt to suppose, longing to go hence. To many and many a one the spell of life here is broken, not to be renewed. No more "flowers on the earth," no more "singing of birds" for them. Flush of spring and wealth of summer are over, and the fading of the leaf is not unwelcome, and the white mantle of innocent snow, the winding sheet of the year, will be best of all. Amid the noise and strife of our great cities, on the crowded way, or in the busy shop, you might find not a few who love the invisible company, who long for the unseen life, and whose souls rise now and again with a great desire, like ships lifted on a mighty tide, towards the haven where they would be.

And all these comings, need we say? are presages of the *final personal coming by death* into the "general assembly and church of the first-born in heaven." We speak often and think of death as a going away, and picture to ourselves the spirit passing into vast solitudes, friends and dear familiar scenes all left behind, as it looks out upon the first reaches and roundings of the everlasting journey. Some thoughtful writers have dwelt much on the loneliness of death,[1] until one has felt intensely solitary in the prospect. They have fixed upon

[1] John Foster and Robertson of Brighton.

the fact that each of us must meet death *alone*, and, of course, that is true, at least as regards earthly companionships. But that even then we shall be absolutely alone is only conjecture; and if we must conjecture, I for one would rather take the other side, and believe, that since God gives us company here from the moment of birth to the moment of death, He will have other company awaiting us there, so that we shall take no step in loneliness or dread, but enter at once and easily into the higher fellowships, and go forward with a cheerful confidence through the valley of transition.

We believe, as the words of the Apostle indicate, that our friends who have gone have thus "come." They have made no lonely journey; their going from us has been a coming to their heart's home. They say to us, "We are come now, indeed, to what we have loved and longed for and purposed to win, to the heavenly Jerusalem, to angels worshipping and ministering, to many companions of our pilgrimage perfected now, to Him whom, having not seen, we loved so long."

Knowing this, we yield them up willingly, although not without natural sorrow and tears. We are glad for their sakes. We sorrow only for ourselves. We remember their firm faith, their cheerful piety, their open hand, their heavenward lookings; and how steadfastly they set their faces to go to the heavenly Jerusalem. The light that hallowed their even-tide seems yet to linger on our way. The words they spoke, the verses of Scripture in which they took delight in their last days, we set up like stones with "Ebenezer" written on them, and often their very presence seems to be about us still. We sorrow not as others who have no hope. We can spare them; we can spare them well: they but enter in before us into the home that is ours as well as theirs: and as we follow them with our faith and love we find it a little easier to resist, while we serve one world, and to rise to another.

But this spiritual arising, this detachment and reserve of the affections in daily life is practically very difficult. Here is the world all about us: we see it, feel it, touch it, every moment. Our duties are in it, and our discipline: God's gifts to us, His messages, His love: and yet we are to rise above it and reserve ourselves for what is far better. The truth is, we are no match for this world in a wrestling bout; we may as well try to overcome the law of gravitation, as try to get the mastery of it so. But we can call in another world by our faith, to redress the balance and weigh it quite to the other side. Then the law of spirit-gravitation draws us heavenwards. We see there the ever-increasing company of those whom we love; our home is more and more where they are; our life is hid with Christ, and we yearn towards that hidden life. We are home-sick. The world ceases to fret and annoy us as it did once. We often leave it and join the general assembly of Heaven; we go excursions thither, sometimes every day, and in a sense all day long. We "come" to it in meditation, we come to it in prayer; we come to it in the purpose and end of our labour even here. We may come to it so much, so often, and so pleasantly, that the last coming of all may be very natural and easy—the faces of our beloved ones on earth growing dim, and their voices sounding distant—as we are drawn sweetly into other company, and into the presence of Him who Himself is our Eternal Rest.

XXX.

The Lot at the End of the Days.

"But go thou thy way till the end be: for thou shalt rest, and stand in thy lot at the end of the days."—DANIEL xii. 13.

THESE words contain undoubtedly the dismission of Daniel from his whole life-work, and may therefore be applied to any one who has been working well for God, and has now gone to rest. This divine allowance and release from earthly toil has, of course, close connection with all the things that go before, those sublime things that constitute the substance of the book of Daniel. The first five or six chapters are historical, and record things in which the greatest kings and empires of the time were concerned, and in which Daniel himself was a chief actor. The succeeding chapters are chiefly prophetical, sketching the course of history through the ages; foretelling the coming of Christ and the establishment of the kingdom of God in and by Him; describing the troubles and persecutions of the Church; the wide diffusion of knowledge, the last conflict, the resurrection of the dead, the doom of the wicked, and the rest of the righteous at the end of the days. The text, therefore, taken in its connections, may well and fitly bring before our view

The majesty and greatness of the providence of God. There is no subject perhaps which we are so apt to dwarf and belittle in our ordinary conceptions as the subject of the world-providence of God. We require to place ourselves, so to say, in position to see it. Just as it requires some bodily exertion to go up a hill or to reach a mountain-top, so it requires some mental exertion to place ourselves so that we can take a true and wide view of the providence of God. There are always a few men who are climbing hill-sides and standing on mountain-tops; but a much greater number are in the fields, on the highways, or in the cities. There are a few who look out occasionally on the various and far-stretching domain of providence; but to the multitude, life is, partly by necessity, partly also by their own choice, toil and strife, and narrow round, and limited view. The forces and necessities of life would be too strong for us all, and we should all be dragged down and kept low and common, and made at length almost brutish, if it were not for the elevating influence of Christianity. The Bible lifts men up. This book of Daniel is a magnificent climbing-ground. It gives us a succession of far-reaching views. It shows us the continuity of history, the connection of one thing with another, the development of one thing out of another, the plan of God in it all.

The grandeur of God's plan appears in this, that at

any one time all that exists in the world is a part of it; every kingdom and every person being in some way within its scope; and in this also, which is still more striking, that the living world at any one time forms but a part, and a very small part, of the whole providence of God, is but one term in the statement or in the working of the vast problem, which will be finished only "at the end of the days."

God says not only to individuals—to each of His own servants, when he has done his work—" Go thy way." He says it to communities of men and witnesses for the truth. He says it to churches. He says it to generations. He says it to worlds—to one world after another: "Go thou thy way." What power of will and thought is His which can develop itself in fulness only through all the worlds and along all the ages! How great is His patience, which waits and is never weary, until the evil is vanquished and the good is triumphant at last! And how vast is His providence, by which the whole is wrought out! All thoughts and plans and systems of man, all passions, all pursuits, all births and deaths of individuals and of nations, all histories of races,—everything is in the providence and plan of God. Some things are inserted and sustained directly by Himself, some things by the exercise of the free choice of His creatures; but everything is ruled and used for the accomplishment of His ultimate and perfect will.

How little is Individual Man.
Is it not as if with some sublime consciousness of

the greatness of His own providence — covering the world, stretching along time, reaching up to heaven, filling at length eternity and infinitude—that God says to Daniel, in dismissing him, "*But go thou thy way.* I have said enough to thee, more than thou canst understand. I have got from thee all the little service I require. Thou hast done thy small and short work. Pass on, that others may take thy place. Linger not on a scene where thou art no longer needed. Say thy farewells, and be gone." We do not press this thought, because if it is in the passage at all it is not very strongly in it. But perhaps we may just catch the echo of it. At any rate it is a thought which naturally arises in the mind by contrast. When we look at the great structure of providence rising slowly and dimly to our sight, its walls stretching away in the far distance, its towers rising up into the sky, all unfinished, and when we turn from this spectacle to look at any man, however great and distinguished he may be, it is as if we turned from gazing on a vast cathedral to look at an ant carrying a grain of sand to help to rear the pile, or a fly shaking the dust from its wing in aid of the work of the builders. "Lord, what is man that Thou art mindful of him, or the Son of man that Thou visitest him?" Man "whose foundation is in the dust, who is crushed before the moth, who is altogether vanity."

And yet *God is mindful of man.* He does visit the son of man, talks with him, dwells with him, works in in him, and works by him for the accomplishment of

His own great purposes. After all, there is a sense in which a fly is more than a cathedral; for it is living, organised, capable of motion and of a kind of thought, and is therefore more in the scale of being than any form or size of inanimate matter. On this principle a man, living, intelligent, immortal, is more than the whole providence of God. It therefore may be expected that God *will* look to and tenderly regard the sons of men. Dust and ashes in his earthly life, man is a child of the Father of spirits, capable of holding with his Father, loving conscious fellowship, capable of entertaining God's thoughts within him, of adopting them as his own, of seeking to put them in force in his life, and of being thus a co-worker with God in the work of the ages. Therefore, although a man should be humble in utmost lowliness, because he is frail and because he is sinful, because his earthly life is but a shadow, and because at his best and greatest he must always be infinitely less than God, yet it may be expected that God will know and hold in His regard all His children, even those who have been rebellious and disobedient. As for those who have loved and served Him, who have cherished His thoughts, and lived on His grace, and who have been happy in His kingdom, and valiant for His truth on the earth, they will be regarded with a Father's love and pity. He will deal gently with them. He will hide them beneath the shadow of His wings. He will keep them unto life eternal.

So He deals with His servant Daniel. "Go thou thy way." "Thou art weary and I will give thee rest.

Thou hast done thy work; go now and claim thy recompense. It is natural that thou shouldst fondly linger and look behind, and think of unfinished purposes and works, and long and pray for permission to stay and finish them. But it is better not. Leave all that to me. I will gather up the fragments of your life-activity, so that nothing at all shall be lost. I will cast all your living energies where they shall meet and mingle with the energies of other lives, and travel along the ages towards the day of fruition. Thou shalt lose nothing at the length. Thou shalt be too late for nothing that is best. 'Thou shall stand in thy lot at the end of the days.'"

So God speaks to every one of His dying children. "Go thy way. Thy day's work is done. I have watched thee at it all the day long. It is not in some ways so much as thou hast thought it; in other ways it is more. I alone know what thy work has been. I have known thy secret purpose, and I have reckoned *that* in thy work. I have taken thy very failures and sown them as seed in the ground, to spring to harvest after thou hast left the field. I have taken thy formalities, thy poor pretences, thy vain glory, thy bigotry, thy selfishness, and thrown them aside so that they shall never be found. And so it is. Thy life is over here. Thy work is done. The good and the evil alike are all wrought, and thou hast nothing to do but to go. And I bid thee go. Go in trustfulness. Go in peace."

For "*Thou shalt rest.*" To go from earthly labour

The Lot at the End of the Days.

for God is to go to heavenly rest. "Blessed are the dead which die in the Lord, from henceforth, yea, saith the spirit, that they may rest from their labours." Even the earthly part rests in the grave, where the "weary" are "at rest." But the better part, "sleeping in Jesus," is carried to Paradise, to the stillness of the blessed dead, to the waiting yet happy and restful company of sainted souls. We speak of the "future state," might we not more truly speak of the future states? For there seems to be first the state of rest immediately succeeding death, and then the perfected glory at "the end of the days."

Some interpret "sleeping in Jesus" literally; they think that the spirit falls into a state of restful unconsciousness until the morning of the resurrection; that God in this way is laying to sleep His great family, one generation after another, and that when the last generation has gone, it will be morning, and the angel-trumpet will awake them all. There is nothing unphilosophical in this theory, for if we can sleep and be as dead during six or seven hours of the twenty-four here, we might, if God wills it, sleep from the hour of death till the day of judgment, and the long ages would appear no more than a watch in the night. The practical extinction of time is not difficult to imagine. No length of time is anything when compared with eternal duration. He that falls asleep in Jesus may sleep safely through all the remaining ages of time, and still have undiminished eternity to live in. It will be as God ordains; and His ordination will be best. But He seems to have in part told us how it is to be. To sleep in Christ is not to be unconscious. It is, we are told, to be "in Paradise." But Pandemonium would be the same as Paradise to one who was utterly unconscious. To be in Paradise must be to be sentient, percipient, happy. It is, as Paul puts it, to be "with Christ, which is far better." But it can hardly be "better" to him who knows nothing consciously about it. The meaning seems to be, "thou shalt rest," and know that thou art resting. That is the first part of the promised reward, and the more we think of it, the more we shall see how fit and meet it is.

Take the earthly analogy. What is so welcome to a tired worker from the fields, when night falls, as rest? Or to a traveller who has come over the mountains, and been on the way since the sun rose, until now that he has set? Would you propose to such wearied men some new enterprises, asking them to join you at once in some new endeavour? They would say "No, we are tired now—let the night be gone, we will speak with you in the morning." Such and so welcome is the rest of the grave, and the sleep of death to God's children when they are weary. There are some who seem in death to pant after the full blessedness, and to long for the light of the beatific vision, and the raptures of the new song; but I think to the greater part of God's dying children, "thou shalt rest," is a more welcome promise, at least at first. The shadow of the Almighty is sought for a while, ere coming into His full glory. I believe the real feeling is, with most of those who depart from toil and strife here, with a good hope through grace—" I would rather not go up at once, into full, shining, rapturous heaven. I would rather slip quietly into some shaded realm, and rest awhile among the waiting ones. There I shall be safe. I shall be able to think of all that is past, and to prepare for all that is to come. I shall be with Christ, resting from my labours in and for Him, while He watches over the issues of them, and gathers up their fruits. Let me rest! Let me sleep in Jesus! Let me go my way quietly—the way all my fathers have gone—under the sweet shade of the great promise, "Thou shalt rest."

Of course, this rest after the work of life will be more or less to each, according to the labours that have preceded it. If a man loiters in the field half the day, and leaves almost half his work undone, I warrant you the shadow of the oak-tree near his home will not be very soft and pleasant to him at night. He who does what his hand findeth to do with his might through life's working day, will go to his heavenly rest with a satisfaction and a zest which loiterer and laggard can never know. I say through life's working day, for there is no rest here. Sometimes, but not often, there seems to be a foretaste of it in this life, a tranquil eventide, when the saint is seen resting on this side death. But it is to be much observed that most of the strongest labourers in the kingdom of God work on till nightfall, and any little visions they themselves have of evening serenity, and any plans or efforts they make for the attainment of it, are generally disappointed. Dr.

Chalmers had a strong desire for a calm evening after his busy, gigantic life, and had provided for it in his own imagination—had retired from this and that—had called his house at Morningside "The Refuge," when—Death came one morning suddenly. With the pen in his hand, working still, and thinking of some little rest on earth, he was carried, in a few brief moments, into rest indeed.

This rest at death is preparatory to something far more complete at the " end of the days." Then—when the whole vast system of earthly providence is wound up, when the purposes of God in it are accomplished, when He has revealed Himself fully to men, when the world has had its day, and the shadows of its evening have come, when each one of the race has lived through his mortal probation, and sown the seed of which the harvest has now come ; when all God's servants have been called home from the field; when the gleaning angels, the last of the reaper band, shall gather up from the darkening fields of Time the separate ears of corn and carry them home to the garner; when all the little rills of human life flowing into the rivers of the centuries, shall have confluence in the great wide sea of unbounded duration; when all the forces and tendencies of universal human history shall converge in a second fulness of time; when the lustre of the crown shall cover all the shame and darkness of the cross; and the meeting of the Sons of God in the realm of victory and peace shall extinguish the several sorrows of the

The Lot at the End of the Days.

pilgrimage ; when the curtains of limitation shall be drawn aside, and, far and high through universal space, the new heavens shall shine, and at our feet shall bloom the new earth, the dwelling-place of righteousness : *then* shall each man, woman, and child stand in their " own lot."

I think that the reference here is chiefly to the righteous—the phraseology seems to point to their destiny—to that of Daniel, and such as he. " *Thou* shall stand in thy lot." Thou shall rest first, until the night is over, and then stand up in the morning as a man refreshed with sleep. The other class are not described as standing—rather we see them " fleeing," " hiding," crying to rock and mountain to cover them. They have chosen to belong to the dispensation that passes, and they pass with it; while diligent, godly, faithful souls "stand" with all that is permanent and divine. Certainly in great strength the term "*stand*" expresses the completeness, and above all the permanence of the New Life. It is said no longer, "Go thy way," as a changing dying creature: no longer " Thou shalt rest," after labour, in some repeated friendly sleep, as of a new death, while other battles are fought, while earth and heaven go surging through another trial, and hell opens once more. " *Thou shalt stand.*" Here at last is fixity of tenure. Here is possession of the incorruptible and undefiled inheritance. Here is the life begun, which has only to develop, and grow, and blossom, and shine in the light of God for ever. "The world passeth away, and the lust thereof, but he that doeth the will of God abideth for ever." And it will be our *own* lot. We shall stand then in that which we are making now. We shall claim that which by our faith we claimed before, and in a measure possessed by our love and hope.

Sower, be not slack! For the reaping day is coming, and "as a man soweth, so shall he also reap." Weaver of destiny! Look to the swift shuttle that flies through the loom of your daily life; let the threads be strong and the colours fair, and the whole fabric fit for immortality. Child of light! Let light be in you, and around you—for see, yonder, on your far horizon, are the first streaks and upward flushings of the coming day!

XXXI.

The Great Hope and its Earnest.

"Now He that hath wrought us for the selfsame thing is God, who also hath given unto us the earnest of the Spirit."—2 COR. v. 5.

WITHOUT attempting anything like a complete exposition of this remarkable passage of Scripture (from the 1st to the 10th verse of this chapter), it will be well to give just so much explanation of it as is necessary to the understanding of this fifth verse. There are many verses in the Bible, and especially in the New Testament, which absolutely refuse to be lifted out of their connection. They form part of a living tissue of truth, and to take them out of it is to do violence and injury to their vital wholeness. It is so with this text.

Let us ascertain, if possible,

First, What "*this self-same thing*" is, for which we are "wrought." Studying the context, we find it to be a certain state of mind; it is a tone, a temper, or rather a certain attitude of mind in regard to many things. We must go back into the fourth chapter to understand this fully. "We are troubled on every side, persecuted, bearing about in the body the dying of the Lord Jesus." So the passage runs. "We are here in a suffering state:

dwellers for a little in, or pilgrims through a transitory world: we carry about with us frail suffering bodies. If we are Christ's, and in proportion as we are Christ's, the world is unfriendly: we are alway delivered unto death for Jesus's sake: death worketh in us:" but also life; we die, and live, as our crucified Lord died and lived: the life of Jesus begins to be made manifest even in our mortal body: we shall rise with Him, fully and visibly at length. We see, by faith, that after all, affliction is but light, comparatively, and short-lived: and that while it continues, it is working for us more and more an eternal weight of glory. We are in no doubt about these things, for *we know*, we very confidently expect, on the strength of evidence that cannot be resisted that all this suffering-work, this trial-work, is temporary, is preparatory to something very glorious about to be revealed—sure to be revealed by death, if we do not reach the revelation in any other way. Christ *may* come before we die, says the Apostle. We do not want to die. Although not afraid of its consequences, knowing what we do of the redeeming power and transforming grace of God, yet we instinctively shrink from it. The tabernacle in which we dwell is indeed frail and crazy, and falling down to dust; and yet it has been for long our only home, and it has served us so well that we would not, if it might be avoided, put it off. We would rather, like Elijah, without putting off the old, put on the new. We would not be unclothed; we would rather be clothed upon, have the vesture of immortality drawn *over* the vesture of decay, that "mortality might be swallowed up of life," that the immortal principle might assimilate to itself, by absorption and life-power, what seem to be the elements of corruption and death. But come death, as it has come hitherto to all,—or come the Lord of life to abolish it, and to give us in the flesh the victory,—we know that we shall never be homeless; if we are driven from one house, it will only be into a better. If we do forsake this earthly tenement, that has so often been shaken by outward storms and internal pains and aches, there is another building, strong, fair, and imperishable! It will come out of the heavens. It will come from the hands of God. He made the first house in Eden of clay. He will make the second of spiritual and heavenly substance. He will give a body to each believer at length, like unto the body of the risen and glorified Lord. Thus we stand; believing, expectant, resolved; sighing, yet singing in heart; groaning, yet exultant and confident; always confident, because we are sure, in whichever way it may be, that we shall soon pass from our present home in the body, and come to our home in the Lord."

Such is the temper and attitude of mind which explains the meaning of this phrase, "*the self-same thing.*" And I think it must be allowed that it is a very great and heroic attitude. It was so for Paul, who described it so well, because he stood in it, and knew all its pangs and its glories; and it is a great attitude for all others who can really assume it. He who can take up the language of a passage like this, and honestly adopt it as the description of the state and feeling of his mind, is a very king, and must be among the happiest of men.

We have around us here and now, the old, old world—God-denying and anti-Christian—which was around the Apostle Paul. It is not changed! It is not changed! Many and many a time have we tried to persuade ourselves that it is—that Time has mollified it, that art has refined it, that science has illumined it, that reason and natural religion have got some general sway over it, and that good men now may live in it and pass through it, working and speaking for heavenly truth as they go, at least unmolested, if not regarded even with reverence and silent approbation. *No;* not if they contend earnestly for the faith as Paul did. If they do, they will meet with his experience, enemies will come around them, and trials will gather on their way, and then it will be a great thing to be able to reach and rest in this state of mind, this victorious condition, this "self-same thing" of our text, to be able to say, "Let the world fret and murmur as it will, it gets no victory over me! I stand in Him who overcame the world, and who says to me, and to every trusting soul, 'Be of good cheer.'"

The Apostle seems to have lived in a tough, and in some ways a strong "house;" and yet a house that, after years of toil and hardship, became worn-out and frail, very sensitive and familiar with death-pangs. If it was a great thing for him to triumph over bodily suffering, and to face death, must it not be a great thing for afflicted and suffering people to do the same

The Great Hope and its Earnest. 417

now? The angels looking over the earth to see where are the sublimest examples of courage, find them, where? In the shock of battle, and the fearful onset of man against man? No. Although these, in their own way, and tried by their own standard, are often splendid enough. They find them rather in weary pilgrims, to whom every step is pain, and who yet travel on in good heart and hope; in little rooms where the sick lie, sometimes through long years, waiting submissively for the day of deliverance. They find them in that silent host, which, without sound of trumpet or tread of foot, is always advancing to the death-gate, and passing on and through into what is beyond.

And is it not a great thing, in these times, to be able to look to that "beyond" in faith and confidence, to cast anchor of thought and faith, as well as of desire and hope, in another life? While atheism spreads blackness over the universe; while materialism drags men down to the dust; while heartless philosophies and flippant literatures tell us "it does not matter," and that our wisdom is to live for to-day, to seize the passing pleasure, and to withhold our heart from no joy; in times like these, it is a great thing to stand on the old watch-tower, and to look by faith clearly beyond the visible into the invisible, declaring, "Yes, I see it. *I know* that if the earthly house of this tabernacle were dissolved, I have a building of God, an house not made with hands, eternal in the heavens."

This then is the meaning of the words "this self-same thing." This is the position occupied by a Christian man. The question now occurs. How can any one rise to such a height? How are we to account for such an attitude, corroborated by such experience, in the case of those who assume it? The answer is

Secondly; *That it is wholly the result of a Divine process.*—" He that hath wrought us unto this self-same thing is God." The process is the great process of grace. It is redemption taking effect in the heart. This is no merely evolutionary process. It is not a natural development of the human being. It is not merely that the mind conquers the realms of knowledge; the imagination the forms of beauty and grandeur; the conscience the laws of truth and right. If it were so; if a man had the inborn power to do and be all this, the Apostle in that case might have phrased his statement differently: he might have said, "He who created us, when we were born, for this self-same thing, is God;" or, "He who gave us life, and gave us power to mould and renew our own nature till we rise into all goodness, is God." But he does not say this. His words take another line. "He who hath wrought us"—created us anew in Christ Jesus —"wrought us" as the block of marble is wrought into the shape of the fair figure; as the clay is moulded and fashioned, until the "vessel of honour" appears; as the wood is chipped and planed and carved, till the design of the carver is achieved; as the rough iron ore, taken from the bowels of the earth and indistinguishable at first from common mould, is wrought into burning heat in the fiery furnace; smelted, poured out in a glowing stream, broken, beaten with hammers, cast into the fires again and again, until it is so purified and hardened that instruments of shining steel can be made of it; so are we "wrought" by God. His work is marvellous. He must have wrought a great work in Stephen before he could stand up fearlessly with an angel face, amid the shower of death-dealing stones, and, looking steadfastly up into heaven, say: "I see heaven opened, and Jesus standing at the right hand of God." A wonderful process God conducts to great issues in many a one of less name than Stephen. By truth, by teaching, by Spirit-power, by the discipline of Providence, by loss and pain, and sickness and death, He works. He works always along main lines, amid infinite variety of circumstance, but always with a view to the "self-same thing," and, therefore, in some degree along the same road to reach it; and this is the road. "Whom He did foreknow, He also did predestinate to be conformed to the image of His Son. . . . Moreover, whom He did predestinate, them He also called; and whom He called, them He also justified; and whom He justified, them He also glorified." These, and such as these, if we may say so, are the master-strokes of the divine chisel; these are the main lines of the divine Artist, as He paints the living picture and brings out the image of the heavenly.

"*Foreknown.*"—Ah, how much better is that to me than if I had come into the world by chance, and had to go through it only in the strength of my solitary personality! "*Predestinated*,"—then my poor wavering purpose is not all. There is a strength beneath and behind it, which nothing can resist; and I shall be conqueror and more, at last. "*Called*,"—then my willing heart shall answer; nay, all my life shall give thankful reply. "*Justified*,"—then who is he that condemneth? "*Glorified*,"—then the beauty of the Lord shall be mine for evermore.

We stay not a moment to conjure up metaphysical or philosophical difficulties. We know that the chief difficulties of all deep human thought lie in that very passage—in these very terms which signify and express to us God's greatest work in and for man. But because we cannot solve these difficulties, shall we tell the great Master to stand aside and desist, lest our free-will should be touched, or our poor glimmering reason bewildered? No, no; rather say with an old divine: "If I feel not faith, I may know that predestination is too high a matter for me to be a disputer of. Until I have become a better scholar in the schoolhouse of repentance and justification, which is the grammar-school wherein I must be conversant, I am not ready to go to the university of God's most holy Predestination and Providence."

O Thou who "workest hitherto," work in us all Thy deepest, dearest, greatest work, and let Thy Holy Spirit abide in us, that that work may never fall into decay or be discontinued; but that it may grow and rise from smaller to greater, from less to more, from poorer to richer, until we put on the perfect image, and clothe ourselves with our house which is from heaven!

Lastly. All this is made sure to us, not only in divine promise, but by "*the earnest of the Spirit.*" That is to say, this "self-same thing" means, not merely a hope that something good and great is coming by and by, but that it is in part matter of experience now. A person objecting or doubting might say, "You speak indeed of great things: you speak of 'putting off' a body and of 'putting on' a body, as though it were a mere garment; of rising superior to infirmity, of getting the victory over the grave; of claiming immortality, just as though all this were as sure and evident as any of the things that are happening around us. But is not this, after all, only the language of speculation—religious speculation indeed, but without any basis of fact? Since no man alive has ever put off or put on a body, has ever gone within the veil, or drawn one breath of the immortal life, all we can say is: "It may be true, or it may not be true." "Nay," we reply, "the question does not stand quite so. There *is* One who has been within that veil, and who returned thence to make us sure of our immortality." But apart from this. These things are not merely matters of speculation and hope, but also of experience and realisation. It is a paradox, but it is true, that we have already entered into the heaven towards which we are yet always travelling, and which we shall not fully reach but through the door of death.

There are estates in this world which you can enter truly enough by crossing a river, or going over the summit or ridge of a chain of hills. You are then in the estate, and if you know the proprietor, and he knows you and accounts you his friend, you have some feeling of safety as you travel on over moor and moss, through gloomy forest, and dark defile; but if you are going to the mansion, *that* is twenty or thirty miles distant perhaps, and many adventures may come to you by the way. Still, if you walk well—and walk right on—through the swollen streams—swimming the river if the ferryman is not there with his boat—not stopping for every dog that barks, or sheltering from every shower that falls, but pressing always on,—why then, just about sunset perhaps, the western sky all gold, sweet evening breathing peace over the earth, you will see the towers of the castle whither you are going. And the landscape will begin to soften and glow; the grass is greener now; the trees are more select; the road, how smooth it is, compared with some of the first miles you trod! And then you pass the great iron gate, and lo! yonder in the doorway, is your Friend who has sent for you, and who is lord of all the way by which you have come.

Such is our heavenly way. Every step of it is on King's ground. We are in heaven when we begin to live to heaven's King. Yes. To be "called," and to answer, and arise, and come, is to enter heaven. But it is a wide estate, far wider than many people think. It has in it the less and the more perfect. But this peculiarity belongs to every one who treads *any* part of its ground, that they are all going from the less perfect to the more perfect; they are all in heaven as to state, yet all travelling to a further heaven—and aiming, and striving, and looking, and longing, and praying as they travel—and *this* is "the earnest of the Spirit :" this is the witness in the man himself that he has "passed from death unto life," and that he shall win the life immortal at length. This is the evidence of that of which some say there is no evidence ; and even on-lookers can see it, in the patient, hopeful, faithful lives of Christian men. *It is here* in every such life. Not much of it at first, but more will come—and more. First the toilsome uneven way, with its "by-path meadow" sometimes, and its "doubting castle," but the land of Beulah is reached at last. "First the blade, then the ear, then the full corn in the ear." First faith, then perseverance, then victory in death, then heaven and eternal glory.

THE END.

www.ingramcontent.com/pod-product-compliance
Lightning Source LLC
Chambersburg PA
CBHW051740300426
44115CB00007B/637